CIVIL WAR IN ULSTER

CLASSICS OF IRISH HISTORY
General Editor: Tom Garvin

Other titles in this series:

P.S. O'Hegarty
The Victory of Sinn Féin
with an Introduction by Tom Garvin
(1998)

Walter McDonald
Some Ethical Questions of Peace and War
with an Introduction by Tom Garvin
(1998)

CIVIL WAR IN ULSTER
ITS OBJECTS & PROBABLE RESULTS

Joseph Johnston

edited by Roy Johnston
Foreword by Tom Garvin

University College Dublin Press
Preas Choláiste Ollscoile Bhaile Átha Cliath

First published 1913
This edition first published by
University College Dublin Press, 1999
© Roy Johnston 1999

ISBN 1 900621 30 4
ISSN 1393–6883

University College Dublin Press
Newman House, 86 St Stephen's Green, Dublin 2, Ireland

Cataloguing in Publication data available from the British Library

Typeset in Ireland in Baskerville by Elaine Shiels, Bantry, Co. Cork
Printed in Ireland by Colour Books, Dublin

CONTENTS

The Ulster Volunteers at Larne Harbour landing the German arms and ammunition from the *Mountjoy* on 24 April 1914. From the drawing by S. Begg published in *The Illustrated London News*, 2 May 1914. (National Library of Ireland)

FOREWORD
Tom Garvin

Civil War in Ulster was written at the beginning of the Irish crisis of 1912–23. This crisis resulted in the partition of the island in 1920 and the emergence of the two political entities now known as Northern Ireland and the Republic of Ireland, the latter controlling the bulk of the island as an independent state and the former being a subordinate entity within the United Kingdom. This early twentieth-century crisis was also accompanied by considerable levels of violence, and was connected closely to the general European crisis that produced the Great War of 1914–18.

Late nineteenth-century Ireland had experienced profound social, political and cultural change. The great disaster of the Irish Famine (1845–48) triggered a stream of emigration from the island, mainly from rural Ireland, to America, Great Britain and Australia. Uniquely in the demographic history of western Europe, the population of the island of Ireland fell from nearly nine million in 1844 to about four million in 1900. One ideological theme of Irish separatism at the end of the century was 'race death', or the final depopulation of Ireland and the complete replacement of the Gael by the foreigner. In reality, demographic recovery was about to occur, and has occurred, but did not really happen for fifty years; even at the end of the twentieth century the population of the island is somewhat under six million. It is, however, a very different population; then, it was rather poor, Irish-speaking or just becoming literate in the English language, now it is rather rich, literate, English-speaking and increasingly post-Catholic and, perhaps, post-nationalist.

The great Irish Famine triggered cultural changes, perhaps particularly changes in the political culture of the general population. An apparently begrudging acceptance of British rule was replaced by a sometimes mild, but sometimes aggressive, refusal to accord legitimacy to the rule of the London parliament in Ireland. An ancient disaffection from English or British rule gained a force that it had not quite had earlier. Nationalist and Catholic propagandists were able to build on the perceived negligence and alleged irresponsibility of the London government and propose political independence as the ultimate solution for Ireland's ailments.

Linguistically, the Famine hit Irish-language communities particularly hard, and the ancestral language declined even in western and southern regions where it had been strongest in pre-Famine times; Ireland had been effectively bilingual since the sixteenth century, but appeared to be heading towards a monolingual English-speaking condition by the 1880s.

Religiously, the Famine was connected with another cultural revolution. Most Irish people outside eastern Ulster had always been at least nominally Catholic and had looked, again in theory, to the See of Saint Peter in Rome for spiritual guidance. However, it was only in the years after the Famine that they became perhaps the most religiously observant and generally obedient Catholic people in the world. Furthermore, the emergent post-Famine rural Ireland of small- and middle-sized family farms proved to be a very effective source of the vocations to the priesthood, the nunneries and the clergy in general. By the end of the nineteenth century the ratios of clergy to people of the Catholic population of Ireland were the highest in the world. Ireland had evolved into a sort of Catholic Tibet.

Irish landlordism received its final comeuppance at the hands of the Land League (1879–81), led by two leaders of genius: a peasant Catholic from the western county of Mayo (Michael Davitt) and a Protestant landlord from the eastern county of Wicklow (Charles Stewart Parnell). Thereafter the land of Ireland fell into the hands of what had been a quasi-feudal tenancy but which rapidly transformed itself into a piously Catholic, incipiently democratic, free-farmer society.

Literacy in the English language became widespread, and popular nationalism of a markedly Catholic flavour was preached by a burgeoning popular and nationalist press.

Protestant northeastern Ireland ('Ulster') watched the progress of the Catholic majority on the island with increasing unease and even alarm. Much of its population was of Scottish Presbyterian descent and dated from seventeenth-century settlements. A sturdy, reformed, anti-Catholic Christianity informed much of Ulster Protestantism, as it still does a century later.

The growing political strength of Catholic Ireland made it obvious that, sooner or later, pressure would be exerted by Irish leaders on the British government to concede local devolved self-government to Ireland. Such a proposal was anathema to British conservatives, but was looked upon with sympathy by many liberals, often in the form of 'Home Rule all round', or devolved parliaments not only for Ireland but for Scotland and Wales as well.

In 1906 a Liberal government came to power, and a Home Rule bill for Ireland was prepared. Elements in the British Conservative Party, the Irish Unionist branch of that party and the armed forces prepared to resist Home Rule, if necessary by force. The German government, fishing in troubled waters, lent its good offices to both sides in the Irish conflict. As the Home Rule bill threatened to become law, Ulster Unionism turned militant. In 1912 a Provisional Government of Ulster was formed, as was the Ulster Volunteer Force. Guns were smuggled into Ulster, and a Solemn League and Covenant was signed by hundreds of thousands of young men.

Meanwhile, among the nationalists a demonstration effect was occurring. Since the Famine, a minority of nationalists favoured a revolutionary solution to Ireland's problems, and a secret organisation known as the Irish Republican Brotherhood (I.R.B. or Fenians) had existed since 1858, financed in particular by embittered Irish emigrants in the United States. The crisis of 1906–12 gave the I.R.B. its chance, and it used entryist tactics to infiltrate nationalist organisations such as the Gaelic League, the Gaelic Athletic Association and what was to become the separatist Irish Volunteers of 1913, later to evolve into the Irish Republican Army (I.R.A.). In effect, the Ulster mobilisation accelerated mobilisation in the rest of Ireland. The outcome in the long run was the end of British rule in Ireland outside the northeastern area ten years later, amid much bloodshed.

Joseph Johnston, writing before the European catastrophe of 1914, naturally could not imagine such a violent set of consequences. The Europe he lived in was innocent beyond modern belief in that the Great War which was to occur was almost unimaginable. Similarly, the idea that a peaceful and bucolic Ireland, enjoying a modest prosperity, could be on the brink of great violence was discounted by all reasonable people.

Tom Garvin is Professor of Politics in University College Dublin. His most recent book is 1922: *The Birth of Irish Democracy* (Dublin, 1996).

INTRODUCTION
Roy Johnston

The republication of my father's book, at what is once more a watershed in the history of these islands, may help to place again on the agenda a constructive nation-building role for Irish Protestants, by giving them the chance to re-discover and assess the role of the Larne gun-running and the Tory armed conspiracy which prevented their participation in a peaceful constitutional process, of a similar kind to the recent developments in Scotland and Wales.

The book has to be seen in the historical context of the political forces then at work: the Home Rule movement, Irish-Ireland, the Ulster situation, Liberalism and Toryism in England, and in particular in Oxford where my father was a student from 1910 to 1912. Having observed the developing threat of civil war, my father then wrote the book rapidly, publishing it in November 1913.

BIOGRAPHICAL SKETCH

My father Joseph Johnston (I call him J.J. from now on, for brevity) was born in Castlecaulfield Co. Tyrone in 1890. His father John Johnston was a schoolteacher and farmer, his mother Mary Geddes. The family had been settled in Ireland since 1620, and an ancestor William Johnston had served in the siege of Derry. They were of working farming colonial stock, like most of the Presbyterians who came from Scotland.

There were six boys and two girls in the family. The elder of the girls died. J.J. was the youngest son. All seven survivors had university education, in most cases with the aid of scholarships. Of J.J.'s five older brothers, four went into the Indian Civil Service; the other became a medical doctor in London. The education trail led in most cases from Dungannon Royal School to postgraduate work in Oxford, either from Trinity College, Dublin, or from Queen's College Galway.

J.J. came up to Trinity College, Dublin, in 1906 and studied Classics, taking his degree with large gold medal in 1910. He went on to Oxford and took a second B.A. degree (in *literae humaniores*) which was conferred in October 1912.

The environment in Oxford where J.J. was a postgraduate was highly politicised; the debates[1] in Lincoln College and in the Oxford Union were an entry-point into the understanding of the the issues of the time – Home Rule for Ireland being one such, votes for women being another. J.J. supported votes for women in Lincoln College debates. He undoubtedly would have attended Oxford Union debates on Home Rule, addressed by Augustine Birrell, Chief Secretary for Ireland, and later by Sir Edward Carson, the leader of the Irish Unionists, but there is no record of his participation. The Lincoln–Balliol political set with which he interacted was decidedly Liberal, even Socialist, and included Lionel Smith-Gordon, who worked subsequently in Plunkett House for the Irish co-operative movement, and G. D. H. Cole, the economic guru of the 1945 Labour Government, who visited J.J. in Ireland in 1946.

A significant influence from the University academic staff was likely to have been H.A.L. Fisher,[2] whose book, *The Republican Tradition in Europe*, published by Methuen in 1911, would have been a current discussion topic. Both Fisher and my father were interested in the opportunities presented by the Albert Kahn Foundation;[3] J.J., however, upstaged Fisher by winning a Travelling Fellowship in 1914.

J.J. returned to Trinity College Dublin where he sat for the Fellowship examination, becoming a Fellow in 1913. Having achieved this relatively secure position, he felt able to defend Home Rule publicly against the Tory armed conspiracy, the political origins of which he had observed during his period in Oxford. His *Civil War in Ulster*, published in November 1913, is a polemic against Carson and the Tory leaders who were responsible for the Larne gun-running. He was among the few who appreciated the full destructive significance of this event in its time.

At the time J.J. wrote the book his thinking appears to have been dominated by his Trinity College, Dublin (T.C.D.) and Oxford experiences, and he seems to have been only marginally aware of what was going on with nationalists such as Arthur Griffith, Bulmer Hobson and D.P. Moran, and their respective papers *Sinn Féin, Irish Freedom* and the *Leader.* His main contact with the world outside T.C.D. was probably with intellectuals like AE (George Russell), also Horace Plunkett and the co-operative movement. J.J. was instrumental in starting a consumer co-op for the supply of groceries to the Trinity students living in rooms, and this aroused the ire of the Dublin traders, as reported in the June 1913 issue of Hobson's *Irish Freedom.*

After writing the book, and seeing it published, J.J. embarked on a world tour as an Albert Kahn Travelling Fellow[4] which occupied him during 1915, and later in 1916, as the Fellowship procedures were disrupted by the war.

His actions after 1916 were concentrated on attempting to invoke a Canadian model, not unlike what eventually emerged as the Free State. In this context he contributed to the debate in the Liberal press in Britain, via pseudonymous articles in the *Manchester Guardian.* He also supported developments within Trinity College in which Sinn Féin's objectives could be aired politically (such as in the Thomas Davis Society).[5]

After 1922 his efforts were directed towards attempting to prevent the worst effects of Partition, keeping intellectual contacts in existence between opinion-leaders in both parts of the country, and specifically in attempting to keep alive a co-operative approach to Irish rural economic life, as pioneered before the War of Independence by Horace Plunkett and the Irish Agricultural Organisation Society (I.A.O.S.).

His career in the Free State and subsequently in the Republic is for me a continuing research topic, with a future publication in mind. Between his experience and mine, we span the century. This early episode, which set the scene for what followed, forms part of an early chapter. It is worth publishing now because of the contemporary political developments, as part of the case for a positive Protestant role in the development of a multi-cultural Irish nation.

One final note on the family: apart from the older brothers, four of whom were in the Indian Civil Service,[6] the youngest and only sister Anne did a law degree in Trinity College, and entered the civil service in Dublin, pre-1914. She is on record, in the company of Douglas Hyde and others, in the group photograph of the 1912 Ard Fheis of Connradh na Ghaeilge, which is on display in the Hyde museum in Frenchpark. She stayed on in Dublin in the civil service, making her career there. With Thekla Beere and others, she was a founder-member of an Oige, the Youth Hostels Association, in the early 1930s.

So, on the whole, the family tradition was Protestant and Irish, looking to Ireland as its home, as an integrated whole, for which they sought Home Rule, while identifying with the British Empire, which they regarded as heading progressively towards Dominion-type independence.

THE HOME RULE MOVEMENT

The Home Rule for Ireland movement included both Catholics and Protestants. The third Home Rule bill was introduced in the House of Commons by the Liberal Government in 1912. A meeting of the All for Ireland League in the Cork City Hall on 31 March 1910, with the Earl of Dunraven presiding, an event recorded in the memoirs of the then Prime Minister, Herbert Henry Asquith, gives something of the flavour of the discussions leading up to the bill. Dunraven represented that sector of the landed gentry which identified with and lived in Ireland. His family had been associated with the foundation of St Columba's College, nearly a century earlier, which had been established to teach Irish to the sons of the landed gentry, the better to understand their tenantry. On the platform were William O'Brien M.P., who had launched the All for Ireland League that year, and Tim Healy K.C. M.P., at one time a supporter of Charles Stewart Parnell. The call went out for an all-party conference, to consider a federal system for the whole of the United Kingdom. The Home Rule bill was attacked as being bad financially; everything of any importance was reserved, but it was thought that the Ulster rank and file would accept a wise measure of Home Rule. The Ancient Order of Hibernians (A.O.H.) was seen as the enemy: '. . . must a man, before he dare call himself an Irishman, have a pass from Mr. Devlin?'[7]

In a visit to Dublin on 19 July 1912, Asquith remarked sarcastically that while it was apparently acceptable to the Tory press for '. . . Sir Edward Carson to go to Belfast, to Dublin and to Cork, breathing fire and slaughter, no member of the responsible Executive may, it would appear, go anywhere or say anything . . .'. He received a massive welcome and made a robust speech in favour of Home Rule and ridiculing Partition. He could not help, however, becoming increasingly aware of the way in which the military establishment, in particular Lord French, was briefing the King, and he became more inclined to pay attention to this than to Liberal business interests, including Harland and Wolff, the Belfast shipbuilding firm, which supported Home Rule. On 11 August 1913, King George V wrote to Asquith suggesting the Partition of Ireland; again on 22 September he wrote expressing concern at the threat of army officers' disaffection (this would have been the first indications of what became known as the Curragh Mutiny of March 1914). These influences were to insulate Asquith against the arguments of supporters of Home Rule for Ireland as a whole.

There is much to done by historians to recapture the full potential of Home Rule for a united Ireland, initially as a partner in the British Empire, but increasingly in a position to assert its independent interest through a Dublin legislature. Parallels with present-day Scotland and Wales need to be teased out. The indications are that, as well as being inclusive of the interests of the Protestant community, it would have offered an environment within which the co-operative movement would have been able to thrive, making the bridge between agricultural and industrial production, and the needs of the consumer, with a democratic control system in charge of economic development.[8] Co-operative literature at that time was full of discussions of this kind, which subsequently could not be realised because of Partition. The consumer co-operative movement was strongest in Belfast, while the movement in what became the Free State was strongest among the producers in Munster.

ULSTER AND THE LARNE GUN-RUNNING

Ulster local newspapers in the latter part of 1913 reveal a growing triumphalist campaign supporting armed resistance to what they regarded as the 'Home Rule Peril'. Many were syndicated under the '[*placename*] *Telegraph*' label and one finds the same orchestrated material surrounded by local news variations. Volunteer training camps on landlords' demesnes are reported with enthusiasm. There are scare stories about victimised Protestants in the South: letters from Cork signed by 'Southern Protestant'—'Ancient Order of Hibernians terrorises Protestant postmaster', boycotts, and abductions of Catholic servants who converted to Protestantism.

A Liberal pro-Home Rule meeting in Ballymoney was, however, reported, exceptionally, in full by the *North Antrim Standard* on 30 October 1913. Elsewhere it received disparaging treatment, with more space given to discrediting it than reporting on what was said. This meeting was a local reflection of the politics which J.J.'s book was aimed to support. The hall seated 400, and only Protestants were admitted, so that it could not be said it was packed by Catholic Home Rulers. It was addressed by Sir Roger Casement,[9] by Captain White,[10] by Alice Stopford Green[11] and by Alec Wilson J.P., the son of Walter Wilson, a Director of Harland and Wolff. There was a named platform party of some 40 or more of the great and the good: J.P.s, clergy, local councillors from near and far, including the Rev. J. B. Armour,[12] J. Goold-Verschoyle, Robert Carson, James Hanna U.D.C., W.D. Hamilton J.P., J.L Taggart J.P.

The meeting passed a resolution protesting '. . .against the claims of Sir Edward Carson [the leader of the Irish Unionists] and the self-constituted Provisional Government of Ulster to represent the Protestant community of north-east Ulster in the policy they have announced of lawless resistance to the will of the Parliament of Great Britain and Ireland and, further, hereby pledges to offer such opposition as the law permits or enjoins to the arbitrary decrees of an illegal and entirely non-representative body.'

The Ballymoney meeting generated a deputation to Asquith. J.J.'s book would have been targeted at supporting this process. The deputation was reported in the *Belfast News Letter* of 26 November as including Professor Henry of Queen's University of Belfast, Alec Wilson, David Campbell of the Belfast Trades Council and Captain J. White among others. There is in the Asquith papers[13] a memo from Professor Henry dated 18 November 1913, pointing out that the 'volunteers' opposed to Home Rule were landlords' retainers and dependants; in Saintfield, of 1600 Presbyterians only ten had joined and there was said to be substantial Liberal Home Rule support among Presbyterians. This memo in the Asquith papers is printed but of uncertain origin with marginal scribbles. It must have been part of the documentation of this deputation, which otherwise appears to have left little on record.

There are many indications that the British Establishment was actively conniving at the armed Ulster conspiracy, as a means of undermining a Liberal Government which they considered a threat to the Empire. Consider, for example, the evidence of Sir William Harcourt, a civil servant servicing the Imperial Defence Committee in the period 1911–14, whose papers are accessible in the Bodleian Library. There is simply no reference, at the time it happened, to the Larne gun-running on record at this level; they were more concerned with things like the strategic threat of the then current Channnel Tunnel proposal. This is a case of 'the dog that didn't bark'. They knew it was going on, approved of it, and simply put nothing on record.

The treatment of the Home Rule issue at successive Conservative Party conferences[14]—Leeds 1911, London 1912, Norwich 1913 – shows the intensity of concern increasing. In 1912, there are echoes of the sabre-rattling of the Blenheim call to arms, rising to a peak in 1913, when calls went out for organising armed English volunteer participation, in an atmosphere of hysteria. The *Spectator* article in the Appendix to this book provides an example of the contemporary 'hype' and was timed to influence the 1913 conference.

The details of how the Larne gun-running was organised, and the political background, as seen from a current Unionist perspective, have been well documented by A.T.Q. Stewart in *The Ulster Crisis* (Blackstaff 1997). One can only conclude that the Tory conspiracy to prevent Home Rule by arming the Orangemen was the beginning of the end of the Empire that they aspired to defend. If Home Rule had gone through without Ireland being partitioned, the Irish nation would have evolved as a pluralistic participant in the British Empire. The Larne gun-running, however, gave the go-ahead to the Irish Republican Brotherhood (I.R.B.) and led to the 1916 Rising in the form it took, with Partition as one of the outcomes. Had there been no 1916, the resistance to the First World War, as expressed in parallel but in different traditions— socialist and republican—of James Connolly[15] and the I.R.B., would have focused on opposition to conscription, which would have been strongly on the agenda by 1918 and which would have been opposed by all people in Ireland, giving rise to a united Protestant and Catholic anti-war national move- ment, and reviving the potential of 1798 for national-democratic revolution. This Catholic-Protestant unity has tragically, per- haps, begun to rediscover itself in the commemoration of the Irish in the 1914–18 war, as expressed in the memorial at Messen. It would have been more solidly based had unity emerged in opposition to the war.

I have always been appalled by the extent to which the significance of the Larne gun-running was misinterpreted by the I.R.B. in 1914. Besotted as they were with the Fenian tra- dition of physical force as a 'principle', they welcomed the

Larne gun-running uncritically. James Connolly's scathing attacks on this spurious 'philosophical position' were ignored. The I.R.B.'s illusions were shared by Bulmer Hobson and by Arthur Griffith. Hobson as early as October 1912 was promoting the idea that '. . . the present campaign in the North . . . will turn out beneficial . . . drinking in the doctrines of physical force . . .'; he seemed to think that anti-Redmond Ulster policy would support a 'new Patriot Party'. By May 1914 he was welcoming the Larne gun-running, and saying that '. . . we must profit by the Carsonite example . . .'. Griffith in *Sinn Féin* on 2 May wrote that '. . . the Ulster Volunteers did well when they violated the English edict . . .'.

The Larne gun-running was in fact the most evil and destructive act in Irish history of this century, and the Tory Party in Britain, under Balfour's leadership, was to blame for it.[16] If it had not taken place, the emergence of a pluralistic Irish nation would have been as peaceful as the emergence of Norway from Swedish domination.

An interesting question raised from studying the Asquith papers is how the Government view was switched, overnight, from fulminating about 'treasonable conspiracy' to concern about the level of customs and import licences. What was in the coded exchange of messages that must have persuaded Asquith to draw in on the 'treasonable conspiracy' approach? Why was the import of arms for the purpose of threatening civil war against the enactments of Parliament merely allowed to subside to the level of a 'customs' matter?

J.J. always regarded the Larne gun-running as one of the factors leading to the start of the First World War. Importing guns by the shipload, in 1914, from Germany? At Tory instigation, and with Imperial Defence Committee connivance? Was this not treasonable? The instigators ended up in the Government, so presumably treason when it succeeds is no longer called by that name.[17]

I was able to find two reviews, both of late November 1913. The *Derry Standard* on 28 November gives grudging recognition to the quality of the book: '. . . we feel bound to say that Mr Johnston has handled the subject without any of the cant, hypocrisy and misrepresentation which mark the purely nationalist attempts to place Home Rule . . .in a favourable light . . .'. The *Derry Standard* goes on to admit that they prefer '. . . people slavishly attached to their priests than an Ireland given over to free-thinking and anti-Christian ideas . . .'.

The *Dungannon News* on 27 November gives an extensive hostile nit-picking review, in which none of the key concepts is picked up. The reviewer is clearly a competent hatchet-wielder, and J.J. gets the attention due to a local who had made good, but had subsequently gone to the dogs. '. . . What has the Duke of Abercorn . . . to gain by shouldering a rifle in defence of the Union?. . .'. Volunteer triumphalism is hailed as altruistic. He goes on to remark that '. . . the Donaghmore Nationalists passed a resolution . . . that they look to Home Rule to override any local government of which they do not approve . . .', thus raising the bogey of Catholic nationalist exclusivist politics, as promulgated in papers like the *Leader*.[18] The *Dungannon News* gave short shrift to the October Ballymoney Liberal rally, and they must have felt it necessary to nip in the bud any support for this position which might be generated by local sales of J.J.'s book. Despite this, I have handled a tattered copy in a Tyrone Protestant farmhouse, in recent years.

We are not able to rewrite history, but we can draw conclusions from it, and in situations where nations are emerging, try to set up processes to support their emergence without violence. In a global situation where world wars are becoming 'unaffordable', there are increasingly resources available for the avoidance of minor wars, and these need to be deployed, with good advance warning, in such a way as to avoid the type of situation which has occurred in post-Yugoslavia, and in the many African States where the boundaries were defined under various imperial systems.

If my father's 1914 book turns out to be of any use in helping to define the background to studies of such situations, as well as in the current Irish situation, this re-publishing will have been doubly worth while.

CODA

I feel I should add an anecdotal coda. The year was 1966, and reappraisal was going on of the 1916 Rising. I found myself on a platform at Murlough, Co. Antrim, representing the Dublin Wolfe Tone[19] Society at a commemoration of Roger Casement,[20] in the company of Conor Cruise O'Brien,[21] then recently returned from his time at the United Nations, and carrying some of the aura of his work in the Congo, for which he had been demonised by the British media, becoming in the process for a period a hero of the Irish Left. Eoin (the 'Pope') O'Mahony[22] was presiding. He introduced me as the son of Joe Johnston, adducing my father's 1913 publication of *Civil War in Ulster* as relevant background for the occasion. I had not briefed him, having at the time been only marginally aware of this book. This in fact drew to my attention this aspect of my father's background, and for that I am grateful. There is here a hint of convergence of all-Ireland Protestant Home-Ruler experience through the Wolfe Tone Society's initiative. We were indeed beginning in the 1960s to lay the basis for reconstructing the inclusive 'Protestant, Catholic and Dissenter' nation adumbrated by Wolfe Tone, in the context of our attempt to politicise and demilitarise the republican tradition. This process was wrecked by the storming of the defenceless Falls Road by the B-Specials in August 1969, and the consequent emergence of the Provisional I.R.A.

EDITOR'S NOTES

1   The editor is working on a biographical project and would be
    interested in hearing from historians or others interested in the
    period. He has collected much information on this and other
    subjects touched on in this introduction. Please write to Dr Roy
    H.W. Johnston, Techne Associates, P.O. Box 1881, Rathmines,
    Dublin 6, or, preferably, e-mail him at rjtechne@iol.ie.

2   See note 1 above.

3   The Albert Kahn Foundation was based in Paris and was
    dedicated to developing a global network of liberal intellectuals,
    having potential as opinion leaders, in opposition to the perceived
    threat of world war. It remained in active existence subsequent to
    the war, though its funding source dried up after the 1929 crash.
    It was taken over by French public funding sources, and remains
    in existence at 10 quai de 4 Septembre, 92100 Boulogne, as a
    museum and library.

4   See note 3 above.

5   There is nothing about the Thomas Davis Society in the Trinity
    College Dublin archive. The editor would welcome contact from
    anyone having records or memoirs of it (see note 1 above).

6   See note 1 above.

7   Joseph Devlin (1871–1934) re-established the Ancient Order of
    Hibernians and was its President (1905–34).

8   Geoffrey Dawson, then editor of *The Times*, visited Ireland in
    October 1911; he met a variety of people including Sir Horace
    Plunkett, George Russell and Canon Hannay, and picked up a feel
    for this positive perception, as well as how it was under threat from
    Ulster, and how this threat was totally underestimated by Plunkett.
    See also R.A. Anderson, *With Plunkett in Ireland* (Dublin, 1983).

9   Sir Roger Casement, from Ballycastle Co. Antrim, had espoused
    the Home Rule cause after his experiences of the workings of the
    imperial system while in its service. He was subsequently associated
    with the attempt to get arms from Germany in support of the
    1916 Rising, for which he was hanged.

10 Captain Jack White, of Whitehall near Ballymena, had served in
    the Boer War, in which his father played a leading role. His
    autobiography, *Misfit* (London, 1930), shows him untypical of the
    landed ascendancy. He helped to found the Irish Citizen Army
    with James Connolly in 1913 (see note 15 below).

11 Alice Stopford Green was the widow of J. R. Green the historian;
    she had become an historian in her own right, having published
    The Making of Ireland and its Undoing (Dublin and London, 1908),
    Irish Nationality (Dublin and London, 1911), and *The Old World*

(Dublin and London, 1912). See also Leon Ó Broin *Protestant Nationalists in Revolutionary Ireland: The Stopford Connection* (Dublin, 1985).

[12] Kenneth Armour, son of J.B. Armour ('Armour of Ballymoney') read a paper in 1966 at a seminar in Dublin organised by the Wolfe Tone Societies, as part of the then attempt to resurrect an all-Ireland democratic tradition inclusive of the Protestant community. For more on J.B. Armour and many other Protestant Home Rule supporters see Flann Campbell, *The Dissenting Voice* (Belfast, 1991).

[13] See note 1 above.

[14] See note 1 above.

[15] For the role of James Connolly in this context see C.D. Greaves, *Life and Times of James Connolly* (London, 1961). Connolly's collected polemical writings for this period were edited by Desmond Ryan and published by Three Candles, Dublin, *c.* 1949.

[16] Much background to these events can be found in George Dangerfield's 1935 book *The Strange Death of Liberal England* (republished in 1997 by Serif, London). See also Catherine Shannon, *Arthur J. Balfour and Ireland* (Washington D.C., 1988), principally chapter 5, where background to the Larne gun-running is given in some detail, and Dangerfield's *The Damnable Question* (London, 1976).

[17] I am indebted to Gary Peatling (Oxford) for unearthing the fact that this political assessment was articulated by several nationalists during and after the war; see W. O'Brien, *The Irish Revolution and How it Came About* (London, 1923), pp. 186, 222–3, ch. 12, etc.: R. Lynd, *Ireland a Nation* (London, 1919), pp.10–18: J.J. Horgan, *Parnell to Pearse: Some Recollections and Reflections* (Dublin, 1948), pp. 327–37: A.S.Green, *Ourselves Alone in Ulster* (London, 1918). Also in the British radical liberal press: see *The Daily News*, (26 February, 1918), p. 2, (14 April 1917), p. 2: *The Nation*, vol. 22, (9 February 1918), pp. 587–8.

[18] *The Leader*, edited by D.P. Moran, was the mouthpiece of aggressive, exclusivist Catholic nationalism. See Conor Cruise O'Brien's *Ancestral Voices* (Dublin, 1994) for critical comment.

[19] The Wolfe Tone Societies (Dublin, Belfast and Cork) had emerged politically from the Wolfe Tone Directories set up in 1962 on the initiative of Cathal Goulding, then I.R.A. Chief of Staff, to organise events based on the bicentenary of the birth of Theobald Wolfe Tone (1763–98), commonly called the father of Irish republicanism, and originator of the aspiration to unify 'Protestant, Catholic and Dissenter under the common name of Irishman'. The process of politicising the republican movement in the 1960s was rooted in this aspiration, and the Wolfe Tone Societies attempted with

some successs to catalyse it. The 1963 seminars in the Mansion House included one with Hubert Butler as main speaker. The meeting which led subsequently to the foundation of Northern Ireland Civil Rights Association took place in 1966 in War Memorial Hall in Belfast on the initiative of the Wolfe Tone Societies. There was significant liberal Protestant participation, and Kadar Asmal, then leader of the Irish Anti-Apartheid Movement and now a Minister in the South African Government, was among the speakers.

[20] See note 9 above.

[21] Conor Cruise O'Brien was at this time flirting with politicising left-republicanism as his channel for entry to politics; he was under active consideration by Sinn Féin as a candidate for Mid-Ulster, for the seat subsequently taken by Bernadette Devlin. This episode, and other aspects of the process, touched upon in note 19 above, are ongoing topics of research by the writer (see note 1 above).

[22] Eoin (the 'Pope') O'Mahony was well known at the time as a 'character', conversationalist, writer and broadcaster, primarily on topics relating to genealogy. He welcomed the chance to preside at public events, and was in demand for this purpose, because he always knew everything about the seed, breed and generation of everyone on the platform and could introduce them entertainingly.

NOTE ON THE TEXT

The text of this edition is that of the original book published in Dublin by Sealy, Bryers & Walker in 1913. It is complete and the author's own punctuation and footnotes have been retained.

Some explanatory notes by Roy Johnston, which are numbered in the text, are located at the end of chapters.

The Appendix was not included in the original edition.

CHAPTER I

INTRODUCTION.—OBJECT IN WRITING.

It is stated by responsible politicians that if the project of granting Home Rule to Ireland is persisted in, the result will be civil war in Ulster. Public meetings have been held, addressed by Members of Parliament, and even members of former administrations, in which people have been told that the preservation of their civil and religious liberties will probably require a resort to arms. Rifles and bayonets have been imported, where it has been possible to avoid the vigilance of the Customs authorities, and placed at the disposal of certain political societies; drilling has been openly indulged in, while what is intended as the future Provisional Government has already assembled. Almost the whole of the press on one side reports these proceedings with approval, and occasionally publishes leaders warning the authorities of the crisis that will be precipitated if any attempt is made to interfere with them.[1] By a document which was circulated on rather short notice in almost all the Protestant Churches last year, the support of the leaders of religion has been obtained in advance.[2] The consequence is that civil war is placed before the country as something so much of the nature of an obvious duty on the part of anyone who disapproves of the Home Rule Bill or any of its provisions, that nobody pauses to consider if it is really necessary, if it is likely to succeed, and what its consequences will be. These are comparatively trifling details to leaders whose connection with Ulster mainly consists in running down from Dublin or London once or twice a year to address political meetings there, or more recently to inspect guards of honour, but the matter is one of vital importance for the writer,[3] whose home happens to be in a district which is likely to be a centre of whatever disturbance there may be, and who has hitherto managed to live in peace and harmony with his neighbours, without regard to their religion or politics, as have most of his relatives, some of whom are now being supplied with arms, and instigated to kill or get killed in whatever manner may seem most conducive to bringing about a change of Ministry.

He, therefore, proposes to consider a few of the reasons usually given in justification of a resort to force, and some of the consequences that will probably ensue if this happens, in the hope that by this means something may be done to clear the political atmosphere, and that, if there is a civil war, those who take part in it may at least know what they are fighting for, and what results they are likely to bring about by doing so.

So great is the power of the phrase-maker that probably the expression rendered famous by Lord Randolph Churchill, when he informed the world that "Ulster will fight and Ulster will be right," would be considered by the ordinary man a full and complete answer on all the points I have suggested. It is, however, even more dangerous to put one's trust in phrases than in princes, and Palmerston's brilliant epigram that tenant right meant landlord wrong conduced to a superficial treatment of one of the most serious of Irish problems, which was the cause of untold misery in Ulster as well as the other parts of the country. A blind assumption of the correctness of the principle laid down in the other phrase may lead to consequences even more disastrous, and it will be one of my principal objects, instead of taking the truth of this proposition for granted, to examine the grounds on which it is based.

It will probably be conceded that there are some things which, while desirable in themselves, may be purchased at too high a price, and that war, and especially civil war, is such a very high price, that the advantages to be obtained, or the disadvantages to be avoided, would have to be of an overwhelming nature in order to justify it. A great many people do not like the Insurance Act, but nobody dreams of heading a revolt on account of it. The English Nonconformists did not like Mr. Balfour's Education Bill, but they confined themselves to passive resistance, and most of them have tired even of that. The South African Republics look better when painted red on the map than they did in their former colours, but there is considerable misgiving as to whether the change was worth £250,000,000 and 20,000 lives. The advantages of retaining the present system of government in Ireland, assuming it can be retained indefinitely, the difficulties of which will appear later on, would have to be very great indeed, and the drawbacks of the system proposed to be substituted to be of a most serious character, before a resort to arms if seriously intended would be justifiable. If not seriously intended, and the whole thing is a mere attempt to frighten the British electors by threats which there is no intention of putting into execution, the conduct of those who would deceive their followers in Ireland, in order that they may deceive the public in Great Britain, would seem too reprehensible for belief, were it not that it has acknowledged precedents in connection with the same question. The biography of Lord Randolph Churchill shows that while he was repeating on the platform "Ulster will fight and Ulster will be right," in his letters to Lord Salisbury he described this course as playing the Orange card, and having by the help of the Orange card got his party and himself into office, he had no hesitation in recommending a policy of governing Ireland through the instrumentality of the Catholic Bishops. In view of the fact that political leaders, however much they may find it desirable to talk about taking their followers into their confidence, cannot do so without showing their hand to the other side, and consequently risking their game, even if their projects were always such as would secure the approval and co-operation of their supporters, it is necessary sometimes to take their statements with a certain amount of salt, sometimes to read between the lines of them, and sometimes to consider what is unsaid rather than what is said. There is the further difficulty expressed by the proverb, that it is easier to raise the devil than to lay him, that in spite of the fact that the Covenant was so worked as to surrender practically into the hands of one man the right of private judgment on the part of those who signed it, his control over his followers may prove to be imperfect, and the latter having got arms in their hands may proceed to use them without orders, or in a manner for which they will find few apologists in the House of Commons. There is, it seems to me, a good deal more risk of anarchy than of civil war, but as the consequences of this would be even more mischievous, this circumstance affords small consolation. There exists, however, plenty of good feeling and commonsense in the province, if it could only find a voice, which I hope it will, if I succeed in showing any considerable section of the population even a glimpse of the dangers in which they are likely to be involved, if the threat to resist Home Rule by force of arms is carried out.

Fortunately, or perhaps unfortunately, nobody in Ulster nowadays has any conception of the horrors of war, and, above all, of civil war. Yet a very scant acquaintance with history, or even a casual reading of the recent newspapers, will show anyone that these horrors are very real and very great. Apart from all question of the loss of life in action, any war involves much expenditure of money, great destruction of property, and cessation of, or very grave interference with, the commercial and industrial life of the nations engaged in it; in addition to all this a civil war involves the temporary destruction or paralysis of the institutions of government. In the state of affairs that ensues, the worst elements of the population find occasion to gratify their most criminal instincts. Neither life, property, nor female honour is safe. The leaders of the Ulster movement may think that they have their men under complete control and discipline, but the whole teaching of history goes to show that you cannot overthrow the settled institutions of government without giving free rein, at any rate for a time, to the forces of disorder. In addition to all this, religion has been so mixed up with politics in the discussion of this question, that riots among the lower classes are bound to break out, and a sort of "civil and religious" warfare will reinforce the elements of hooliganism which exist in every community.

Consequently, when we are told that civil war is the only alternative to accepting the Home Rule Bill, and that Ulster has made up its mind it will have the former rather than the latter, it is surely worth while to inquire whether of the two evils Ulster is really choosing the lesser, and whether her choice may not result in her obtaining both, and in a very aggravated form, since the position of those who have taken to arms unsuccessfully is necessarily for some time very unpleasant. The real truth seems to be that the horrors of civil war are entirely ignored, or, at any rate largely minimised, and the evils ensuing from the acceptance of the Home Rule Bill by Ulster are exaggerated beyond all reasonable limits. My own opinion is that if Ulster appeals to force, she will do more harm to herself than the Home Rule Bill could possibly do if it were ten times as bad as it is represented to be. With the analogies that are usually supposed to justify this course I shall deal in the following chapter.

EDITOR'S NOTES

[1] See Appendix, p. 195.
[2] I have been unable to trace this document and would welcome a copy or a pointer to its possible location.
[3] Johnston's family was then living near Dungannon, a mixed district.

CHAPTER II

COMPARISON WITH 1688. THE SUPPOSED DANGER TO PROTESTANTISM.

I begin by stating clearly that I make no attempt to support the doctrine that it is better to submit to any form of government rather than rebel. There are times when rebellion is a clear duty. It is generally agreed that the Protestants of Ireland were justified in their rebellion against the government of King James II, as the outlook was so uncertain, and the king's attitude so notorious, that a too great regard for legality on their part might have led to the loss not merely of their privileges but of their liberties.

It certainly was a doubtful issue then whether Protestantism or Roman Catholicism was to be the official religion in Great Britain and Ireland, and in those days not to be of the official religion was a much more serious matter than it is now, when the principles of religious toleration have been almost universally accepted, and nearly every town of a few thousand inhabitants has the chapels of at least four or five different religious bodies. All the progress of two hundred years cannot be wiped out in a day, and the common argument that the civil and religious liberties of Protestants are in danger requires something more than a reference to the events of 1688 to justify it. Let us compare the state of things then and now.

In those days Protestantism was in very real danger. France was the most powerful country in Europe, and France was strongly Catholic. Even in England the Protestant interest was infinitely less strong then than now. The king was a Roman Catholic. The people of England had on three previous occasions—under Henry VIII, Queen Mary, and

Queen Elizabeth—shown their willingness to acquiesce in the religion of the Court, and, the King's power being then far greater than it is now, they might possibly in any case have been dragooned into compliance. The population of England differed by only a few millions from that of Ireland, and Ireland was predominantly Catholic. If King James had won in Ireland, he would have carried the war into England and Scotland, and if successful would have established his religion as the State religion. The Irish Protestants by their resistance at Derry and Enniskillen prevented the success of that scheme. They were thus instrumental in keeping the upper hand for Protestantism, not only in Ireland but in England and Scotland as well. Is there any analogy in the present condition of affairs? The population of Great Britain is now ten times that of Ireland, and only three fourths of Ireland is Catholic. Great Britain is at present predominantly Protestant. The British Empire has come into being, throughout which the principles of religious toleration are recognised, while the majority of its inhabitants are Protestants of one kind or other. France is strongly anti-clerical, a Protestant empire has been established in Germany, and the political system of Europe has ceased to turn on questions of religion, or indeed in most cases to take any account of it at all. Consequently Protestantism is in no danger in Great Britain or anywhere else. Even if Catholicism were as strong in Europe as it was in the seventeenth century, while Ireland remains an island and Britain commands the sea, Protestantism in Ireland can be in no danger. The next largest naval Powers at the present day being Germany, which is Protestant, and France, which is anti-Catholic, under no conceivable circumstances is Protestantism in Ireland in any danger of being seriously interfered with, quite independently of the fact of such interference having gone out of fashion.

The Irish Parliament which it is proposed to create is a strictly subordinate Parliament, dependant for income and its very existence on the Imperial Parliament, in which there is an overwhelming Protestant majority. Consequently, however bigoted Irish Catholics may be, and most people who live

among them find them easy enough to get on with, so long as
they agree to differ on matters of religion, it would be the
height of bad policy on their part to indulge in any action
which might be construed as an injustice to Protestants—active
persecution is out of the question—and self-interest, if nothing
else, will induce them to steer a fairly straight course; no
Protestant seriously apprehends that he will be interfered with
in the exercise of his religion unless it should take the form of
attempting to convert Catholics, which is a somewhat risky
proceeding even under present conditions. An attempt on the
part of Catholics to convert Protestants would lead to equally
unpleasant consequences; but, so far as I am aware, such
attempts are never made except in the single case of the off-
spring of mixed marriages with which I shall deal separately.

What the Irish Protestants really fear is, not that they will
be persecuted in the exercise of their religion, but that they
will be excluded from public appointments, and will be
subject to petty acts of administrative unfairness. I think that
the probability of either of these two events taking place is by
no means proved, but let us assume for the sake of argument
that they do take place to some extent. When reduced to this
form, it seems almost superfluous to inquire if it is worth while
to plunge the country into civil war in order that a few
Protestants rather than Catholics shall hold public appointments. What difference does it make to the average Protestant
whether Mr. Campbell or Mr. I. O'Brien is Lord Chancellor,
or Sir E. Carson or Mr. Moriarty Attorney-General?[1] The
number of public appointments in the direct gift of the
Government is not by any means unlimited, while in regard
to those under the control of local bodies, if the question of
religion exercises any influence in filling them, it will do so
whether there is Home Rule or not. A civil war based on this
ground is rather in the nature of locking the stable door after
the steed is stolen, and to have been effective should have
been fought when the Unionists passed the Local Government
Act of 1898. After all, the average Protestant, not possessed of
aristocratic connections, can console himself with the reflection
that so far as he is concerned, it makes very little difference

who holds the appointments, since in any case it will not be he, and may even venture to hope that it will be easier to overcome the handicap of religion in the future than it has been to overcome that of the absence of blue blood and aristocratic connections in the past. I shall show presently that, although the Local Government Act has been in force for fifteen years, there is still a very considerable number of Protestants in the service of the local bodies in those counties where the majority of the population is Catholic, whereas it is a notorious fact that in predominantly Protestant parts of Ulster hardly a single Catholic is employed in a position carrying a decent salary. For posts of hewers of wood and drawers of water, there is of course no discrimination, and even the most zealous political Protestants take anybody they can get. Would the Catholics be held justified in rebelling against the Union on the ground that it has deprived them of their fair share of appointments in Ulster, or even in Ireland as a whole, which was the case until the last few years, and still is to a very large extent? To ask such a question is to answer it.

There remains the question of administrative unfairness. It is not a subject on which one can dogmatise, for the simple reason that it is almost entirely a matter of opinion, and there are hardly any materials to go on as to the extent to which it will take place, or whether it will take place at all. I would point out, however, that even if in certain cases the persons in authority are so ill-advised as to indulge in it, the scope of their action will be limited by law, public opinion, the presence of a large number of Protestant members in the Irish Parliament, and, in the last resort, by the presence of representatives of the Irish Protestants in the British Parliament, whose future attitude towards the Irish Parliament will largely depend on the wisdom and ability with which it conducts its business. There are many reasons, financial and otherwise, why an Irish administration should keep on good terms with Westminster, and to go out of its way to fulfil the dismal prophecies of the opponents of Home Rule would be an act of folly of which the Irish leaders are hardly likely to be guilty. Acts of administrative unfairness can be indulged in by local bodies as well as by governments, but their number must have been extremely rare, or more would have been heard of them at a time when every such incident furnishes political capital of the highest quality, and supplies the concrete instances which pass current as proofs of a general argument.

As I write, I notice a statement by the Right Rev. Dr. Plunkett, Protestant Bishop of Tuam, in his address to the Protestant Synod, in which he is reported to have expressed the conviction that under Home Rule it would not be the fault of the Catholic people of the West if the happy relations that exist between them and their Protestant neighbours did not continue with increasing warmth. I do not know the politics of Dr Plunkett, or whether he has any, but it is a notorious fact that the intensity of the apprehension said to be felt by Irish Protestants varies almost directly according to their numerical preponderance. If anyone doubts this, let him compare the tone of a Unionist paper published in Dublin, such as the *Irish Times*, with that of one of the Unionist papers published in Belfast. In other words, where the Protestant element in the population is most feeble and most unprotected against injustice, it is sympathetic or indifferent, while where it is in overwhelming preponderance, and well able to take care of itself under all circumstances, it is violently hostile. Do the Ulster Protestants ever ask themselves if they are not to some extent to blame for this estrangement of feeling? Does the public celebration with bands and banners of victories over their fellow-countrymen in the past tend to promote racial harmony? I have yet to learn that the British inhabitants of the Transvaal flaunt in the faces of the Boers the surrender at Paardeberg, or that those in Canada treat the French Canadians as an inferior race on the strength of the victory on the Heights of Abraham. Do the French Republicans go out of their way to remind the population of La Vendée that they crushed them 120 years ago when they happened to take the other side in the civil dissension that then prevailed, and are prepared to do it again as often as necessary?[2] The fact is that principles and methods are applied in Ireland, which in any other part of the world would be considered, to put it mildly, the height of bad taste, and, in view of the manner in which they keep open old wounds, would probably be sternly suppressed by law.[3] In the South and West, where nothing of this sort takes place, the two sections of the population usually live in harmony and friendship. It is only in the North, and only, I might almost add, at certain seasons in the year, that the relations are strained. If the Protestants of the North were to follow the example of one of the Bishops of their own Church, and treat the rest of the nation as fellow-countrymen and not as hereditary enemies, the result would probably surprise them. Their present attitude reminds one irresistibly of the words of the French naturalist—"this animal is very vicious; if one attacks it it defends itself".

Assuming, however that Protestantism is in as much danger now as it was in 1688, the question remains are the Unionists of Great Britain to be relied on to defend the interests of Protestantism? The Roman Catholics of Great Britain who are not of Irish descent are Unionists almost to a man. The English Catholic peers voted against the Home Rule Bill in the House of Lords. The Catholics of England oppose Home Rule because, as they say, if Ireland obtains Home Rule the influence of the Roman Catholic Church in Ireland will be lessened. The Duke of Norfolk, the chief Roman Catholic peer in Great Britain, is a Unionist. His brother, Lord Edmund Talbot, is Chief Whip of the Unionist Party. The following extracts from his speeches will therefore, I hope, be received in Ulster with the respect due to his position, even if it should lessen that for the men who meekly take their orders from him when in England but become good political Protestants the moment they set foot in the province for whose interests they feel such great concern. Lord Edmund Talbot is reported to have stated as follows:—

"Things of a most offensive character, things displaying most narrow-minded ignorance and bigotry, had been uttered and written against his (the Catholic) religion by those who were undoubtedly strong opponents of Home Rule, not by responsible leaders of the Unionist Party, but by what he might term the third-rate type of lecturer, who found it conveniently easy to dilate in anger and venom on matters of religion, either through incapability or lack of intelligence to understand the question as a whole."

In a speech at Liverpool on the 22nd October, 1912, the same speaker is reported to have expressed the following sentiments with reference to the probable effect of Home Rule on the position of the Roman Catholic Church in Ireland:—

"If I am compelled to look on the question as a Roman Catholic from a Roman Catholic point of view alone in regard to its bearing on Roman Catholic religion in Ireland, then I say without hesitation, looking at the actual Bill now before us, that I can hardly conceive any greater disaster to the Roman Catholic religion in Ireland than that this Bill should become law."

The South African war has scarcely escaped the memory of present-day Ulstermen. The Boers were Dutch, or French Huguenots, by descent, and Presbyterians in religion. Except for a slight Scotch element on his part they belonged to the same race as William of Orange, and were of the same religion as practically one-half of the Protestants of Ulster. When that war was just begun, the Lieutenant of an English county, presumably a Unionist, expressed sentiments of such a kind about President Kruger and the psalm-singing characteristics which he shared with many Ulster Presbyterians, that I cannot refrain from quoting them. They should form interesting reading for those who have signed the Ulster Covenant, and those who held special services in connection with it. He said:—

"Neither you nor I believe in these perpetual appeals to Providence in the wrong place and at the wrong time. Neither do we believe in these continual quotations from Scripture. We do not believe, either you or I or anybody else here, in the man who holds the Bible in one hand and the Mauser rifle in the other. And another bit of advice I should like to give you is this—if you meet a gentleman, a somewhat aged gentleman, whose name begins with a K, anywhere down Pretoria way, I ask you to make him sing Psalms out of the wrong side of his mouth, and as to his cant, drive it down his throat with a dose of lyddite and three inches of bayonet to keep it there."

It is now pretty generally admitted that that war was quite unnecessary and was a huge mistake from first to last. It was brought about by a Unionist Government in the interests of some South African financiers and mine owners, most of whom were not even Christians. The South African Boers were and are one of the most intensely Protestant peoples on earth. It is hard to believe that the party which wantonly forced on a war with a people of the same race as William III and the same religion as the Scottish Covenanters, and did so, moreover, at the bidding of financiers, many of whom were German Jews, has or ever had any special enthusiasm for the cause of Protestantism as such.

The Unionist party in England is admittedly the clerical party. They used their position in 1902 to pass an Education Bill establishing the principle of denominational education in English primary schools, and did so with the assistance of the votes of Irish Unionist members, who in this respect, as in many others, did not reflect the feelings of their constituents. This Bill outraged the feelings of Nonconformists in England, and the Protestantism of English Nonconformists is just as strong as that of Irish Unionists. While the Unionist Party in general suffers from the odium of the passing of that Act, Irish Unionists will appeal in vain to English Nonconformists to help them in their present difficulties.

But it is not merely in English affairs that the Unionists are a clerical party. The whole of Irish primary and secondary education is run on denominational lines. This is perhaps as much a result of the circumstances arising from the Union as of deliberate policy on the part of the Unionists, but I have yet to learn that the Unionist Party when in power made any attempt to check the influence of the priest in education, be he Catholic, Episcopalian, or Presbyterian; or when in opposition made any protest against its continuance.

Not only is this the case, but the Unionist Party has before now made appeals to the Roman Catholic Bishops in Ireland, and, there is reason to believe, even to the Vatican itself, in order to win over to their side the influence of the Roman Catholic Church in Ireland.

In 1886, on the rejection of the Home Rule Bill and the return of the Conservatives to power, an agrarian agitation known as the "Plan of Campaign" was started in Ireland. Whether Rome was actually appealed to by the British Government is an open question; there are good grounds for believing that such an appeal was made, unofficially of course. At any rate one Mgr. Persico was sent by the Holy See to Ireland in July, 1887, to investigate and report. The result was a rescript from Rome, issued in April, 1888, condemning the Plan of Campaign and boycotting, on the ground that they were contrary both to natural justice and to Christian charity.

This was not the only occasion on which the Unionist Party tried to utilise the authority of the "priest in politics." In a letter quoted in the "Life of Lord Randolph Churchill" (vol. ii, p. 4, Oct.14, 1885), we read how that statesman proposed to Lord Salisbury to win over the Church to Unionism. He writes:—

> "I have no objection to Sexton and Healy knowing the deliberate intention of the Government on the subject of Irish education, but it would not do for the letter or communication to be made public, for the effect of publicity on Lancashire would be unfortunate . . . It is the bishops entirely to whom I look in future to mitigate or postpone the Home Rule onslaught. Let us only be enabled to occupy a year with the education question. By that time I am certain Parnell's party will have become seriously disintegrated. Personal jealousies, Government influences, Davitt and Fenian intrigues, will be at work upon the devoted band of eighty. The bishops, who in their hearts hate Parnell, and don't care a scrap for Home Rule, having safely acquired control of Irish education, will, according to my calculation, complete the rout. That is my policy, and I know it is sound and good, and the only possible Tory

policy." And again he wrote:— "My opinion is that if you approach the archbishops through proper channels, if you deal in friendly remonstrances and active assurances . . . the tremendous force of the Catholic Church will gradually and insensibly come over to the side of the Tory Party."

But in 1886, as "the tremendous force of the Catholic party" had not come over to his side, he "decided to play the Orange card, which, please God, will prove a trump." When he came to Belfast and raised the famous cry in the Ulster Hall that "Ulster will fight and Ulster will be right" he had only just returned from making overtures to the "Scarlet Woman."

When we consider the position of the Roman Catholic Church in Irish education to-day in the light of the above revelations of Unionist principles and policy, it is not difficult to see that the real Rome Rule party in Ireland is not the Home Rule party, but the party which is determined at all costs to maintain the Union, and finds this the most practical means of doing so.

In future when Unionist speakers wax eloquent about the twin causes of Protestantism and the Union, Irish Protestants will, I hope, be in a better position to estimate the value of such statements.

In view of the facts adduced above, it is surely not too much to assert that the Unionist Party as a whole has no genuine enthusiasm for the cause of Protestantism as such, and that if they seem at present to lend a sympathetic ear to the religious fears of Irish Protestants, it is only because they have in view some ulterior object which they hope to gain by the exploitation of those fears. Is it not possible that once more, as in 1886, the Unionist Party has "decided to play the Orange card, which, please God, will prove a trump." It is surely worth while for the Ulster Protestant to inquire what are the reasons why English Unionism is at present apparently so enamoured of his Protestantism. The reasons will appear in the sequel. It is also worth his while to enquire what are the evils he proposes to avoid by accepting the role of a card in the Tory pack.

The idea that Home Rule will lead to the wholesale oppression of Protestantism as such in Ireland is generally scouted in responsible circles and in the debates on the Home Rule Bill in Parliament has been disclaimed by the recognised leaders of the Unionist Party. The *Cork Constitution* of May 2nd, 1911, which is a Unionist paper circulating in the South of Ireland, and which may be supposed to know what it is talking about, in quoting a statement in a letter from a Tipperary Quaker to the effect that "whatever legislative changes might take place, there would be nothing to prevent Protestants and Roman Catholics from living harmoniously together," added the following:— "Few will be found to take serious objection to this statement, for it is not so much religious as political intolerance that is feared by the minority in Ireland."

In other words, a Nationalist body, whether County Council or Parliament, will elect Nationalists to places of power and emolument, just as Unionist County Councils and Parliaments elect Unionists. It is only natural that the respective political parties should prefer to advance their own adherents to positions of which they have the gift. If this is political intolerance, practically all party government is political intolerance, and political intolerance is the keynote of the English constitutional system as it is worked at present.

Under the Local Government Act of 1898 opportunities for such intolerance were given to the Catholics in the greater part of Ireland. The Irish Unionists before the passing of that Act declared that they feared it worse than Home Rule. According to the "A.B.C. of Unionism" their fears were justified. "In the three provinces outside of Ulster there are only fifteen Unionists on the twenty-four Co. Councils of those provinces. The Nationalists number 684. In Ulster, where Unionists are better able to hold their own, the division is about equal, as between Unionists and Nationalists."

This, like many other political arguments, sounds very impressive till one comes to analyse it, on which it appears that in Ireland, as elsewhere, people prefer to elect as their representatives those who are in sympathy with them, rather than those whose views are opposed to theirs, and that the mass of the Irish electors are Nationalists. In Ulster the number of persons elected on each side is roughly in proportion to the number of voters belonging to each political party. Ireland would indeed be an isle of saints were any other result possible. The question is not whether Unionists are not elected as such where the majority of the voters are Nationalists, but whether Protestants are excluded merely on account of their religion. Of this there is no evidence, and the analogy of the Irish representation in Parliament, where nine of the Nationalist members are Protestants, while Parnell, for many years the idol of a large part of the country, was one, goes to show that religion in itself is no bar in Ireland any more than it is in Britain, and that the essential thing in each case is to find constituents with whose views and aspirations one is in sympathy, or who can be persuaded to that effect.

But the real question is not so much whether Protestants get elected to local bodies where the Nationalist element predominates, as whether Protestants as such are excluded from public appointments in the gift of such bodies. In fairness it must be admitted that the existing local bodies took over the staffs appointed under the former regime, under which, I fear, a preference was in many instances given to Protestants. Since 1898, however, these local councils have had the power of dismissing their former officials as well as of making new appointments. So far from carrying out wholesale dismissals of Protestant officials, the Nationalist councils have in every case treated them fairly, and have in more than one case given them substantial increases of salary. An inquiry into the subject of appointments made since 1900 revealed the following state of affairs:—In the case of 176 public boards—County Councils, City and Town Councils, Urban and Rural District Councils, and Boards of Guardians—since 1900 187 public appointments have been given to Protestants. Not only so, but nearly 400 Protestants have been elected as members of those bodies. The case of the Clonmel Corporation is very striking. I append a list of the Protestants who have been appointed by that body since 1900:

Borough Analyst,	£10 per year	
Consulting Gas Engineer: 25 guineas	”	”
” ” ” 30 guineas	”	”
Assistant Gas Manager,	£120 ”	”
Head Master Technical School,	£200 ”	”
Art Master Technical School,	£125 ”	”
Commercial Teacher Technical School,	£125 ”	”
Manual Instructor Technical School,	£155 ”	”
Secretary and Headmaster Technical School,	£260 ”	”
Veterinary Surgeon for Corporation horses,	£15 ”	”

Clonmel is, it must be borne in mind, in a county where Roman Catholics form nearly 95 per cent. of the population.

Is it too much to hope that what Clonmel does to-day the rest of the country will do to-morrow or the day after? Or even if it should not, is it so very unjust that people who have been almost entirely excluded from public appointments for 350 years should follow the example of their opponents in acting on the principle that charity begins at home? If this is a sufficient ground for civil war, the United States would have one after each Presidential election involving a change of party, when there is a redistribution of appointments practically from top to bottom in the whole public service, and all the Irish rebellions that have taken place would have been held justifiable if the leaders only had had sense enough to have stated their case properly.

The direst results were apprehended from the Local Government Act of 1898, so much so that the Unionist Party thought it necessary to protect at least one section of the population from the consequences of its own revolutionary legislation, by stereotyping the amount of the landlord's contribution to the rates and transferring it to the tenant, whose rent was reduced by a corresponding amount; while at the same time an Imperial grant of £750,000 was given in aid of Irish local finance.

As a matter of fact, the terrible oppression and waste that were apprehended from the action of the local bodies never took place. So far from having mismanaged everything, as it was alleged they would, the Local Government Board Reports bear witness to their efficiency. That for the year 1903, when, be it noted, the Unionist Government was still in office, states:—

"The general administration of the Local Government Act by County and District Councils continues on the whole to be satisfactory, and the manner in which the several local bodies transact their business calls for no special observation. The collection of rates has been efficiently carried on. Very great and very creditable improvements have taken place in the care of the sick."

There is no need to look up official reports for evidence of this; the fact is patent. Anyone whose memory extends back for ten or fifteen years cannot fail to have noticed the great improvement in roads, in hospitals and dispensaries, in sanitation and all departments of public effort, that has taken place during the period. Why, at least until the experiment has been tried, should it be assumed that Ireland is almost unique amongst the civilised countries of the world in having an inherent incapacity to govern itself? It has never had the chance of trying, as even when it had an independent Parliament, the executive was not subject to the Parliament, but was controlled from England, and the trouble that led to the loss of its legislative independence was largely due to the action of the executive in going its own way, in total disregard both of the Parliament and of the public opinion of the country. The Irish Unionists feared the Local Government Act worse than Home Rule, and their fears turned out to be entirely groundless. Those in regard to Home Rule may turn out equally so, and at any rate, unless the Nationalists possess greater cohesion among themselves than they do at present, they have quite a respectable chance of being able to play the same part at Dublin as the Nationalists have done at Westminster, and control the situation by the possession of the casting vote. They would probably be a very influential party under any circumstances, and further on I shall indicate a modification in the scheme of representation which I have no doubt their leaders could obtain for the asking, which would lead to such a distribution of political power that Ulster not merely would have nothing to fear, but in combination with the moderate elements in the other provinces would generally be in a position to rule the country. Are Irish Protestants so wanting in self-confidence and in regard for their own dignity that they must spend so much of their lives in shouting before they are hurt that nobody any longer troubles to listen to them? If they possess even half the virtues their leaders claim on their behalf, they will come out on top under any circumstances, and would be extremely ill-advised to put themselves in the wrong by taking the violent measures they are asked to do, until it is seen whether any necessity for them is likely to arise.

EDITOR'S NOTES

[1] The only one of these names remembered now is Carson; the list includes one then prominent Catholic and one Protestant notable for each position.
[2] The Protestant community in Portadown, in the infamous Garvaghy Road context of the 1990s, might usefully consider this key paragraph and the one which follows.
[3] Under the current Race Relations Act in Britain it is unlikely that dominance-asserting parades of whites would be allowed in the black communities of London.

CHAPTER III

SOME GENERAL CONSIDERATIONS ON THE RELATIONS BETWEEN CHURCH AND STATE, AND AN OUTLINE OF THE ARRANGEMENTS ELSEWHERE. THE NE TEMERE AND MOTU PROPRIO DECREES.

A great deal of what is written about the danger to Irish Protestantism and Irish Protestants under Home Rule depends on the failure to distinguish between the theoretical claims of most religions and the practical applications of them. Most religions—the Roman Catholic is by no means the only one— if carried to their extreme logical conclusions, as they unfortunately were a few hundred years ago, would produce extremely awkward consequences both for their own followers and for those outside their pale. In the interval, however, the common-sense of mankind has been at work, and gradually a sort of working arrangement has been evolved, by which those parts of a religious theory which are impracticable are quietly dropped or suppressed, just as numerous ancient statutes are never enforced because they have become obsolete, though still technically the law of the land. When Parliament can find the time, it occasionally repeals some of these obsolete and unworkable statutes, but as it is part of the convention of a religion that it is always right and entirely right, it cannot afford to act like Parliament, which spends most of its time in attempting to correct its own mistakes, since it is not allowed to admit that it has ever made any. Consequently a little rummaging in the historical lumber-room of the other side will always supply abundant material to any politico-religious leader who finds it convenient to create a panic. I quite admit that the theoretical claims of the Church of Rome are very great, and merely enquire where at the present day it is able to give effect to them, even where practically the whole population are members of its communion. I search the map of Europe in vain. Certainly not in France, where the Government is strongly anti-clerical. Not in Italy, the Catholic people of which have in recent times deprived the Pope of his temporal power, and between the government of which and the Vatican there is a standing feud. Not in Portugal, where the relations between the Government and the Church are even more strained than in France or Italy. Even in Spain, which prides itself on being the most Catholic country in Europe, there is complete liberty of conscience. Why should it be assumed that in Ireland alone all the progress of the last three hundred years will count for nothing, and that Irish Protestants will suddenly find themselves, when the Home Rule Bill becomes law, caught up and dumped down in the middle of the sixteenth century? Especially when their co-religionists in the South and West, who might be expected to be there already, assure them there is nothing to be frightened about. It may interest those of my readers who are Presbyterians to learn that the theoretical position of their own Church is held by a competent observer to be just as hostile to present day ideas of civil liberty as is that of the Church of Rome. I would invite attention to the following extract from Mr. Andrew Lang's essay on the "Mystery of the Kirks" in his "Historical Mysteries", Nelson's edition. If the fact that Mr. Andrew Lang[1] was not a Presbyterian, and was not particularly sympathetic towards Presbyterians, is held to destroy the value of his criticism, the same objection will apply to most of the Protestant criticism of the attitude of the Roman Catholic Church. He writes:—

"Now, the fact is that the Church of Scotland has been, since August, 1560, a Kirk established by law (or by what was said to be a legal Parliament), yet had never, perhaps, for an hour attained its own full ideal relation to the State; had never been granted its entire claims, but only so much or so little of these as the political situation compelled the State to concede, or enabled it to withdraw . . .

"The position was stated thus, in 1851, by an Act of Declaration of the Free Kirk's Assembly: '*She holds still, and through God's grace ever will hold,* that it is the duty of civil rulers to recognise the truth of God according to His word, to promote and support the Kingdom of Christ without assuming any jurisdiction in it, or any power over it . . .'

"The State, in fact, if we may speak carnally, ought to pay the piper, but must not presume to call the tune . . .

"Knox's ideas, as far as he ever reasoned them out, reposed on this impregnable rock, namely that Calvinism, as held by himself, was an absolutely certain thing in every detail. If the State, or 'the civil magistrate', as he put the case, entirely agreed with Knox, then Knox was delighted that the State should regulate religion. The magistrate was to put down Catholicism, and other aberrations from the truth as it was in John Knox, with every available engine of the law, corporal punishment, prison, exile, and death. If the State was ready and willing to do all this, then the State was to be implicitly obeyed in matters of religion, and the power in its hands was God-given; in fact, the State was the secular aspect of the Church. Looking at the State in this ideal aspect, Knox writes about the obedience due to the magistrate in matters religious, after the manner of what, in this country, would be called the fiercest 'Erastianism'. The State 'rules the roast [*sic*, R.J.]' in all matters of religion and may do what Laud and Charles I perished in attempting, may alter forms of worship—always provided that the State absolutely agrees with the Kirk.

"Thus, under Edward VI, Knox would have desired the secular power in England, the civil magistrate, to forbid people to kneel at the celebration of the Sacrament. That was entirely within the competence of the State, simply and solely because Knox desired that people should not kneel. But when, long after Knox's death, the civil magistrate insisted, in Scotland, that people should kneel, the upholders of Knox's ideas denied that the magistrate (James VI) had any right to issue such an order, and they refused to obey while remaining within the established Church . . .

"Thus we see that the State was to be obeyed in matters of religion, when the State did the bidding of the Kirk, and not otherwise . . .

"The idea of Knox is that in a Catholic State the ruler is not to be obeyed in religious matters by the true believers; sometimes Knox wrote that the Catholic ruler ought to be met by 'passive resistance'; sometimes that he ought to be shot at sight. He stated these diverse doctrines in the course of eighteen months. In a Protestant country the Catholics must obey the Protestant ruler, or take their chances of prison, exile, fire, and death. The Protestant ruler, in a Protestant State, is to be obeyed in spiritual matters by Protestants, just as far as the Kirk may happen to approve of his proceedings, or even further, in practice, if there is no chance of successful resistance . . ."

But even Knox, living in the sixteenth century, did not allow his theories to run away with his common-sense or his natural feelings on the subject of right and wrong. In this connection I would invite attention to a further extract from Mr. Andrew Lang.

"Knox knew the difference between the ideal and the practical. It was the ideal that all non-convertible Catholics 'should die the death.' But the ideal was never made real; the State was not prepared to oblige the Kirk in this matter. It was the ideal that any of 'the brethren,' conscious of a vocation, and seeing a good opportunity, should treat an impenitent Catholic ruler as Jehu treated Jezebel. But if any brother had consulted Knox as to the propriety of assassinating Queen Mary, in 1561–67, he would have found out his mistake, and probably have descended the Reformer's stairs much more rapidly than he mounted them."

Is it unreasonable to suppose that Irish Catholics in the twentieth century will draw a similar distinction between the ideal and the practical?

The Church of England, owing to the nature of its relation to the State, and its being hedged in on almost every side by

Act of Parliament, is usually more moderate in her claims, but even she, I shall point out later on, has on some subjects adopted an attitude which, whether right or wrong, shows that the difficulties represented as being likely to arise in consequence of the claims of the Roman Catholic Church are of a general, not of a special nature, and may arise in connection with any Church, and under any system of government.

It is also assumed quite unnecessarily and in most cases erroneously, that when the claims of a person's religion and country come in conflict, it will be the country which will suffer. This was the basis of the laws excluding Roman Catholics from public employment, because the Pope claimed a power of releasing subjects from their allegiance, and hence it was argued Catholics must be bad subjects. The logic was excellent but for the fact that the assumptions were wrong, and the policy embodied in these Acts is now universally admitted to have been an unwise one, and has been thrown overboard by everybody. Lord Howard of Effingham, who commanded the English fleet sent against the Spanish Armada, which sailed against England with the Pope's special blessing, was a Catholic. All throughout the centuries, until within the last 60 or 70 years when the Pope lost his temporal power, kings and princes were fighting against him temporally while professing obedience to him spiritually, and I cannot recollect any instance where their subjects refused to follow them. Catholic soldiers fought for King William, and some Protestants for King James, including the head of the house of Abercorn of that day, and so topsy-turvy was the state of things at that time, as compared with the simplicity they have assumed since in popular imagination, that the sympathies of the Pope were actually on William's side, and the Catholic Court of Austria had prayers said for the success of his expedition. Coming to quite recent times, in 1881 the Pope issued a rescript condemning a public subscription then being raised for Mr. Parnell, and which at the time stood at £8,000. By the end of the year it had reached £37,000, hardly all of the balance of which can have been contributed by Protestants. General Sir William Butler was a Catholic, but he took part in the Red River expedition, which suppressed a rising of Canadian Catholics. Nor when he was in South Africa did the difference in religion between himself and the Boers imbue him with prejudice against them, and if his advice had been listened to, instead of that of persons more nearly approaching them in religion, Consols would probably be somewhat higher than they are at present.

Who have been the Irish leaders during the last two hundred years? Except O'Connell, who is pretty well forgotten,[2] practically all the principal ones have been Protestants. Is the regard for the memory of Grattan, or Lord Edward Fitzgerald, or Wolfe Tone, or Henry Joy M'Cracken, or Robert Emmet, or John Mitchel, or any of the others who worked or died for Ireland any less on account of the fact that they differed in religion from the majority of the people of the country they tried to serve? What regiments distinguished themselves most in the Boer war, and have always done more than their share of whatever fighting was to be done anywhere in the British dominions? They are recruited from the "hereditary enemies" about whom we hear so much in Ulster.

In view of the many great services of the Irish to the Empire abroad, they might be given credit for a little patriotism at home, provided they have a country in which they can take a legitimate pride, and not one in which the surest road to the highest positions in the State is to refer to them on every possible occasion in the most insulting language that political rancour can suggest.

Most of the subjects I have dealt with are matters falling within the knowledge or observation of my readers themselves, and all that has been necessary has been for them to divest themselves of traditional prejudices, and look at the questions from the point of view of an impartial outsider. Where this is not the case, I wish to ask them as little as possible to take anything on trust, and so propose to give extracts from authorities when practicable. I shall, therefore, insert here a number of quotations from a work of recognised rank, "A Political History of Contemporary Europe," by C. Seignobos,[3] of the University of Paris, English translation, second edition,

London, 1904, which will show the position of some of the principal Catholic countries of Europe in regard to religious liberty. Describing the settlement following the Restoration of 1814, he writes:—

"The two great Catholic monarchs preserved State control of the Church and religious liberty. Austria pre-erved Josephism with toleration, France the Napoleonic Concordat with equality of creeds. They restored neither compulsory unity of faith, nor independence of the Church; France did not even restore the religious orders nor the Church domains that the Revolution had destroyed. . . .

"In Germany, the Church of the times before the Revolution was not restored; not only the ecclesiastical principalities, but the convents, remained suppressed. The plan of a single regulation for the whole Confederation fell through. A new Church with new districts was established by special agreement between the Pope and the govern-ment of each state. Bavaria alone gave to this agreement the form of a Concordat (1817); it recognised in the Church the 'rights and privileges which appertain to it by divine order and canon law', but the Concordat was promulgated with an edict similar to Napoleon's organic articles, which, in spite of the protest of the Pope, guaranteed religious liberty. In the other German States, the Church was organised by a series of Papal bulls concerted with the governments. Everywhere the government preserved its power over the Church, and even continued, as in the eighteenth century, to interfere in the regulating of details in purely Church matters, liturgy, festivals, and pilgrimages.

"The Restoration re-established only an impoverished and subordinated Church."*

The Italian attitude on the subject is described as follows:—

"The Italian Government has adopted, since Cavour's time, the motto of the Catholic Liberals—a free Church in a free State. It tried to introduce the Belgian system in

* Seignabos (1901), p. 690.

Italy. On the one hand, it suppressed all that remained of the old compulsory Church authority, Church courts, tithes (1866), and established full religious liberty; later it adopted civil marriage; it suppressed the majority of the convents, and secularised the Church estates, replacing them with salaries for the secular clergy. On the other hand, it abolished the former subjection of the Church to the State, leaving the Pope free to appoint bishops, and reserved to the clergy their honorary privileges. But, as the Pope refused to negotiate, this organisation, though established in fact, remained unrecognised by the Church.

"The occupation of Rome in September, 1870, greatly aggravated the conflict. The Government, by the *law of guarantees*, promised to let the Pope enjoy the personal situation of a sovereign in his palace of the Vatican, to grant him an annual compensation for his lost revenues. . . . But Pius IX, declaring himself morally a *prisoner*, refused to negotiate . . . The conflict became a chronic one, and has not yet ceased."*

The principles of civil and religious liberty have, up till recently, made less progress in Spain than in any other Catholic country in Europe. Nevertheless, even there non-Catholic religions are very far from being proscribed or persecuted, and the relations of Church and State have not always been harmonious:

"In Spain, the conflict was violent after the revolution of 1868; for the first time in Spain unity of faith was officially abolished; the Constitution of 1869 proclaimed the public liberty of non-Catholic beliefs; then the clergy having opposed the government, the Cortes established civil marriage. Pius IX openly sided with Don Carlos, the legitimate King, and the breach was complete between the Holy See and the Spanish Government until the restoration of 1874. The Pope consented to recognise the government of Alphonso XII; but he did not secure the complete

* *Ibid.*, pp. 707–8.

restoration of unity of faith, and protested against the Constitution of 1876, which granted toleration of private worship for non-Catholics."*

Elsewhere Seignobos writes that

> In Spain: "The Cortes, finally elected in January 1876, and composed of ministerial deputies, voted the Constitution, including Article I: 'The Apostolic Catholic religion of Rome is the national religion; the nation assumes the obligation of supporting religion and its servants. No one is to be disturbed on account of his religious opinions nor for the form of his worship, provided he does not violate the respect due to Christian morality.'"†

Austria preserved *Josephism* up till 1848. In that year this system was abandoned, and the ecclesiastical authority became paramount; in 1867, however, a new Constitution was established which guaranteed complete religious liberty. Various laws were passed asserting the control of the State over the Church, and the Pope attempted in vain to annul them by means of his apostolic authority. According to Seignobos:—

> "The Austrian Government maintained its laws, affirming the right of the lay power to modify by its own sole authority even a regulation made in common with the Church authority. ". . . The conflict continued in the laws of 1873, and Austria returned to the system of Joseph II, but without restoring the old forms of State guardianship. The Church found itself in much the same position there as in France, except that it retained its control of marriage and records of population."‡

The whole situation has been put in a nutshell by the Protestant historian, Lecky, where he says, *vide* his "Clerical Influences,"⁴ as republished by Maunsell and Co, Dublin, 1911, page 24. This essay was written in 1861, but the state of

---

* *Ibid.*, p. 709.   † *Ibid.*, p. 316.   ‡ *Ibid.*, p. 708.

things described still exists, and is being carefully kept alive in the interests of class ascendancy:—

> "Unfortunately, however, there exists in Ireland a topic that effectually prevents discontent from languishing, or the sentiments of the two nations from coalescing. Sectarian animosity has completely taken the place of purely political feeling, and paralyses all the energies of the people. This is indeed the master curse of Ireland—the canker that corrodes all that is noble and patriotic in the country, and, we maintain, the direct and inevitable consequence of the Union. Much has been said of the terrific force with which it would rage were the Irish Parliament restored. We maintain, on the other hand, that no truth is more clearly stamped upon the page of history, and more distinctly discernible from the constitution of the human mind, than that a national feeling is the only effective check to sectarian passions. Nothing can be more clear than that the logical consequences of many of the doctrines of the Church of Rome would be fatal to an independent and patriotic policy in any land—nothing is more clear than that in every land, where a healthy national feeling exists, Roman Catholic politicians are both independent and patriotic . . ."

We are living in the twentieth century and not in the sixteenth. The religious fears of Irish Protestants form the driving force in their opposition to Home Rule for Ireland. If there were no religious difficulty practically every Protestant would be a Home Ruler. Protestants are told that their civil and religious liberty will be endangered if Ireland obtains Home Rule. Surely it is impossible to hold that opinion unless the real state of affairs in the South and West of Ireland is ignored, and the whole development of political life in the last three centuries in every country of Europe is deliberately put out of sight. One of the objects of this work is to make it no longer possible to ignore these factors and to show the fallacy of the argument that Home Rule and Rome Rule are identical. On the other hand, many competent observers are of the opinion that the state of things is just the other way about, that it is the artificial nature of the political system which causes the Roman Catholic Church to have so much influence in Ireland, and that with the grant of Home Rule Irishmen will emancipate themselves from excessive ecclesiastical control in the same way as the other Catholic nations of Europe have done. This view would seem to be shared by the authorities of the Church itself whose enthusiasm for Home Rule seems to vary inversely with their rank, while the attitude of the Pope can hardly be described even as one of benevolent neutrality, and he has sometimes been actively hostile to the movement.

Before quitting this part of the subject it is necessary to say a few words about the Papal edict on the subject of mixed marriages, known as the "Ne Temere" decree, a mere reference to which will, I fear, be thought by many of my readers to be a sufficient answer to all I have contended in the foregoing pages. Let me state at once that I strongly disapprove of it, and shall welcome the day, if ever it arrives, when a British Ministry can secure its withdrawal—it has not been enforced in Germany—but that day will not be brought any nearer by the presence of 103 rather than 42 Irish members at Westminster, most of whom are hardly to be expected to support a Government in the exercise of any pressure directed towards this object. In regard to this, as in regard to many other things, the present system is directly injurious to Protestant interests. While, however, I consider it a matter for regret that the decree has been promulgated, I would point out that it in no way indicates a double dose of original sin on the part of Irish Catholics, and that it is as unreasonable to blame them for it as it would be to hold me responsible for the last resolution of the General Assembly of the Irish Presbyterian Church on the subject of Home Rule. They cannot always control their ecclesiastical superiors any more than I can. I would also point out that it does not affect Protestants except in the case of mixed marriages performed otherwise than in a Catholic Church, the number of which is extremely limited. While I regret the attitude the Roman Catholic Church has adopted in this matter, as it has furnished a new element of bitterness in my native country when the old animosities were dying out, I am forced to admit that it is difficult to see how she could adopt any other. According to her theory marriage is a sacrament, and can only therefore be administered by one of her own priests. It follows that a marriage not so performed is from the religious point of view no marriage at all, and consequently one of the parties to it who is a Roman Catholic cannot be admitted to the privileges of the Church as long as he or she is living in what is technically a state of sin. If the Church has the right of formulating her own terms for admission to her communion, it is difficult to find any flaw in this position, though it may work extreme hardship in individual cases. This is by no means the only case in which hardship is likely to arise where people marry into surroundings different from those to which they have been accustomed without considering all the contingencies that are liable to arise. The position of the wife in a marriage in disregard of the Ne Temere decree is absolutely unassailable in civil law if the necessary formalities have been complied with; and her case is much less unfortunate than that, say, of a British girl who marries a Frenchman in Britain and finds that in France it is invalid because he did not take the consent of his parents, or one who marries an Indian and finds he has two or three wives already, or is entitled under his personal law to take two or three more should he feel inclined to do so. Though the Church of England does not regard marriage as a sacrament, it is noteworthy that some of her ecclesiastical authorities are adopting a position exactly similar to the Roman Catholic one in regard to certain classes of marriage, such as the re-marriage of divorced persons and marriage with a deceased wife's sister. The following extract from the *Daily Mail* of June 17th last, will show that it is not the Roman Catholic Church only that does not always see eye to eye with the legislature, and that Protestants as well as Catholics can get into trouble with the spiritual authorities for exercising their civil rights in a manner the Church, or a particular Bishop of it, does not approve:—

"*Sacredness of Marriage.*—Throughout the diocese of Chichester the following pronouncement on the subject of marriage, passed by the Diocesan Synod and promulgated by the Bishop (Dr. Ridgway), has been made in every church: 'That, inasmuch as there is a growing divergence between the marriage law of the State, which legislates from the standpoint of human expediency for its citizens, and the marriage law of the Church, which regards marriage as a God-made relation and legislates for its members only, it is the duty of the Church: (1)To resist all encroachments on the sacredness of marriage as a danger to the foundations of society; (2) To refuse to solemnise marriages in church for those who desire to be married in disobedience to the marriage law of the Church; (3) To subject those of her Communion who have contracted marriages contrary to the Church's law to such discipline as the Bishop shall determine to be just and salutary.'"

If action of this nature is an encroachment on the civil power, it is even more reprehensible on the part of an ecclesiastic of the State Church than on that of one entirely independent of the State and unconnected with it. And yet while the one case is the subject of denunciation on scores of political platforms, the other has not even the honour of a front page in the *Daily Mail*, but is relegated to the column of local and provincial news. Why do not the political Protestants so anxious about ecclesiastical aggression begin by taking measures to check it in the case of their own Church? The principle at stake is the same, and owing to the connection of the Church of England with the State, it is much easier to find a means of raising the question in regard to it, and of forcing the position taken up to be abandoned if invalid.

As a matter of fact, in adopting the attitude she has done the Church of Rome is only following the example of the Church of Ireland, and the spectacle of Presbyterian clergymen joining with their Episcopalian brethren in denouncing an attitude which it has required an Act of Parliament to restrain the latter from adopting towards them, must afford considerable gratification to the cynical philosopher. If it is possible for anything to give them a sense of political and historical perspective, I would commend to their attention the following extract from "A Champion of the Faith: Rev. Henry Cooke, D.D., LL.D., his Life and Work," by Rev. W. T. Latimer, B.A., the well-known authority on the history of the Irish Presbyterian Church:—

"The Armagh Consistorial Court decided, in 1840, that a marriage between a Presbyterian and an Episcopalian, performed by a Presbyterian minister, was illegal. In 1841 a man convicted of bigamy appealed against the verdict of the jury on the ground of the marriage having been celebrated by a Presbyterian minister, although between a Presbyterian and an Episcopalian. In the Queen's Bench, three of the judges were for liberating the prisoner, and two for his condemnation. The question was carried to the House of Lords. Here the Law Lords were equally divided, which caused the decision of the inferior Court to be upheld and the marriage to be pronounced invalid. This decision caused great alarm among the Presbyterians of Ulster. Public meetings were held. An address by Dr. Goudy, of Strabane, was printed, and widely circulated. In February, 1842, Government gave notice of introducing a Bill to legalise all marriages of this kind, which had been already solemnized. But, as the Bill was merely retrospective, Dr. Cooke convened a special meeting of Assembly, by which it was condemned. Presbyterians were now thoroughly aroused to contend for their rights. Many meetings were held; intense excitement prevailed, and at last Government gave way. In 1844, another Bill was passed, which granted Presbyterians all that they demanded, so that marriages celebrated by clergymen of our Church are legal, if *one* of the parties united be a Presbyterian."

Another decree, that entitled Motu Proprio, has excited some attention, but I shall not waste time in discussing it, since it does not affect Protestants at all, and even in regard to

Catholics it has been held by one of their own Bishops, Dr. O'Donnell, Bishop of Raphoe, that in Ireland it has been suspended by the operation of custom.

With regard to both decrees I need only add that whatever hardships they involve are quite independent of whether Home Rule is passed or not, and it is difficult to see how it will make any great difference to the working of them.

EDITOR'S NOTES

1 Andrew Lang was a prolific popularising writer on topics relating to religion, mythology and folklore, from the 1880s to the 1920s. There are all of 178 titles on record in the TCD Library.

2 Daniel O'Connell forgotten? Perhaps this reflects the Trinity College environment of 1914, from which J.J. had not yet fully emerged.

3 Charles Seignobos *Histoire Politique de l'Europe Contemporaine* (Paris: Coulommiers, 1897) was translated and published in London in 1901; there was a popular edition in 1915, and a reissue in 1939, so it was a work of some standing and durability.

4 W. E. H. Lecky's "Clerical Influences" was a short essay written in 1862, when he was 23; he later dismissed it as crude and exaggerated. It was however resurrected and re-published in 1911, in the context of the Home Rule movement, with an introduction by Francis Cruise O'Brien and W. E. H. Lloyd in which they ranked it among Lecky's best works, the central argument being that ill-feeling between Catholics and Protestants was a direct consequence of the Act of Union. The youthful Lecky makes the case, based on experience abroad, that a national parliament would turn the attention of all sects towards national needs, rather than being preoccupied diversely with London and Rome.

CHAPTER IV

OBJECTS OF ULSTER'S RESISTANCE.—HOW FAR THE ENGLISH UNIONISTS ARE LIKELY TO SUPPORT IT.—POSSIBILITY OF THEIR PASSING A MEASURE OF HOME RULE THEMSELVES.— SUPPOSED CONSPIRACY BETWEEN THE WELSH AND THE IRISH.—REASONS FOR WELSH DISESTABLISHMENT.—DIFFICULTY OF DROPPING HOME RULE OUT OF THE LEGISLATIVE PROGRAMME.—ARROGANT CLAIMS OF THE HOUSE OF LORDS.—AIM OF UNIONIST POLICY, AND METHOD OF GIVING EFFECT TO IT.

It will be fairly apparent from the foregoing that religion has been brought into this controversy largely as the handmaid of politics, that Irish Protestants are being frightened by a danger which exists mainly in the imagination of their so-called leaders, who are quite willing to take equally great risks when their own party is in power, and that on the strength of this supposed danger they are being hustled and goaded into the adoption of a course the dangers of which are very certain and very great. What is the object of Ulster's threatened resistance? The first object, which it is generally recognised will not be attained, is that a General Election should take place before the Home Rule Bill is finally passed into law. Failing this, Ulster Unionists desire that a General Election should take place before Home Rule Bill is put into operation. This is an object which they may or may not attain. Assuming that they attain it, what good will it be to them unless the Unionist Party is returned to power? If the Unionists are not returned to power, they will no longer support Ulster if she goes to extremes in resistance to what will then be an Act of Parliament.

It is, no doubt, true that Mr. Bonar Law has more than once made use of language like this—"I can conceive no lengths to which Ulster may go in resistance to Home Rule in which she will not have the support of the Unionist Party of Great Britain." Mr. Bonar Law has thus signed a blank cheque on behalf of the Unionist Party for any conceivable amount of anarchy and disorder in Ulster. But Lord Lansdowne, the other leader, or rather the real leader of that Party, has refused to countersign it. Speaking in the House of Lords on the Second Reading of the Home Rule Bill on July 14th, he said:—"If the country want this Bill we are ready to let them have it." But in addition to that, it is clear to the intelligent reader of Lord Lansdowne's speech on that occasion that the Unionist Party in England is not opposed to any or every form of Home Rule. One of Lord Lansdowne's chief objections to this Bill is that it is an obstacle in the way of devolution and federation: "We believe it will not bring you one step nearer to a large and more complete measure of Devolution, which *so many of the best friends of Ireland may desire to see*"—(Lord Lansdowne himself, Mr Wyndham, and Lord Dunraven were among these in 1904).—"The Government have thought out their scheme of federation about as much as they have thought out their scheme for the reform of your lordships' House; but whenever that scheme is produced, *I, for one, am ready to treat it with the utmost respect and with every desire to find a solution of the problem of decentralisation.* But then, let me say, even with regard to their Bill, do not let it be supposed that our attitude is merely an attitude of obstruction. If the country want this Bill we are ready to let them have it; but we ask you to put the question to the test. *We are ready to abide by the decision.*"

What is this but a clear indication of preparations for the inevitable? Home Rule will be accepted so long as it is not called Home Rule, or so long as the Unionist Party can save its face by being in a position to say they have bowed to the will of the country. In the face of language like this, Ulstermen would be very ill advised to place too much reliance on

messages from Mr. Bonar Law because he happens to be the
nominal leader of the party in the House of Commons.
Nobody ever thought of him in connection with the position till
he was selected, and it is a fairly open secret that the principal
reason for his selection was that the other persons with greater
claims could not agree among themselves. A leader selected
for the occasion like this has a far weaker position than one
like Lord Lansdowne or Mr. Balfour, whose families have supplied statesmen for generations and rule the country by a sort
of hereditary right, and who besides were Cabinet Ministers
before Mr. Bonar Law was even a member of Parliament.

Are Irish Unionists going to lay down their lives in order
that they may have Home Rule under one name rather than
another?

Even if a general election is forced before the Home Rule
Bill is put into operation, and the Unionists return to office,
it is by no means certain we shall have heard the last of
Home Rule, though the name Home Rule may be supplanted by another of less unpopular associations. But what
are the chances that the Unionists will come back? They
have managed to alienate every progressive element in the
United Kingdom. By their persistent refusal of the Irish
National demand they start with 80 Nationalist votes against
them. Scotland is and always has been strongly Liberal. The
Welsh have been alienated by their opposition to the Welsh
Disestablishment Bill, which is treated as something outside
the pale of discussion, and fought far more fiercely than the
Home Rule Bill has been. It ought to be no part of my
business to discuss this Bill, but so much rhetorical, or, I
might almost say, hysterical, nonsense has been talked about
the infamous conspiracy between the Welsh and the Irish,
that, to put the Irish question in its proper perspective, it is
necessary to clear away some of the hypocrisy and misrepresentation that surrounds the other one. I shall begin by
reference to a few well-known historical facts. Up till the
sixteenth century England, like the rest of Western Europe,
belonged to the Roman Catholic Church, though its kings
occasionally displayed an amount of independence in temporal

matters that should be very comforting to those who say that
Home Rule means Rome Rule. By various Acts of Parliament
passed in the reigns Henry VIII, Edward VI and Elizabeth,
the connection with Rome was severed, and the Church of
England, including that of Wales, assumed something
approaching its present form, though for a considerable time
its regulations were less rigid than they are at present, and it
was quite possible for a minister with a Presbyterian or
Nonconformist ordination to hold a living in it, while now I
fear the mere idea of such a thing would be considered far
more sacrilegious than that of Welsh disestablishment itself.
Under James I and Charles I the royal influence was used to
mould the Church more into the model of that of Rome;
under the Commonwealth it was decided to abolish Episcopacy
and make the religion of England Presbyterian, which accounts
for the fact that some of my readers have had in their youth
to struggle with a catechism prepared by an Assembly of
Divines at Westminster. On the return of Charles II, a very
strict Act of Uniformity was passed, with the result that on St.
Bartholomew's Day, 1662, nearly two thousand rectors and
vicars (about a fifth of the English clergy) were expelled from
their churches and their dwellings as Nonconformists, and
were henceforth subjected to persecution very similar to that
which the Catholics in Ireland suffered fifty years later. It is
only from this date that the Church in Wales has been of its
present form, and all the endowments it has received since are
left to it. As to those it derives from an earlier period than
this, its sole title to them is an Act of Parliament, and what
Parliament can give Parliament can take away, and if it chose
to take the endowments of the Welsh Church now and give
them, say, to the Primitive Methodists, its act would be of
exactly the same nature as what it did originally when it
transferred them from the Catholics to the Protestants.

Of course I am aware that the theory of the Church of
England is that the Reformation was not a change, but
merely a casting off of the corruptions and accretions which
had overspread the practices and beliefs of the early Church.
As, however, every other Christian body that I have ever

heard of, with the possible exception of the Salvation Army, makes a similar claim to be the present-day representative of primitive Christianity, it can hardly expect this claim to be admitted by its rivals, or that the fact of its making it should seem to them a valid ground for its recognition by the State rather than themselves. Moreover, to anyone acquainted with the history of the Reformation in England, and the manner in which the Church of England as by law established came to assume its present form, if he believes it to be the guardian of absolute truth, as I admit many good men do, it must indeed seem that Providence sometimes uses strange instruments, and that there is something very like divine authority for the principle that the end justifies the means.

Owing to various causes, one of which was that for a long time the English clergy holding Welsh livings did not take the trouble to learn the language of their parishioners, the Welsh people have drifted away from their National Church and are now mainly Nonconformists. This fact is strongly contested by the opponents of disestablishment, but if, as is alleged, the majority of the Welsh people are Churchmen, it strengthens the case rather than weakens it, as the last ground for the maintenance of an established Church disappears when its own members do not want it. Reference is frequently made to the good work the Welsh Church is doing, and to the fact that its disestablishment will benefit nobody, but this is not to the point so far as the Welsh Nonconformists are concerned. The real cause of difficulty is that the prevailing theory of Anglican orders requires the possessor of them to look on a Nonconformist minister very much as the holder of a medical diploma does on an unqualified practitioner, and the fact of his being a clergyman of a State Church seems to imply an admission on part of the State of the validity of the claim.

A clergyman who left the Church of England to become a Nonconformist, the Rev. Stopford A. Brooke, in a published sermon makes use of words which exactly illustrate the characteristics of the Church of England to which the Welsh Nonconformists, and indeed all members of other Churches, object so strongly. He says of the Church of England:—

"It has systematised exclusion, and supported caste in religion. It has forced the whole body of Dissenters from its forms, to suffer under a religious and social stigma. Its claims separate from itself and strive to keep down, large masses of men whose spiritual life is as deep as its own; nor does the Church recognise their religious movements as on a level with its own. Its standard of the worthiest is not spiritual goodness, but union with itself; this is not the fault of its members, but the fault of its theory; but the fault utterly condemns the theory. Many within the Church have tried hard to do what was right in the matter, to hold out the hand of union to the Nonconformists, but they have failed—and must fail. The theory of the Church is too strong for them."

Thus the Welsh demand is a demand for equality, which the Irish would in any case support on general principles, whether they obtained any political return or not. When all the privileged classes take the same side, it is not called an infamous conspiracy, and there is nothing necessarily immoral in those who have suffered from privilege themselves helping to fight it in the case of others.

The Unionists, however, do not see things in this light, and elect to have all Wales against them as well as most of Ireland and Scotland. They have nothing to hope from the Nonconformists of England, who have not forgotten the Education Bill of 1902. Tariff Reform is so unpopular that the dose has to be reduced to suit the strength of the patient. But even in its attenuated form it fails to commend itself to the British working man, who sees that its disadvantages to himself are many and certain, while the advantages it promises are few, and by no means obvious.

The Unionists rely mainly on the landlords, the Church, and the liquor interest—the mercantile classes are divided, and many of the largest manufacturers are Liberals—and as it gets the support of most of these three classes under all circumstances, it cannot be expected that these forces alone will carry it to victory. If I might presume to tender a little advice to the

Unionist leaders, and there is any prospect of their being able to drive it into the heads of those of their followers who are known as "backwoodsmen," I would recall attention to the homely proverb about the difficulty of catching birds with chaff. It was thoroughly grasped by their great predecessor, Disraeli, when he spoke of "dishing the Whigs," but has fallen into desuetude lately, with disastrous results to themselves. A party that will give no section of the population what it wants, and simply contents itself with maintaining and where possible, extending existing privileges, has very poor chance of success in a country where the privileged are so few and the unprivileged so many as in England at the present day. Therefore, it seems altogether improbable that the Unionists will come back in sufficient numbers to disregard the Nationalist vote. If they come back only in such strength that a Government cannot be formed without the assistance of the Nationalists, it is practically certain that they will come to a working arrangement with the latter on the basis of some scheme of Devolution which will only be Home Rule under another name.

The situation is such that the Government must pass the Home Rule Bill into law unless they are prepared to abandon the whole of their legislative programme except the Scottish Temperance Bill, which the House of Lords, in a fit of unexpected generosity has let through in a mutilated form. It is not as if the Government majority belonged to a single party and Home Rule were the only question about which a bitter controversy is raging. The Government majority is a coalition majority, and Welsh Disestablishment holds the field along with the Home Rule Bill and the Plural Voting Bill. These three measures must stand or fall together. If the Government gives up Home Rule, the Nationalists may retaliate by refusing to support them on the question of Welsh Disestablishment. The House of Lords has obligingly played into the hands of the Nationalists. If it had passed the Welsh Disestablishment and the Plural Voting Bills, Home Rule alone would have remained, and those of the Government's supporters who are more interested in Disestablishment and Plural Voting than in Home Rule would no longer have had so much interest in the Home Rule Bill, and having got all they wanted themselves, would have had less objection to risking a General Election. By failing to pass the Welsh Disestablishment Bill, the House of Lords has, barring miracles, ensured the passage of the Home Rule Bill as well This shows scant consideration for the interests of the Irish Unionists, who, however, are probably misled by a false sense of perspective, and imagine themselves to be the backbone of the party instead of simply a card in the Tory pack, as a Conservative leader in an unguarded moment once described them. The piquancy of the situation is added to by the fact that Irish Protestants, as a rule, are absolutely indifferent on the subject of Welsh Disestablishment, while those of them who are Presbyterians or Nonconformists ought, according to their own principles, and the attitude they adopted when the same question was pending in regard to Ireland, to be in favour of it.

The same resolution did duty in the rejection of both these Bills in the House of Lords. They claimed that they ought not to be passed until the opinion of the country had been taken about them. As the only recognised method in the British Constitution of taking the opinion of the country is by a General Election, this amounts to a claim that a General Election should be held for each Bill; for if only one General Election were held for both Bills, it would be impossible to say how much Welsh Disestablishment and how much Home Rule had to do with determining the result. The Unionist leaders have frankly admitted this, and, so far as I can follow their argument, it seems to be that the oftener elections are held the better, since the Government thereby keeps more closely in touch with the will of the people. It always creates some suspicion to find people more royalist than the king, and this strange anxiety on the part of the champions of the House of Lords for consulting the people at every step would have possessed more weight if they had displayed it when in office themselves, and had not overlooked the importance and necessity of doing so till they happened to be in opposition.

This claim, reduced to its lowest terms, is that a hereditary and partisan assembly should have the right to force an election on every measure about which it differs from the representatives of the people.

As the House of Lords differs from the House of Commons in regard to almost every measure introduced by the Liberal Party, this would practically mean a general election two or three times a year; when so stated the proposal is seen to be an absurdity. If the House of Lords had regarded the Home Rule Bill as the terrible monster that the rank and file of Irish Unionists are taught to regard it, they would have sacrificed even the Church in Wales with the object of defeating it, and no Irish Protestant would have shed a tear on account of that sacrifice. The House of Lords had it in its power to make Home Rule the all-important issue by passing all the other Bills in regard to which they differed from the Government. If they had done so, their demand for a General Election on the question of Home Rule would have been a demand for one General Election only, and would have had some chance of being listened to. By demanding an indefinite number of General Elections, and by the declaration of the Ulster leaders that they will never accept Home Rule whatever be the decision of a General Election, the whole case for demanding one on this issue has been destroyed. It is thus practically certain that there will be no General Election until both the Home Rule Bill and the Welsh Disestablishment Bill are on the Statute Book. What is the policy of Ulster Unionism in view of this state of affairs? Will they try to force a General Election before the Home Rule Bill is put into operation? They have no power to do so, but, supposing for the sake of argument that an election is held, it is by no means certain that the Unionists will come back with either the power or the will to repeal absolutely the Home Rule Bill. A tie will not help them much, and what is more likely is that the coalition will return with a majority, however small, in which case they will have to proceed to put the Home Rule Act into operation. The avowed policy of Ulster Unionists in this event is that they will refuse to obey the laws of the Home Rule Parliament and to pay its taxes, and will set up Provisional Government of their own, or rather the Provisional Government which their friends have by this time thoughtfully provided for them, will announce that its proceedings are no longer dress rehearsals, but are to be taken seriously on pain of high treason.

What is the object of this policy? Its authors have kindly explained the object, which is practically the only point about the scheme they have explained. Besides the unfortunate consequence of the principle that familiarity breeds contempt which leads to a passion for breaking all on the part of those who have had too much to do with the administration of them, and a very natural ambition to sit in the seats of the mighty, if only for one week, its objects are, we are told, to make the administration of the Home Rule Act impossible, and to force Parliament to repeal it. With the prospects of securing these results I shall deal in the following chapter.

CHAPTER V.

ERRONEOUS ASSUMPTIONS UNDERLYING
PLANS FOR REFUSING TO ACKNOWLEDGE
IRISH PARLIAMENT.— EXAMINATION OF
DETAILS OF IRISH REVENUE.—PROPORTION
OF TOTAL REVENUE A PROVISIONAL
GOVERNMENT MIGHT BE ABLE TO SEIZE.—
PROBABLE CONSEQUENCES OF ATTEMPTING
TO DO SO.—ARMS, EQUIPMENT, AND TRAINING
OF ULSTER VOLUNTEER FORCE.—SUGGESTION
THAT BRITISH ARMY WILL REFUSE TO FIGHT
THEM.—IMPORTANCE OF ULSTER TO THE
UNIONIST PARTY.

The policy outlined above is founded on a lamentable
ignorance of the details of the Home Rule Bill, and a
perfectly unjustifiable assumption that the Government will go
on doing exactly what suits the Provisional Government best.

According to the terms of the Home Rule Bill, the collection of taxes is, and is likely to remain for some time, an
Imperial service. Moreover, the taxes when collected will in
the first instance be paid into the Imperial Exchequer. The
Irish Home Rule Government is to receive a fixed sum in any
case, and the amount does not depend in any way on the
ability of the Imperial Government to collect taxes levied
in Ireland. Consequently the Ulster Unionists cannot refuse
to pay the taxes of the Irish Parliament, because the Irish
Parliament will not be demanding any taxes from them, at any
rate not at first, and as the Imperial Executive is responsible
for their collection, Irish Unionists if they refuse to pay will be
directly confronted with the Imperial authority. But what

taxes can they refuse to pay? I have before me a statement of the Revenue accounts for Ireland for the year 1911–12. The two chief heads of Revenue collected in Ireland are Customs, £3,013,000, and Excise, £5,668,000. Putting these aside for the present, the next head is Estate Duties, £936,000. Not all of this is collected in Ulster. A refusal to pay this tax would affect the legality of the ownership of an estate. Is anyone who has come into an estate going to be so foolish as to refuse the payment which is necessary in order to obtain his title, or pay the tax to an authority which cannot give him a legal receipt for it or a valid title to the property?

Such a person may conceivably find that he may have to pay the tax a second time and a number of penalties or additional charges as well, if the Provisional Government should break down or spend the money on its own purposes, and be unable to credit it to the Imperial Government at the adjustment of accounts—that is if any are kept, which is unlikely.

The next item is Stamps, which bring in £326,000, not all of which, presumably, is collected in Ulster. These also affect the legality of business transactions, and the same remarks apply to them. Next comes Income Tax, £1,206,000. This is the most hopeful, or rather the least hopeless item for the organisers of the Provisional Government. Taking this amount in detail, we find that under the head of Lands and Houses £381,000 were collected in the year in question. Assuming that half of this tax is collected from people resident in Ulster, which is probably a greatly exaggerated estimate, this leaves a possible £190,500 for the Provisional Government to collect if those who pay this tax are foolish enough to give it to them. An amount of £30,000 is derived from the occupation of land; let us give the Provisional Government £15,000 of this, also probably an overestimate; £29,000 are obtained from Government Stocks, etc. As the Government in question is the Imperial Government, whose taxes Ulster Unionists are refusing to pay, I doubt very much whether it will give Ulstermen the opportunity of refusing to pay this tax, and it may be taken as certain that payment of interest will be withheld as long as the payees are in revolt, and if I were one

of them I should also consult my lawyer, if one can be found
who is not also a political leader, as to whether here is not
also a possibility of the principal being confiscated. Such
things have happened before, though in a less enlightened age.
In any case, of this amount the Provisional Government is
likely to get little but the ciphers at the end of the figure, and
if the Imperial Government likes to be vindictive, by con-
fiscating the capital amount, it might recoup itself for most
of its other losses at one fell swoop. On account of Public
Companies, Foreign Dividends and Coupons £430,000 are
realised, but as much of this tax is deducted at the source it
would be unsafe to count very much on the possibility of
refusing payment in this case. Trades and Professions bring in
£216,000. Let the Provisional Government have half of this,
which is also probably a very liberal estimate. The official
salaries of public officers, etc., account for £41,000. I doubt if
the Provisional Government will lay its hands on much of this.
In any case, as the Government officials will either be withdrawn or taken over by the Provisional Government, this can
only be deducted from the salaries it is itself paying to them.
If this should take place, the classic instance of the town the
inhabitants of which lived by taking in each others washing
will fade into insignificance before this illustration of the
financial skill of the "hardheaded men of business" the Ulster
people are so fortunate in having found as their leaders.

Non-official salaries bring in £71,000. Let the Provisional
Government have half of this, which is far too much if all the
manhood of the province is engaged in fighting, or even in
drilling. The total revenue of the Provisional Government thus
amounts to £349,000. The next item of taxation levied in
Ireland is the Land Value Duties. The only one of these which
Ireland pays is the Mineral Rights Duty, and it brings in the
princely sum of £1,000. Let us give the Provisional Government
£500 from this tax. That brings its revenue up to £349,500.

Miscellaneous revenue stands at £110,000 for the year in
question. As £79,000 of this comes from Fee and Patent
Stamps, and Fee Stamps are paid in the course of litigation,
and litigation in the law courts of an Ireland governed by a

Home Rule Parliament is presumably to cease so far as Ulster is concerned, I suspect that there will not be much revenue derived from this tax. Of this £110,000, £29,000 is entered under the heading "Expenses of Administration of Local Loans." I am afraid it will be difficult to tap this source of revenue. There are one or two other items of miscellaneous revenue which are small and unimportant.

The Postal, Telegraph, and Telephone services bring in £947,000, £97,500, and £62,000 respectively. These are services, however, where the expenditure usually exceeds the income, and as they will have to enter into competition with motor cyclist despatch-riders equipped with heliographs and Marconi apparatus for home communications, while, as I shall show later, the etiquette of war requires that those with the enemy's country should be suspended, the loss on their working is bound to be even greater than it is at present. Crown lands bring in £22,500. As the people of Ulster profess that they are still loyal to the Crown, they can hardly well take possession of its lands, and even though their patience should be tried too far, and they find it necessary to make a change in this respect, the recognised principle is that the lands go with the office, and without the consent of the new ruler, which evidently cannot be given till he is selected, the income from this source cannot be regarded as available for the ordinary purposes of administration.

Apart from Customs and Excise, therefore, the total revenue of the Provisional Government will be at the most £349,500. Is this enough to pay for the government of 1,581,696 people of whom nearly half will be unwilling subjects, or rather open rebels against its authority? The total population of Ireland in 1911 was 4,390,219. The cost of governing Ireland in 1911–12 was £11,533,500. At a moderate estimate, the share of Ulster is not less than 3½ millions in time of peace. Sir Edward Carson will have to make his machinery very perfect indeed, or ask his followers to put their hands very much deeper in their pockets than they have hitherto done, if he is going to make ends meet in time of war. Since the above words were written a capital sum of a million pounds as an indemnity fund has been called for and much of it has been promised. True, the generous donors have endeavoured with some success to transfer their liabilities to underwriters in London, but I fear that even heavier demands will have to be made on the loyalty of the men of Ulster on the financial resources of London insurance agencies, if they are going to meet all the liabilities of the Provisional Government they propose to have in office during a time of civil war.

But what about Customs and Excise? Over $8\frac{1}{2}$ millions are collected under these heads alone, and it is often asserted by Unionists that two-thirds of this amount is paid by the Unionists of Belfast and the North of Ireland. Everybody outside a lunatic asylum or a political platform must know that taxes of this kind, wherever collected, are simply passed on, and ultimately paid by the consumer of the commodity on which they are levied. The Connemara peasant who smokes Gallaher's tobacco really pays the tax which is collected in Belfast by Customs and Excise officials. All that is proved by the fact, if it be a fact, that two-thirds of the Customs and Excise revenue is collected in Belfast, is that Belfast is the great distributing centre for commodities like tea, sugar, and tobacco, not only for the North of Ireland, but for a large part of the Midlands and West as well, while it is also the seat of large distilleries. At first sight this may seem a fortunate circumstance for the Provisional Government, but perhaps it is not so fortunate as it seems. What form is the refusal to pay Customs and Excise duties going to take? Will Ulster Unionists drink no tea or whiskey and deny themselves the solace of a pipe or cigarette? That policy might lessen the revenues of the Imperial Treasury, but neither would it put money in the coffers of the Provisional Government; besides it suffers from the distinct disadvantage of being perfectly legal. If the Provisional Government is to get its Customs and Excise and the Ulster Unionist his dutiable articles of consumption, there is only one way of rendering this possible. The Provisional Government must seize the Customhouses and distilleries at Belfast, Londonderry, Newry and every other place where there is a considerable collection of Customs and Excise revenue. Now, it unfortunately happens that a great many of these places contain garrisons of British troops, who might possibly be indifferent spectators of what goes on in a municipal building such as the Town Hall, but can hardly be expected to look on while unauthorised persons seized Government buildings and Government property, whether they do so under the aegis of the Union Jack or the Nine Stars of Ulster. The Provisional Government says it is preparing for all contingencies, and one contingency I hope it will not overlook is that of its amateur Customs and Excise officers finding the performance of their duties obstructed by some hundreds of British soldiers and a few Maxim guns. What about Mr. Asquith's nod, it may be asked? This will be discussed in detail later on, but in connection with the present subject it may be pointed out that such action on the part of the Imperial Government would be one of defence not defiance, and, like the military training to which the people of Ulster are submitting themselves at present, so far as the hours of labour in the factories or the pressure of agricultural operations permit, would only be in the nature of a justifiable precaution against eventualities.

It is to be hoped that in these circumstances nothing will happen beyond a formal protest, and the lodging of a claim that the points at issue be referred to the Hague Tribunal, but should anybody be so ill-advised as to try and rush one of these places, the misfortune of a man whose loyalty manifested itself in an attempt to seize His Majesty's Revenue and Revenue Offices will meet with scant sympathy on the other side of the Channel. Moreover, in case the Imperial Government should wish to keep up an appearance of generosity and the Provisional Government desires to have the Custom Houses, it may well be allowed to have them. The Customs can be collected almost as easily on the quay or in the landing shed. Should the Provisional Government prove unreasonable, and insist on having possession of everything up to the water's edge—nothing has been said about its having a fleet, so presumably it can go no further—it can be allowed to have that, too, on the trifling condition that any port where this is done shall be declared closed. It is unlikely that shipping will disobey the orders of the Imperial Government, and in any case half a dozen gunboats or steam launches will be sufficient to enforce compliance.

The only circumstances in which the Provisional Government is likely to be in a position to collect Customs will be when there are no Customs to collect. It is to be hoped this situation will appeal to Belfast. The vast and profitable distributing trade which it at present enjoys will be diverted to Dublin, Dundalk, Drogheda, and Sligo. The merchants of those places will rejoice; but what will the "hardheaded business men of Belfast" say? It does not require much of the gift of prophecy to foretell that in a very short time a special meeting of the Chamber of Commerce will be called, and the Provisional Government will be denounced in language almost as vigorous as the same body on a former occasion made use of with reference to the Home Rule Bill.

It will be equally easy to take measures to guard the distilleries, and if any Unionist loses his life in an attempt to rush them, his motives will be liable to be misconstrued. It will be difficult to make any political capital out of such an occurrence for the benefit of the Unionist Party in Great Britain. Even if a few distilleries do remain in the hands of the Provisional Government, their possession is likely to add to its difficulties quite as much as to its revenue. The fixing of the amount of duty is a matter in which it is quite impossible to please everybody, and between the teetotallers who may probably want to take advantage of the situation to close them down altogether, and those of less strict principles who may possibly think the general confusion a good opportunity for having as much liquor as they want for little or nothing, it will be anything but easy to hold the balance evenly. Whatever course is adopted is sure to produce dissatisfaction in some quarter, and the Imperial Government can afford to look on with equanimity while the various sections of the supporters of the Provisional Government attempt to impose their views on this question on all the others.

In most places in Ulster Excise duties will thus be collected as usual, though possibly under military protection, and the

Customs revenue which was formerly collected mainly at Belfast and other ports of Ulster will continue to be collected by the Imperial Government at those places, or will be collected at ports outside the influence of the Provisional Government. The Imperial Government will be put to very little inconvenience. It may not get in all the Income Tax, but it can afford to await the inevitable collapse of the Provisional Government before collecting the balance of £349,000. If the refusal to pay this tax has taken the form of refusing to make the return necessary for assessment, the harvest for the Imperial Government will be indeed rich; the penalty for this offence is £20, and treble the duty chargeable. On the other hand, the Income Tax payers who have paid their Income Tax to the Provisional Government will have the uncomfortable feeling that they may be called on to pay it a second time, with a considerable additional amount in penalties of various kinds, to the properly constituted authorities. The merchants of Belfast and Derry will be wondering whether after all any sort of lawful Government, even a Home Rule Government, is not better for business than the Provisional Government. The Imperial Government can allow this state of affairs to continue indefinitely while it enjoys the spectacle of the supporters of its rival cutting off their nose to spite their face, and incidentally benefiting their "hereditary enemies" by diverting most of their business to them.

The total Irish revenue collected in 1911–12 was £12,489,000, and if Excise and Customs are excluded, as I have shown they almost certainly will have to be, the amount that can be intercepted by the Provisional Government is a mere drop in the bucket. Customs it cannot possibly hope to collect, and in regard to Excise the utmost it can hope for is that it will succeed in collecting that on the articles consumed in the territory obedient to it, which at the outside will not be much more than one-eighth of Ireland, and even this is extremely doubtful. Will this be sufficient to bring to its knees the Government of a country which only the other day has been able to vote the Irish landlords a nice little present of £12,000,000 under the head of a bonus on land purchase?

Anything the Provisional Government can do will not merely not cause any serious embarrassment to the Ministry, but will not even affect their prestige if they adopt the proper attitude in dealing with it. All that will be necessary will be to explain that the Liberals are just as devoted as the Unionists to a policy of generosity to Ireland, but have been so impressed by the criticisms of the latter on the Insurance Act that they consider the method of imposing heavy taxation on Ireland, and then returning an even larger amount in subsidies, involves unnecessary cost of establishment, that under the former system the cost of Irish administration has grown till it now considerably exceeds the revenue, and consequently they have decided to meet everybody's objections and effect considerable economies at the same time by discontinuing simultaneously the collection of taxes and the granting of subsidies in such parts of Ireland as prefer the other method. Even if the British elector is not entirely convinced by this show of reasoning, he has grown so accustomed to having to pay an exorbitant amount for every fresh policy in regard to Ireland, that he is very unlikely to discover that anything abnormal has happened. The whole situation seems to have been described between two and three thousand years ago by Æsop, the author of the well-known fables, in the story of the fly and the bull, a translation of which is as follows:— "A fly having settled on the horn of a bull and having sat there a long time, when it was about to leave asked the bull if now he wished him to go away, to which the latter replied: 'I neither knew when you came, nor if you depart shall I be aware of the fact.'"

Assuming, however, that the Provisional Government successfully overcomes all these difficulties, there still remains a rock on which it has a very good chance of splitting. One would have expected that such champions of the rights of objectors would have contented themselves with taking over that part of the country where the people are either sympathetic or indifferent, and would have left alone the remainder of the province where the great bulk of the population is Nationalist. But not so, the farce has to be kept up that

Ulster is Unionist, and the flag of the Provisional Government bears the Nine Stars of Ulster, though a majority of the Ulster Members of Parliament are actually in favour of Home Rule. What is there to prevent a similar state of things in the Parliament of the Provisional Government if it is elected on the same franchise and for the same constituencies? Catholics cannot be excluded without an unmerited slight on the Chief Unionist Whip, and those who have been so eloquent in their denunciations of the alleged political influence of the Ancient Order of Hibernians, can hardly confine the franchise to members of Orange Lodges and Unionist Clubs. And in case the nationalist majority in the Ulster Parliament should decree its own extinction, and amalgamation with the Parliament at Dublin, how can those object who are still lost in admiration of an exactly similar measure 113 years ago, even though the majority was not a spontaneous one, but a large proportion of the members composing it had to be bribed or driven into the course they adopted. Well may the poet say, "Uneasy lies the head that wears a crown," when the possessor of it is a usurper, and there is a danger that the majority of his subjects are in favour of the legitimate ruler.

If, however, the constituencies are jerrymandered, or the non-Unionist inhabitants of Ulster actually disfranchised, there still remain some difficulties for the Provisional Government which may well prove insuperable.

The Provisional Government can be given full scope so long as it makes no attempt to govern, and remains a mere voluntary association collecting subscriptions, which it prefers to call taxes, from those who are foolish enough to pay them. The trouble will arise when it begins to deal with the half million or so of inhabitants of the province who, though they have signed no Covenant to that effect, may safely be depended on to refuse to pay its taxes or obey its laws. What is it going to do in regard to them? Is it going to ignore them? If so, and it is only its own supporters who have to pay taxes, while other people pay none, the grim determination of Ulster will be exposed to one of the most insidious attacks it has yet had to undergo, and the desertions among its followers are likely to be so considerable as to cause very serious difficulties, both military and financial. Is it going to disregard all its own contentions about the rights of minorities, and attempt to compel obedience on the part of those who will not recognise its authority?

If it attempts to do so, will they not have as good a moral right to resist as Ulster Unionists say they have to resist the decrees and refuse to pay the taxes of an Irish Parliament, since the impositions of the latter would be at least legal, while those of the former would not? If any unwilling subject refuses to pay a tax levied by the Provisional Government, will they put him in gaol? In that case, as there will probably be the taxpaying members of a population of at least 500,000 against whom such measures will have to be taken, the gaol accommodation of Ulster will require to be largely increased. Will they seize his property? If he is a farmer, for instance, will they drive off his cattle? If they do so he will naturally object, and probably express his objections in deeds as well as words. If he makes use of a blackthorn stick for that purpose, how often will those amateur tax collectors allow him to brandish it in dangerous proximity to their heads before they fire? Presumably all this sort of work will have to be done by the Ulster Volunteers in the absence of any special staff for this purpose. In the eye of the law such conduct is robbery, and where shooting takes place will be murder or attempted murder. Yet it is the only way by which the Provisional Government can make itself a reality and not a mere sham. The forces of the Crown are bound to interfere to protect in the exercise of their legal rights those who object to illegal taxation. If any Ulster Unionist loses his life in an encounter with the forces of the Crown in connection with a matter of this kind, the usual rhetoric about shooting down Ulstermen whose only crime is their loyalty will have to be considerably modified, and a formula will have to be devised which renders it intolerable oppression to interfere with anybody who is doing what seems right in his own eyes or those of his self-constituted rulers, however much the rest of the world may object to such conduct.

No political capital can be made out of an occurrence such as this. The first duty of a government is to maintain law and order. The Government will have the whole force of British public opinion behind it in whatever measures it may find necessary to take in order to secure the non-adherents of the Provisional Government in the exercise of their legal rights, and to protect them against its exactions. No one expects that the Imperial Government will proceed against the Provisional Government for merely proclaiming itself as such. So far as the Imperial Government is concerned, they may proclaim a Provisional Government once a week in every town and village in Ulster, and they will probably be afforded police protection in doing so if there is any likelihood of disturbance. But once they begin to attempt to govern, in other words, to perform acts which legally will be robbery and intimidation of those who refuse to acknowledge it or contribute towards it, the Provisional Government will become simply an illegal society, and will be proceeded against like any other. The Imperial Government will not be ill-advised enough to attack the Provisional Government at the outset; it will only interfere in order to protect those whom the Provisional Government is attacking. The attempt to throw the responsibility for any trouble that takes place on the authorities will thus be unsuccessful and the sympathy of the British elector will be sought in vain. Granting, however, that the Ulster Unionists succeed in pushing matters to extremes, and that the law is powerless to protect the lives and property of the minority—are the resources of civilisation exhausted? It is idle to appeal to the success of the defenders of Derry or to the difficulty which the British Army experienced in conquering South Africa. The circumstances are very different in the case of Ulster. I see it is admitted by their own leaders that Ulster Unionists cannot resist the whole might of the British Army. It would have been more to the point if they had considered whether they can resist the whole might of the R.I.C., which is an army in everything but name. Have any of the Ulster Volunteers ever examined the rifles of various types that have been supplied to them?[1] Do they know anything about the difference between

black and smokeless powder, and the efficiency of the one as
compared with the other? Do they know anything about the
velocity and trajectory of modern small bore rifles with
smokeless powder as compared with the more ancient type? Is
it a fact that many of the rifles they have been given are over
30 years old, are manufactured to take a black powder
cartridge, and so cannot have much more than half the
range, and a still smaller proportion of the accuracy, of
modern rifles, and in fact are only fit for selling to Somalis or
for serving out to black police in Central Africa or something
of that kind? Even assuming that the Volunteers were
thoroughly trained in the use of them, which they are not, to
ask any persons so armed to stand up to either soldiers or
police possessing modern weapons is equivalent to requiring
them to commit suicide. If they have got some rifles of a more
modern type, will they take the same cartridge? Certainly not,
if the one was built for black powder and the other for
smokeless. And what arrangements have been made that at
any point where there is fighting, there will be a sufficient
supply of the right kind of cartridges? Assuming that the
rifles are perfect, and that no difficulty arises about the use of
more than one kind of ammunition, have they got sufficient?
Has it ever struck anyone to form an estimate of the amount
of cartridges blazed away in even a small engagement, or the
difficulty that modern armies have in keeping the firing line
supplied with ammunition? Even if infinite reserves of ammunition have been laid in, the size and weight of black powder
cartridges makes it impossible for an Ulster Volunteer to
carry more than about half what he might have done if
modern rifles had been supplied. Should the ammunition run
short after the trouble begins, is the Imperial Government,
holding command of the sea, likely to allow it to be freely
imported from abroad? British military rifles of the latest
pattern can be supplied by the Army and Navy Stores at £5
each, and of the long Lee-Enfield pattern at £4 10s. each, and
doubtless if ordered in large quantities there would have been
a substantial discount on those figures, even if Birmingham
Unionism had not seen fit to supply weapons at cost price to

those fighting for the common cause. Instead of which, those who are never tired of telling the people of Ulster how they must if necessary sacrifice everything for the cause, in order to save a pound or two on each rifle, have cast to the winds all those principles of encouraging home manufacture which as Tariff Reformers they may be supposed to possess, and have doubtless alienated the sympathy of their friends in Birmingham, who might reasonably have expected the order, by dumping secondhand foreign rubbish which nobody who was contemplating real warfare would have accepted as a gift. Does it never strike any Ulster Volunteer, as he gazes on the venerable weapon which his leaders have served out to him, which in many cases he has to share with about twenty other men, and probably has never fired in his life, that he would do well to pause for a moment, whenever the flood of rhetoric admits of his doing so, and ask himself what is their object. Nothing but the abysmal ignorance of military matters on the part of the mass of the people of Ulster, arising out of the fact that the Volunteer and Territorial systems have never been extended to Ireland, could blind their eyes to the fact that the Ulster army is only an army for show. Since the Boer War a sharp distinction has been drawn between ceremonial parades and training in the actual business of fighting, with which the former has practically nothing to do. As the recruit in the regular army has plenty of leisure for learning all branches of his business, and the tendency in time of peace is all in the direction of smartness of appearance, it is the ceremonial part of the military education which is undertaken first, and as it is much the easiest to arrange for, and can be practised with wooden rifles, or even at a pinch with broomsticks, the drill that the Ulster Volunteers have learnt up till now is mainly of this nature. Does it never strike them as curious that the persons who express themselves highly delighted with their military appearance and efficiency if they can make some sort of attempt at marching east and presenting arms to the Ulster leader, belong to the party that is always complaining about the want of training and the inefficiency of the Territorials? A Territorial, at any rate, has a modern rifle all to himself, he is taught to fire at various ranges up to 800 or 1,000 yards, and is not supposed to be qualified until he can place a shot pretty well where he wants at most of those ranges; he learns to judge distance, to take advantage of cover, and a thousand and one things which cannot be taught in a drill hall or anywhere but in the open country under conditions as similar as possible to actual warfare. Besides, in most cases he goes to camp, or at least attends field days in which large numbers of troops take part, so that they learn to co-operate with each other and act in concert. Except in the case of a few members of rifle clubs, nearly all these elements are wanting in the training of the Ulster Volunteers. How many of them have ever been on a range at all? How many of them with the rifles they have got, but in most instances never fired, could hit the proverbial haystack at 200 yards, much less the head of a policeman or soldier, which is all they will have to aim at in most cases, even if the barrels are not so badly worn as to spoil the accuracy of the shooting, which is usually the case in rifles when they get old? How many of them have had any field training in combination with any considerable number of other people? Even if their rifles were of the very latest pattern, and cost as many pounds as they have done shillings, and they had trained in the use of them till they could hit a policeman at a thousand yards nine times out of ten, what use would they be without artillery, which could mow them down from a distance of three miles, or even from the further side of a hill where they could not even see it. Too much stress should not be laid on Mr. Asquith's nod, which, when the time comes, may be represented as meaning only that the Provisional Government would not be interfered with so long as it remained a purely voluntary association and did not attempt to govern, especially as some subsequent remarks of Lord Morley's on the subject of maintaining order are as hard to reconcile with the popular interpretation of it, as are the discrepancies in the statements of Mr. Bonar Law, Lord Lansdowne, and Lord Curzon in regard to what the Unionists will do about Ulster if they lose again in a general election. Let the Ulster Volunteers read what their own leaders have said about Mr. Asquith's perfidy in postponing the reform of the second chamber, and how he even deceived the King into signing the Parliament Act, and then consider whether, on the strength of a mere nod, which may only have been due to drowsiness, or can be explained away in the manner suggested above or half a dozen others equally good for the purpose of Parliamentary argument, it is safe without artillery, without training, and with rifles about as useful as the muzzle-loaders most of them have always possessed, to take the risk of coming into armed conflict with the R.I.C., not to speak of the British Army.

There is, however, an idea widely prevalent which it is worth while to examine in this connection. We are told that British officers and soldiers will mutiny rather than fire on Ulster Unionists. Ulster Unionists are on very dangerous ground if they are trying to persuade the forces of the Crown to disobey orders. The essential feature of this idea is that the British Army should refuse to carry out a command of the Government of the day. The object of the Ulster leaders is, no doubt, either to frighten the British public or to win its sympathy, it does not matter which, but if there is one constitutional principle more important than another in British public life, it is that the Army shall not be used as an engine of political warfare, and the very suspicion of an attempt on the part of Ulster to bring about a subordination of civil to military authority, will at once alienate the sympathy of every British elector who has any regard for the spirit and traditions of the constitution. The principle that the military shall be subordinate to the civil power is one of its most essential features. Its origins are to be traced in the struggle for popular rights which ended in the overthrow of the Stuarts. It is manifested at the present day in the fact that the law on which the existence of the Army depends, is a law which must be renewed every year, and which in consequence involves the calling together of annual Parliaments. Ulster Unionists will meet with little sympathy in Great Britain if they attempt to undermine the allegiance of the Army. But still more important is the question, are they likely to succeed? Granted there are many Ulster Protestants in the ranks of the British Army, and that many of its officers are drawn from the class which is traditionally Unionist in sympathy, there are also many Roman Catholics both as officers and soldiers. Regiments like the Dublin Fusiliers and the Connaught Rangers are almost entirely Catholic. In fact, I feel sure I am well within the mark when I assert that there are three times as many Irish Catholics as Irish Protestants in the ranks of the British Army. The remainder of the army is recruited largely from the British working classes. The British working man has no sympathy with the religious fears and political predilections of Ulster Protestants. That accounts very largely for their "apathy" on the question of Home Rule of which the Ulster leader complains.

Even if he shared their fears and opinions to the utmost, it does not follow that the British soldier will refuse to shoot them if ordered to do so, especially as his refusal would render him liable to be shot himself for disobedience. British soldiers might be expected to share the opinions and sympathies of the class from which the majority of them are drawn. That class is the British working class. Yet it is a well-known fact that on more than one occasion in the history of industrial disputes in Great Britain, British soldiers have been ordered to shoot down British working men, and so strong is the influence of military discipline, they have obeyed the order. It is scarcely likely they will show a different spirit in dealing with Ulster. The majority of the officers may in civil life be Unionists. The most they are likely to do is to resign their commissions. It would be contrary to all the traditions of the service to attempt to persuade their men to mutiny or to fight on the side of Ulster, and were they to do so, it is unlikely for the reasons I have given that they would meet with any response.[2] The shortage of officers might seem a difficulty, but there are many who think that the army might with advantage be made more democratic, and I am sure it would be possible to fill all the vacancies thus created by promotions from the non-commissioned ranks without any very great loss of efficiency. If this were done, and if the wholesale resignations of officers broke down the caste system which at present prevails, and opened the highest ranks to the private soldier in the same way as the emigration of the Royalist officers did in the French army at the time of the Revolution, this Ulster war would probably be the most popular in which the British Army has ever been engaged. It would doubtless be considered rather hard to have to shoot down Ulstermen whose only crime was that they were proclaiming a Provisional Government, but Mr. Asquith's common-sense and political astuteness, even more than Mr. Asquith's nod, may be relied on to prevent this. The chances are that they will only be called in, if at all, to protect unwilling taxpayers from the exactions of the Provisional Government, or to prevent any attempt on the part of the latter to seize Government property and buildings, and if force is necessary to secure these objects, then force will be used; and if anybody gets killed or hurt in consequence, the only sympathy he is likely to get is that conveyed in the phrase, "Serves him right." An idea is prevalent that after they have fired a volley or two in order to show that they are not to be trifled with, Ulster Unionists need only wave a Union Jack and strike up "God save the King," and the other side instead of returning their fire will at once fall on their necks and join forces with them. Might I point out to those possessed of this idea that in warfare the enemy is the person who is trying to kill you, however identical your sentiments may be in private life.

The opinion of General Sir Wm. Adair, which he expressed at a Unionist demonstration at Whiteabbey on July 21st of this year, ought to disabuse people's minds of any remnants of an idea that British soldiers will not shoot down Ulstermen if ordered to do so, or if they are fired on by them. Sir William Adair said:—

"It was one of the maxims of the Emperor Napoleon that when devising a plan of campaign one should credit the enemy with always doing the right thing. The right thing for the Government to do after it passed the Home Rule Bill was to coerce Ulster into submission, and the right way for them to do it was to employ British troops. As an old soldier it had rather pained him lately to hear and read so many questions as to whether the British soldiers would fire on Ulstermen. Thank God, the British soldier and the British sailor had always done their duty, and he knew they always would. And if they were told that it was their duty to fire on Ulstermen they would fire on Ulstermen. He did not care what Mr. Birrell said, or whether Mr. Asquith nodded his head off. It was their duty to oppose the Government, if necessary, by arms, and it was the duty of the Government to oppose them by all the forces that they could command."

Some pages back I suggested that the men who are being asked to risk their lives and properties in pursuance of the policy that "Ulster will fight" would do well, if their leaders ever gave them sufficient leisure to do so, to pause and ask themselves what their object is, that is if they have an object, and it is not merely a case of the blind leading the blind. The leader *par excellence*, who can hardly object to being described as the uncrowned king of Ulster, since he receives royal honours wherever he goes, apparently without any protest, has talked a good deal about taking his followers into his confidence, but if so there must be some secret code only understood by the initiated, as all that the ordinary person can make out of his public utterances is that they are going to resist Home Rule by methods, all of which possess a certain family resemblance, but which appear to be legal or illegal according to the day of the week on which the speech is delivered.

During the intermediate stage of the platform campaign there was a slight preponderance in favour of illegality, as in three out of four speeches which he delivered then, the language was strongly reminiscent of Kruger's threat that he would stagger humanity, and mere law was looked down upon from such a lofty pinnacle of contempt as can only be explained by the supposition of a too literal acceptance of the principle that "the king can do no wrong," while on the fourth day the Government actually had the good fortune to obtain a legal opinion from such an eminent authority for nothing, and were informed that they could not arrest him as he had done nothing illegal. His conduct is becoming apparently more illegal every day, but it is perhaps not too uncharitable to suspect that a person who can successfully create the impression that he is defying every law in the kingdom, and is laying himself open to prosecution for high treason, which is a much more serious crime than murder, and then is found to have been acting quite legally all the time, should fail to give his followers a correct idea of his aims and objects, I will not say through deliberate intention, but through mere force of habit and delight in his own intellectual ingenuity. Is it not even possible that one who has to spend too much of his time in bewildering and befogging other people, may end by bewildering and befogging himself, and get lost in a maze of words full of sound and fury signifying nothing? Whatever the plan is, assuming that one exists, it is evident that rifles have something to do with it, since money has been spent on purchasing them, and also evident that they have not very much, since most of those purchased are so old and inferior.[3] It is not contended that the Ulster Volunteers would have any chance whatever against the British Army unless it turned and fraternised with them, and I have endeavoured to show that even the R.I.C. might be rather awkward to tackle. What then can the object be? It is difficult to advance much further by direct reasoning, but perhaps something may be done by way of analogy.

War has been described as the sport of kings—no personal allusions are intended—and possibly some light may be thrown on the subject by considering the methods of sport. In countries where there are tigers, one of the most common methods of killing them is to tie a goat or buffalo at the foot of a tree, in the branches of which the hunter conceals himself. The tiger scents from afar a possible supper, comes along, and pounces on the unfortunate animal. While he is so engaged, the hunter from his place of safety in the tree fires, and if he is at all a good shot, kills the tiger.[4]

The similarity between the methods of the Ulster leaders and the eastern hunter has hitherto escaped attention, owing to the fact that the speeches of the former have to be searched for in isolated newspaper reports, and have not yet been published in a collected form. I seem, however, to remember an admission somewhere that the Ulster Volunteers would be no match for the whole British Army, and the evident anxiety that the latter should not shoot back would go to support this view. In his speech at Omagh, I find the great leader reported as saying, "So long as the Government allow us to take that course, and don't interfere with us, there is no reason why we should have a collision; but if the Government interfere with us, I shrink from no collision." In plain English, the Ulster Volunteers are being worked up so that, if the Home Rule becomes law, they are bound to come into conflict with the authorities, and then when in self-defence the police or soldiers have to fire, the leaders, who will occupy a strategic position in the rear similar to that of King James at the battle of the Boyne, will retire to the other side of the Channel and stump the country about the brutality of the Government in shooting down loyal Ulstermen; the wave of indignation so created will presumably sweep the Government from power, the Unionists will return to office, and everybody will live happily ever after, except, of course, those who had to be killed to bring this happy result about, and those who had the misfortune to be dependant on them, unless the indemnity fund is adequate for this and all other purposes. The traditional relationship on the part of Ulster of utility to the Conservative Party will be maintained, but on this occasion instead of being a card in the Tory pack, she will serve as a goat to the Tory huntsman.[5]

This appears to be the real and only conceivable object of the movement, that is, if it has an object, and all the rest is mere decoration and embellishment. Had the leaders been quite frank with themselves or their followers, a considerable amount of time spent in drilling, and whatever money has been spent in buying discarded rifles, might have been saved. Rifles are by no means necessary to get the police to fire on a mob; the same result can be produced by means of stones or bricks, as was demonstrated at Cawnpore the other day, where over forty of a Mohammedan crowd engaged in defending their civil and religious liberties, as they were led to believe they were, by pelting the police with bricks, were shot down just as if they had been ordinary rioters. The description of the incident in the *Irish Times*, a Unionist paper, which has overlooked the parallelism of the two situations alike in the objects aimed at, the methods employed, and the existence in each case of a strong local feeling in favour of peace, and that it was the influence of self-appointed outside leaders—in the Indian case they are called agitators—that turned the scale in favour of a resort to force, may be of interest as showing the manner in which such conduct is regarded when it takes place outside Ulster. The extracts are as follows:—

"An official account of the riot at Cawnpore states that the Mohammedans were excited by scurrilous attacks in the newspapers, and taunts of lack of religious zeal. Strenuous efforts were made by circulars to arouse feeling and to secure a big attendance. The crowd was estimated at about twenty thousand. Fiery addresses were delivered, and the police were received with brickbats and mercilessly beaten. The mounted police were forced to retire. The magistrate finally ordered the police to fire.

"Mr. Dodd, Superintendent of Police, was severely injured. Twenty-four were badly hurt, and one was killed by buckshot in the *mêlée*. One hundred and thirty-one persons are now in custody.

"Eighteen rioters were killed, and twenty-seven wounded.

"Intense depression prevails in Cawnpore, though the city is now quiet."

. . . .

"There can be no doubt that yesterday's riots at Cawnpore were caused by Moslem agitators."

. . . .

"The cry of sacrilege was assiduously spread by the Moslem League, and the news spread. Virtually it can be said that there was no excitement in Cawnpore itself, and the moderate section of the Moslems was arranging a deputation to Sir James Meston, the Lieutenant-Governor, who had undertaken to visit the mosque with them on the 9th inst., and to receive a formal statement their grievance on the same day. Meanwhile local Moslems, taunted by outside agitators with petty religious matters, held a mass meeting yesterday, which had some unfortunate results. It is reported that thirty or forty rioters were killed and wounded, and several policemen were also injured. The occurrence illustrates the danger of agitators playing on the fanaticism of an ignorant crowd."

The rule of the Provisional Government will thus in all probability be characterised by riot and disorder. I reserve for the next chapter a more detailed discussion of the problems with which it will be faced in its dealings both with its own subjects and with the Imperial Government, and the methods it may seek to apply in solving them.

EDITOR'S NOTES

1   This was written before Ulster Volunteer Force were armed with the Larne guns, which were relatively modern weapons.
2   This was written before the Curragh mutiny, which proved J.J.'s judgment wrong, and that of Carson right.
3   See note 1 above.
4   This analogy, and the subsequent Cawnpore allusion, springs from the older brothers in the Indian Civil Service.
5   This, to my mind, is the key paragraph.

CHAPTER VI.

PROBABLE COURSE OF EVENTS UNDER A PROVISIONAL GOVERNMENT.—METHODS OPEN TO THE IMPERIAL GOVERNMENT IN DEALING WITH IT.—EFFECT ON VARIOUS CLASSES IN ULSTER AND ON DUBLIN PARLIAMENT.— EFFECT ON BRITISH ELECTORATE

When the regime of "civil and religious" warfare or rioting has been introduced in Ulster, how will the Imperial Government deal with the situation thus created? Will it resign, or repeal the Home Rule Bill, or commit a breach of faith by disregarding the promise conveyed in Mr. Asquith's nod and ordering British troops to Ulster? These are the only possible courses that seem to have struck the leaders, or which they have considered it advisable to communicate to their followers. Not at all; there is at least one other possible course which naturally would commend itself to a Radical Government averse to war, or to any Government that had sense enough not to play the game of the other side, and that is the method known as a peaceful blockade. All that will be necessary will be to declare that certain parts of the country having set up, or rather having had set up for them by the forethought of their leaders, a government of their own, all communications by sea, rail, post, telegraph, or telephone, except on the public service, are cut off with those localities till the Provisional Government disappears, or its subjects cease to obey it. The Post Office, Telegraphs, and Telephones, being Government departments, no difficulty will arise in their case; it is unlikely the railway or steamer companies will object provided their losses are guaranteed, and in case they do, a few gunboats will be ample to look after the communications by sea, while the organisers of the midnight raid on the Boyne bridge by the motor cyclist corps have obligingly suggested a method of dealing with those by land.

Let us assume for the sake of argument that all the counties and parts of counties that have ever returned Unionist members of Parliament are in revolt, how long do they think they could manage if they found themselves confronted with this state of things? It may perhaps be thought, if the Government adopt tactics of this kind, the matter can easily be brought to a head by marching to Cork—as at one time it was stated the Ulstermen would do, before Mr. F.E. Smith discovered the doctrine of the homogeneous counties, and informed the world and his audience that they had no desire to dictate to the rest of Ireland—or even merely as far as Dublin, and doing for the Irish Parliament what Cromwell did for the English one.

Most of the Ulster Volunteers I have met have carried their ideas of warfare no further than potting a policeman from behind a hedge, or applying whatever force may be necessary to a political opponent to get him to contribute to the revenues of the Provisional Government, while one when asked if he would shoot when the time came, replied with all the emphasis of which he was capable: "Well, indeed I'll not"; but if any of them seriously think of marching to Cork, or Dublin, or even Dundalk, I would commend to his consideration, and that of his leaders, the following extracts from a recent work on military history, called "A Review of the History of Infantry," by Col. E.M. Lloyd, R.E.,[1] which will give him some faint idea of the difficulties he will have to meet with, and the losses he will have to face in the prosecution of any such attempt. Writing of the war between the Federals and the Confederates in the United States, Col. Lloyd says:—

"In the American Civil War the loose organisation, the inexperienced staff, and the thickly wooded country were additional reasons for fighting on the defensive. In the first battle of the war (Bull Run, July 21, 1861) the Federal

regiments which attacked proved incapable of movement under fire. They showed no want of courage, but
they broke into fragments, and their firing was wild. They
gave way before Jackson's counterstroke; but 'the same
want of discipline that had driven them in rout to
Washington had dissolved the victorious Confederates into
a tumultuous mob.'"

In regard to the Austro-Prussian war of 1866, he writes:—

"The difference of arms and tactics caused a striking
disparity of losses in every engagement. At Nachod (June
27) the advanced guard of the 5th Prussian corps (6½
battalions) held its ground for two hours against three
Austrian brigades (21 battalions), giving time for the main
body of the corps to debouch from a defile. The Austrians
fell back defeated, having lost five times as many men as
the Prussians. At Trantenau, on the same day, they were
more successful; the 10th Austrian corps (Gablenz) drove
the first Prussian corps back into the mountains. Yet here
the loss of the victors was nearly four times as great as that
of the troops they defeated."

The following passages from the same work must form
pleasant reading for the possessor of an Italian rifle who is a
member of a force that possesses no artillery, and the cavalry
of which will require a good many fresh recruits if it is to form
even two squadrons, while its training has hitherto mainly
consisted in escort duty:—

"The Austrians were so heavily handicapped in this
war by the difference of weapons that it is hardly necessary
to look further for an explanation of the result. It was in
infantry fighting they failed; in cavalry and artillery they
more than held their own."

Another passage dealing with the causes of the Prussian
defeat in 1806 is also worthy of his attention:—

"Many hard things were said of the Prussian army after
its defeat; but it seems to have been painstaking, zealous,

well drilled and disciplined. The muskets, says Clausewitz, were in a high state of polish, but they were the worst in Europe, and the artillery was inferior to the French. The chiefs were old men. . . ."

The Ulster general is 66, and is therefore a little younger than the Duke of Brunswick, who was 71, but he is a cavalry man, and the London correspondent of the *Irish Times* has blurted out the truth about his qualifications with that delightful candour which makes this paper sometimes so embarrassing to its own party. In its London Letter of September 23rd it is stated:—

"Sir George Richardson has had a distinguished career, and has done very well in subordinate positions, but his experience of high command has hardly been sufficient, in the opinion of his brother officers, to enable him to take control of the Ulster forces."

Therefore, before undertaking a campaign in which they have to assume the offensive, I would strongly advise them to provide themselves with an adequate force of cavalry and artillery, to arm their whole army with modern weapons, and teach it how to use them, if their march is not going to be a mere second edition of that of the Suffragettes from Edinburgh to London. In any case a glance at the Army List will show so many Ladysmiths and Mafekings on the way, that when sufficient detachments are left to besiege them, and to hold down the surrounding country, the chances of reaching Cork vanish entirely, and the number likely to be available to seize the capital will be so small that even if Mr. Asquith's nod prevents him from taking any steps to strengthen the garrison during the week or two that will have to be spent on the march, inexperienced commanders such as they possess will hardly risk such an extremely hazardous operation with raw and badly armed troops, and the force will have to fall back on its own frontier, or even beyond it, since the southern parts of Down and Armagh are mainly Nationalist. The case of the South African Republics illustrates the difficulty of an amateur army in carrying on anything but defensive warfare, and there are certain differences in their respective situations which the people of Ulster would do well to consider before they commit themselves to the policy of a Provisional Government, which if it succeeds can only succeed at the cost of great loss of life and destruction of trade, and if it fails will have made their position ten times worse than before, by having exasperated public feeling and rendered them ridiculous as well as unsuccessful.

For one thing, there is this difference between the position of Ulster and that of the South African Republics. The Boers were practically a self-supporting people. They did not depend on oversea communications for the maintenance of their economic and industrial life. But the position of Ulster is the exact opposite of this. Not only does Ulster depend on railway and steamship communications in order to export the produce of her farms and factories, and import those articles which she cannot produce at home, but she depends on such communications for the very possibility of carrying on her manufactures. There are no coal fields in that part of Ulster over which the Provisional Government is likely to obtain control, unless a shaft at present under construction is finished by then. If the method of a peaceful blockade is adopted, in a very short time the factories of Ulster would be at a standstill, and the factory workers would be out of employment. When this had happened, the theological questions which have hitherto almost monopolised attention would be superseded by more pressing and more practical ones. Would the employers go on paying wages to their workmen while their factories were idle, and they were earning nothing themselves? If not, what are the work-people going to live on? How will the farmers like to have their markets cut off, or rather to be provided with a large home demand for their produce on the part of people who have no money to pay for it? In fact if a large portion of the population are not to starve, a regime of communistic socialism will be an absolute necessity, and the principle "From each according to his ability, to each according to his needs" will have to be applied by persons whose antipathy to socialism is only less bitter than their antipathy to Home Rule. It will, if it takes place, be an exceedingly interesting political and social experiment, but in view of the small progress that such ideas have made in Ulster as yet, it is greatly to be feared that considerations of individual self-interest may begin to make themselves felt. Employers may raise difficulties about paying workers who are idle, while the employed may think they have as good a right to be paid for fighting as for working, and may argue that it is not their fault if there is no fighting to be done. The farmer may conceivably feel obliged to say to both in the words of a recent Irish play, "What about my money ?" Under such circumstances it is almost inevitable that there will be weak-kneed individuals in the camp who will begin to grumble and complain that the campaign is not nearly such a picnic as they were led to believe; when on the top of all these difficulties the Provisional Government is confronted with the problem of collecting taxes from people who are earning nothing, and about half of whom are living at other people's expense, it seems possible or even probable that the heads of the Provisional Government will consider it prudent statesmanship to slip away with that unobtrusive modesty which charac-terises the movements of revolutionaries who have failed and kings whose thrones have crumbled, and which, unfortunately, has been sadly wanting in their attitude hitherto.

The great Ulster leader in speaking at Newbliss, if correctly reported, made use of an argument which, like the proverbial straw which indicates the direction of the wind, allows one to see how difficult it is for lawyer politicians, even when they put themselves at the head of provinces rightly struggling to be free, to shake off the point of view which has become second nature to them. The question he put is this:—

"May I say solemnly and seriously and with all sincerity and from the bottom of my heart one word of warning to those who differ from us, and who, I dare say, especially differ from me? May I ask them this question? Are they certain in their own minds that they can find in this Home

Rule Bill and in this Home Rule policy any material
benefits which can possibly arise to themselves?"

The question is one which cannot be answered in a word or
two, for this reason, if for no other, that the advantage or
otherwise to the nation and to the individuals composing it
will largely depend on whether people determine on the
introduction of the new regime to make the best of things, or,
like the Right Honourable Gentleman and his friends, to
make the worst. In case the Unionists return to power, there
are certain very tangible material benefits such as the salaries
attached to certain legal appointments, and the bonuses
which may be expected to accompany land purchase where
the principle of compulsion is banned as "an unclean thing,"
and there is no way of getting landlords to sell except by
bribing them to do so, but it may be safely laid down as a
general principle that most of these material benefits will stop
short at the edge of the platform, and very few of them will
filter down to the audience. Assuming for the sake of argument that Home Rule will bring no material benefits, or
even some disadvantages, I would recall attention to the fact
that the point at issue appears likely to be, not Home Rule
versus the present state of things, but Home Rule *versus* anarchy
or civil war under the auspices of a Provisional Government,
and I would put the question to ordinary people who have to
live by their business, or their farms, or their labour, and have
no hopes or expectations of Government employment, "Can
they find in this Provisional Government scheme and in this
Provisional Government policy any material benefits which
can possibly arise to themselves?" The business man is told
that under Home Rule he will be crushed by unjust taxation.
It will not be such an easy matter to arrange taxation the
incidence of which will fall entirely on one class. Thanks to
the excellent moral lessons conveyed in the readers provided
by the Commissioners of National Education, most of the
members of the Irish Parliament will be familiar with the story
of the goose and the golden eggs. Few analogies are altogether
perfect, and the points of discrepancy are all in favour of

Ulster, the industries of which could not be suddenly cut off at
one fell stroke like their prototype in the fable, but if they
perish at all can only perish by one of those wasting diseases
which give ample time for treatment, and can often be cured
by a removal of the unhealthy conditions. Besides, will the
Provisional Government be able to live on air, unless it also
consists of that element? And not merely to live, but to carry
on warlike operations, which are always expensive, however
much economies may be made by dispensing with artillery, and
almost entirely with cavalry, and using black powder instead of
smokeless. The utmost that the Tariff Reformers ever hoped for
was to make the foreigner pay, but the Provisional Government
will have improved greatly on this if they make the enemy do
so, and the goodnatured British administration is going to
allow Customs duties to be collected which are to form the
sinews of war to be used against it. Is there not a chance that
the Provisional Government will be compelled to levy
contributions from its subjects, which if levied by anyone else
its authors would have no hesitation in describing as crushing
taxation? And will the damage to credit, and the interruption
of trade, and all the disorganisation that is bound to ensue
from a state even of excitement and disturbance, much more
from civil war, not also involve very great loss, even if no
property is looted or burnt in the course of the operations? A
business man who fails to see that so far as he is concerned, a
Provisional Government and all that it involves is a case of out
of the frying pan into the fire, must possess a brain singularly
well provided with watertight compartments.

We will assume, however, that the business man is
prepared to risk it, but what about those whom he employs,
whether in a superior position, or as ordinary workers? Has
such a person any guarantee that when business is interrupted
and work at a standstill, he will continue to draw his pay, or
that he will receive any allowance whatever? Or that the
result of the civil war may not be to cause such ruin to the
industries of Ulster that he will be thrown out of employment
and have to start life again elsewhere? All these are extremely
practical questions, which one would expect to have seen

discussed when the question of material benefits was being dealt with, but I have been able to find nothing about them in the newspaper reports, and am obliged to console myself with the reflection that possibly they fall into the class of affairs of state which have no doubt been carefully considered in private by the Provisional Government, but which it would be injurious to the cause to divulge at present.

The farmer is in a better position than the other two classes, since a civil war cannot do very much damage to his land, and may even improve its fertility should it happen to be the scene of an engagement, in which connection many of my readers will doubtless remember the following lines which they learned in their school days:—

> . . . "The unreturning brave, alas!
> Ere evening to be trodden like the grass,
> Which now beneath them, but above shall grow
> In its next verdure when this fiery mass
> Of living valour rolling on the foe,
> And burning with high hope shall moulder cold and low."

A farmhouse, however, is just as combustible as a factory, and the contents of a farmyard a good deal more so, while that disagreeable practice known as commandeering to which armies sometimes have resort, will press more hardly on the farmer than on anybody else, since the farmer will be the principal person who has anything to commandeer. From our consideration of the probable condition of the other elements of society, it would appear extremely doubtful if supplies thus taken will be paid for in cash, or by anything but an expression of gratitude or a knock on the head with the butt of a rifle, according to the alacrity the farmer displays in providing what is required of him. At the best, the most that can be hoped for is vouchers or paper money redeemable when the Unionists return to office, and this will involve special legislation. The possibility of such legislation has been overlooked by the British public, and probably by the Unionist leaders themselves, but it would seem to follow from Mr. Bonar Law's pledge, read out at the meeting at Craigavon on 12th July, that in whatever action the Ulster leaders thought fit to take "under present circumstances" they would have the whole Unionist Party behind them. Surely this, if it means anything, means that they will foot the bill? Surely the Unionists who have waxed so indignant over the betrayal of Ulster would not themselves be guilty of conduct which might be construed as a betrayal? The language used by leading members of the party on the subject of the delay in the promised reconstitution of the House of Lords justifies the hope that they at any rate will not attempt to wriggle out of even an implied promise, or one made by mistake through neglect to weigh their words with sufficient care. It may, therefore, be assumed that they will do their duty to Ulster, especially as Ulster would have done its duty to them by cutting with the sword the Gordian knot with which Tariff Reform and other unprofitable adventures have bound them, and restoring them to office when their prospects seemed most gloomy. With the passing of the measure through both Houses of Parliament, however, its success will still be by no means assured, and this owing to a danger its authors have themselves gone out of their way to create.

One of the greatest difficulties that the Ulster leaders have to contend with, unless the fact that at least 45 per cent. of the population are hostile, and a large proportion of the remainder indifferent or apathetic should be reckoned as one, is the necessity of employing principles, which in the case of the inhabitants of the other provinces used to excite their utmost abhorrence; however since the greatest of them[2] was constrained by a sense of duty to accept a brief rumoured to have been marked with four figures in the Marconi case, it is difficult to say how much of this feeling was personal, and how much was the maintenance of a correct professional attitude on the part of an officer charged with the enforcement of the law, and on whose consciousness the existence of that higher law which requires him at the proper time and place to break all laws not made according to his own formula, had not yet dawned. In any case, when a disturbance takes place in one of the other three provinces, the persons taking part in it are rebels and traitors. Transfer the scene to Ulster, and they are loyal heroes preserving their birthright. A corollary to this attitude is that their principles are not of universal application, and must on no account be put into operation by anybody but themselves, or the consequences might be extremely awkward. One such instance strikes me of a difficulty that may very well arise if their views are accepted. In spite of the outcry about dragging the King into politics that was made when, at the time the Budget was rejected, the Government adopted the only means known to the Constitution of putting an end to the deadlock, in the speeches of responsible leaders of the party, His Majesty has been deluged with suggestions to refuse to sign the Home Rule Bill, in other words, to disregard the whole constitutional theory and practice of the last two hundred years, and act on the advice of persons other than his Ministers. The proposal has even received the countenance of the leader of the Opposition, who either despairs of ever obtaining office, or has failed to foresee the difficulties that may be created for him when he gets there, if the precedent he seeks to set up is established. Let us assume that the plans of the Ulster leaders have proved successful, that the blood of the martyrs has had all the magical effect usually attributed to it, that after a short and glorious struggle between the R.I.C. and the Ulster Volunteers the Unionists have come back to power, and Mr. Bonar Law presents for His Majesty's signature the Bill throwing the expenses of both sides in the campaign on the Imperial Exchequer. The King's affection for his Army and Navy is well known, and it is extremely probable that he would feel considerable sympathy for those unfortunate policemen who perished in the execution of their duty. Is it conceivable that in such circumstances he should refuse to sign the Bill, and express the sentiment, which would secure far more universal approval throughout the country than anything he might do in connection with the Home Rule Bill, that those who make war should pay for it? In that case the only remedy of the farmer who has suffered in his person or his property owing to the civil war will be a suit in the courts, unless he receives compensation from the rates on the head of malicious injury; and as those of the Ulster leaders who have not obtained positions which preclude the necessity of private practice will flock to defend their henchmen, while quite possibly the judge who tries the case will be one of them who has gone to the place where good leaders go when they happen to belong to the legal profession, the result is likely to be a foregone conclusion, and the farmer will do well to rebuild his house at his own expense, cease to grumble about his contribution in provisions and supplies to the success of the cause he has, or ought to have, at heart, and in short remember that there is a great deal of truth in the old proverbs about the uselessness of crying over spilt milk and of throwing good money after bad.

In the absence of any detailed proposals as to the course the leaders propose to follow in some of the most elementary contingencies that any government must be prepared to face, I find it very difficult to see what material benefit can arise to anybody in Ulster, except the lawyers and landlords, from the attempted establishment of a Provisional Government, while there would seem to be very serious danger that it may cause very widespread loss, and in a good many cases total ruin.

A touch of humour is added to the situation by the fact that although all this would inconvenience the Imperial Government to some degree, and will inconvenience Ulster Unionists far more, it will not trouble the Dublin Parliament in the slightest; on the contrary, it may be a means of adding considerably to its income in the future if it causes an increase of expenditure on the R.I.C., which remains an Imperial Service for the first six years, and is then to be handed over to the Irish Government, because, no matter how high the cost at which it has been taken over, whatever savings it is subsequently found possible to make, go to the benefit of the Irish Government. I cannot forbear quoting in this connection the opinion of a distinguished Unionist barrister who has written a book on the financial aspects of the Home Rule Bill:—

"This novel system of raising Irish Revenue at the expense of the British taxpayer can be exploited in infinite variety. It would pay the Irish Government to keep up . . . as much agrarian and other disturbance in Ireland as possible during the first six years, and thus compel England to keep up a greater and more expensive Constabulary force. The Nationalists can also contemplate with complacency the determination of Ulster to pay no taxes under Home Rule. England is to be responsible for the collection of the taxes; and the bland idea of the Radical Ministry that they will check-mate Ulster by reserving the Royal Irish Constabulary for British control during the first six years to keep Ulster in hand, and to enforce the collection of taxes there as an Imperial Service, must commend itself to the embryo Irish Chancellor of the Exchequer as excellent statecraft. Ireland must get her six millions to supply the Transferred Services whether any Revenue is raised in Ulster or not raised. The Irish Government is not to be responsible for the peace during the first six years. With a judicious distribution of moonlighting in the South and with Ulster in revolt in the North, there would be a most satisfactory financial outlook for Ireland. The cost of the Constabulary would have to be increased rapidly by hundreds of thousands above its present figure £1,350,000, and then it would be taken over with the transferred sum swelled to the maximum figure."*

Surely this is the *reductio ad absurdum* of the whole scheme of forming a Provisional Government, unless the two parties have a secret understanding, and it is merely a device to squeeze more money out of England?

What are the objects of all this tomfoolery? The immediate object is to impress the British elector, and if possible to force a General Election. So far it may be only bluff. The British elector is not impressed; and a General Election cannot be forced. Even if they do succeed in forcing a General Election, it seems very doubtful if the Unionists will come back to

*Home Rule Finance, by A.W. Samuels K.C., p. 67.

power, and, even if they do, it does not follow we have heard the last of the question of Home Rule.

In regard to this subject the Unionist Party is, and must continue to be, so long as the present system continues, between the devil and the deep sea. One of the clauses in the Act of Union provides that Ireland shall send at least 100 members to the Parliament at Westminster. All the indications point to the fact that at least 80 of them will be Nationalists. Assuming that the remainder are Conservatives, which, in view of the opposition of interests between the usual type of Conservative M.P. and the Ulster farmer or workingman, is a state of things which cannot last for ever, the Unionist Party has either to start with a deficit balance of over 60 votes, or to drive a coach and four through the Act of Union, which has hitherto been treated as its "Ark of the Covenant." The phrase is only intended metaphorically, but as recent events have also given it a more literal significance, it may also be read the other way without objection. Consequently it has either to give away its own case by repealing part of the Act of Union, or to sacrifice most of its chances of holding office. The responsible leaders of the party, such as Mr Balfour and Lord Lansdowne, see this, and would apparently be glad of an opportunity of getting the Irish out of the way if they could do so with any show of consistency. The best that can be hoped for therefore is a respite from, and not a final settlement of, the Irish question.

If they fail to force a General Election, what is their next object? They are going to set up a Provisional Government for "Ulster." They will not desert the "outposts" in Donegal, and doubtless those of Cavan and Monaghan, also, will find shelter under the protecting aegis of their government. On the other hand, if we may believe Mr. F.E. Smith, they have no intention of annexing the rest of Ireland. In his speech at Dungannon he said:— "We have never claimed—the Provisional Government itself does not claim—to dictate to the rest of Ireland." What is more, the Ulster Unionist members twice proposed the exclusion of Ulster from the Home Rule Bill. There are 300,000 Protestant "outposts" in the three southern provinces. Presumably these are to be thrown to the wolves, for without Ulster they can have no representation except by the grace of their Catholic fellow-countrymen. It is more likely that the Ulster leaders know perfectly well that these Southern Protestants will suffer nothing under Home Rule, otherwise the proposals to exclude Ulster, if seriously meant, would never have been made. If Protestants will suffer nothing under Home Rule where they are only 11 per cent of the population and cannot possibly have any representation by their own unaided efforts, what is the danger to Ulster under Home Rule, where the population is about evenly divided, and in many parts the majority of the people are Protestant?

Sir E. Carson in his speech at Dungannon shows how powerless Mr. Redmond would be to oppress Protestants in any part of Ireland:—

"The moment the Home Rule Bill passes, or even when Home Rule is brought into operation, Mr. Redmond will have no soldiers, and he will have no police."

He will have no soldiers at any time, and except for the Dublin Metropolitan Police, who will probably be kept busy enough in the capital unless a great change takes place, he will have no police for six years. In other words, Mr. Redmond can only use police or soldiers for the oppression of Protestants anywhere by permission of the British Government of the day. If actual oppression were proposed, is it possible that the British Government would give that permission? Surely it would be well to postpone the civil war for six years, and by that time Sir Edward Carson and Mr. Redmond, or their successors in the leadership of their respective parties, will have other problems to deal with, and may possibly have formed a Government to restrain the syndicalist tendencies of the working classes in Ireland. At any rate the religious question will have ceased to monopolise attention, as it has already ceased to do in Dublin.

Meanwhile the proposal to set up a Provisional Government for "Ulster" holds the field. In view of the fact that the vast majority of the inhabitants of Donegal, Monaghan, and

Cavan are Nationalists, and the improbability of their being persuaded to accept its rule, I would suggest that the delimitation of the boundaries of the new state should be left to an international commission. No part of Ulster is homogeneous in matters of religion. Even Antrim, Down, and Belfast contain a strong minority of Catholics. If it is proposed to coerce all non-Unionists, the proposal really amounts to a proposal to set up in Ulster, or parts of Ulster, a state of anarchy dignified by the name of civil war. The object of this move would seem to be so to inconvenience the Irish Parliament and the Imperial Government that the latter will have no choice except to force Home Rule on them at the point of the bayonet, or else surrender all along the line and repeal the Act. The success of this policy depends on the Government's acting exactly as its Provisional rival wants it to act. As I have already shown, the Government will not have to send troops to force Home Rule on Ulster, although they may have to defend Government property with soldiers, and use armed force in order to prevent Ulster Unionists from forcing their Provisional Government on those who do not want it. In the last resort they can always bring Ulster to her knees by the method I have indicated or something on similar lines. Ulster Unionists need not expect that British soldiers will fail to do their duty in these or any other circumstances. The Government will be much less inconvenienced by the attempt to carry out this policy than Ulstermen themselves will be, and the Irish Parliament will suffer no inconvenience at all. Consequently it is safe to prophesy that they will fail in this second object also.

One or two of the Ulster leaders have the reputation of being able men in their own departments, and it is difficult to believe that they do not realise that they are practically certain to fail in both their avowed objects. The leader *par excellence* says he does not conceal from himself the difficulties he is faced with in framing his Provisional Government. This is an attempt to make it no longer possible to conceal them from his followers. He has set up machinery for a Provisional Government which he must know is bound to collapse within a week or two after it begins to "govern," as a result of its own inherent absurdity. In the meanwhile Ulster Unionists may profitably employ themselves in pondering the question as to whether the avowed objects of this agitation are its real objects, or whether its real objects have not hitherto been concealed, and the conjecture that I have made as to what they are is not a fairly probable one.

As a result of acute differences of opinion on questions of the interpretation of Christian doctrine, and of a tendency to make lack of unanimity on such points an excuse for appealing to the arm of the flesh, there is always in Ulster a lot of inflammable material which may at any moment take fire. The conduct of the Ulster leader and his lieutenants, and the attitude of mind he has encouraged in his followers with reference to those who differ from them in religion, is not of such a kind as to allay feelings of sectarian bitterness and prevent religious discord from bringing about a state of social disorder. In the original draft of this I had written:—

> "In short, the methods of the Ulster agitators are well calculated to cause riot and disturbance, whether they intend that result or not. It seems likely that the main result of this agitation will be to excite party feeling in Ulster to such a pitch that it will find its expression either in attacks on non-Unionist 'hostages' or in conflicts with policemen or soldiers."

Since then the subject has passed from the region of prophesy to that of history. The usual pilgrimage from Belfast to Derry took place on the anniversary of the Relief. As a result of all the talk about fighting that has been recently indulged in, almost everybody, even the women, carried revolvers, which they blazed away indiscriminately as if they had been so many crackers. At a certain station on the way to Derry the excursion train had to be held up to allow another train to pass, and the celerity with which everybody on the platform succeeded in taking cover shows that perhaps some branches of the military art are more easily acquired than others, and that some modification may be necessary in the conclusions I arrived at when discussing that part of the subject. However, I would seem to have been right about the necessity of learning to aim correctly, as the total casualties were one girl wounded and a telephone wire cut. In Derry itself every opportunity seems to have been taken of trying conclusions with the police, one of whom was shot while engaged in a high-handed attempt to arrest a loyalist who was merely following the universal human instinct of playing with a new toy. Several non-combatants were also shot in the course of the rehearsal of the conditions under the Provisional Government which took place on this and the following days, but it is hoped that with greater practice these accidents will be avoided, and that, in future, nobody will be hit except those wearing His Majesty's uniform. Unfortunately, as most of the leaders were absent on the Continent and elsewhere, the affair was bungled, and, as it happened, nearly all the martyrs were on the wrong side, unless it can be shown that the man killed was shot by the police, which is rather difficult to prove in view of the medical evidence that the wound was of the nature to be expected if caused by an Italian rifle; but as it has now been discovered that the R.I.C. are mainly recruited from the "hereditary enemies," and take much more kindly to civil war in Ulster than they did to evictions in their own country, there is every reason to hope that in a short time a supply of martyrs of the right kind will be forthcoming, and the Ulster leaders, whose present methods differ from those of the suffragettes mainly in the fact that they prefer to obtain their martyrs by proxy, having secured the fulfilment of their own prophesy, will be able to stump England and Scotland and proclaim—"We told the Government so all along, but they would not be warned. They have proceeded on their dangerous course, and now this is the result."

Of course the leaders of the Ulster movement are loud in their protests that they are asking their followers to incur no risk to which they are not prepared to expose themselves. They are, however, mostly lawyers, and one will search the records of history in vain for an example of a lawyer politician who has become a martyr to his political or religious convictions. It is more likely that while heads are being broken in Ulster by irresponsible youths, the responsible leaders of the party will either have important legal engagements on the other side of the Channel, or consider the opportunity a favourable one for enlightening the British public on the subject of the wickedness of the Government. The Unionist leaders require martyrs, but unless the Government plays their game, they will not get the sort of martyrs they require. On the other hand, if the Government refuses to play their game, it can ensure that any Ulster Volunteers who lay down their lives will do so in the course of operations such as illegal tax-collecting which will secure very little sympathy elsewhere, and which, if persisted in in the face of opposition, will turn the whole public opinion of moderate men against this attitude of Ulster, with the result that Ulster, instead of staggering humanity is more likely to make herself the laughing stock of the civilised world, as the scene of the most realistic farce of modern times entitled "The Bluff that Failed."

Thus the promoters of the Provisional Government are likely to fail in all their objects, both those they profess, and those that are kept in modest retirement. Ulster Unionism was spoken of once as a card in the Tory pack. Let us hope that it will have sufficient sense to refuse to play the part of goat to the Tory huntsman. The leaders know perfectly well that the Ulster army is about as fit to face the British Army as a goat is to face a tiger. It will be poor consolation to the dead or dying goat to know that the tiger has been shot, and the tragic nature of its fate will be still further aggravated by the fact that since the episode of the rejection of the Budget, it can have no great confidence in the accuracy of the sportsman's aim. If Ulstermen possess the commonsense with which they credit themselves, they will cease to follow leaders who have either let their promises outrun their performances on the subject of taking them into their confidence, or who are only fit to lead a stage army in a comic opera.

There is, however, some limit to the gullibility of the British public, and there is always the possibility that a majority of the electors may saddle the responsibility for whatever disturbance takes place on those politicians who have abandoned all traditions of constitutional government, and played with imitation rifles, imitation governments, and imitation revolutions, in the midst of a credulous and excitable population, both elements of which are naturally among the most kindhearted people in the world, but are being driven by their encouragement and instigation to fly at each others throats. But, on the other hand, there is always the chance that the British electors may take the other view, and eight years is a long time to have languished in the cold shades of opposition for politicians, over whose heads time has passed like those of others, however much their language and their proposals may seem to bear the stamp of the fiery recklessness of youth. The risk, therefore, would seem to be worth taking from their point of view, though hardly from that of the crowd of followers whose part apparently it will be to be driven forward to draw the enemy's fire.

EDITOR'S NOTES

1   E.M. Lloyd's *Review of the History of Infantry* (London and Calcutta, 1908) was a source of military experience which came to hand, perhaps suggested by the older brother James in India. Lloyd had also written a study of military engineering history, *Vauban, Montalambert, Carnot* (London, 1887).

2   Carson played a professional legal role in the episode known as the 'Marconi scandal'; this was an episode not unlike what we are currently (1999) familiar with as the subject of tribunals of enquiry in the Irish Republic. Marconi himself had nothing to do with it. It related to prior knowledge of a government communications contract on the part of certain politicians. By the way, it is perhaps worth mentioning in passing that J.J. avoids mentioning Carson by name, except when quoting a speech from the record.

CHAPTER VII

BRIEF REVIEW OF IRISH HISTORY, POLITICAL
AND ECONOMIC, FROM 1782–1800.—OPINION
OF PROFESSOR HEWINS, M.P.—FALSITY OF
ASSUMPTION THAT IRELAND OWES ALL HER
PROSPERITY TO THE UNION.—DETAILS OF
THE STATE OF SOME OF THE LEADING
IRISH INDUSTRIES BEFORE THE UNION.

Before dealing with the wisdom or otherwise of the present
attitude of the Ulster leaders any further than can be occasionally inferred from the foregoing pages, I propose to make
a brief historical retrospect of the system of government for
Ireland with which they have identified themselves, and an
examination of how far it has been justified by its results.[1] It is
unnecessary to go back further than 1782, the year in which
the Irish Parliament gained its independence, since previous to
that the operation of Poyning's Law, under which legislation
could only be introduced in it with the permission of the
English Privy Council, rendered it little more than a machine
for registering the decrees of the English Government of the
day. Lest it should be thought my account of the subject has
been coloured by my own views, I shall confine myself entirely
to works of standard reputation as authorities, with a preference
for those written by Unionists and authors who are not Irish.

For the general history of the period I propose to use
O'Connor Morris's "Ireland from '98–'98" a good deal. The
late Mr. O'Connor Morris was a Protestant landlord, and in
politics a Unionist. When he published this history he was
County Court Judge for Roscommon and Sligo. I trust,
therefore, that what I shall write on his authority will be

received as absolutely trustworthy.[2] For the economic aspects of the period in question I shall make liberal use of a book published in 1903 called "A History of the Commercial and Financial relations between England and Ireland from the period of the Restoration," by Miss Alice Effie Murray, D.Sc.,[3] and of the Preface to it by Mr. W.A.S. Hewins, M.A., Director of the London School of Economics, who is one of the leading economists among the Tariff Reformers, and has since become Unionist M.P. for Hereford.

The following extracts from the Preface written by Mr. Hewins for this work will be interesting reading for some of his political friends, whose repertoire so largely consists of the two subjects of their civil and religious liberties and the superiority of British methods of administration to anything that could possibly be evolved in this country:—

"I am the more pleased to contribute a preface to her work because I have long believed that the difficulties of Ireland are due to economic rather than religious or political causes, though in times past, at any rate, the reaction of the latter on the economic development of Ireland and its relations with England has certainly been unfavourable in its effects. I, therefore, welcome every attempt to set forth in an impartial manner the main features of Irish economic history, whether or not I agree with the opinions of the author. There is scarcely any subject of which we are more ignorant or the study of which is more likely to correct extravagant views of British genius in the sphere of economic statesmanship."

In regard to the thoroughness of Miss Murray's investigations and the importance of her conclusions, I would invite attention to the following remarks of Mr. Hewins on the subject, and also to the fact that the work is not a polemical treatise, but embodies the result of the researches which gained Miss Murray the degree of D.Sc. in the University of London.

"The fact that Miss Murray's work won the approval of two such high authorities on the subject of it as Sir Robert

Giffen and Prof. C. F. Bastable is sufficient evidence of its
value. She has not only made use of the available materials,
both books and documents, which are in print, but she has
incorporated the results of much original research amongst
English and Irish manuscript sources."

The idea that most of the difficulties with which Ireland has to
contend arise from the religion or laziness of the native
elements of the population, and that all that is necessary for
her regeneration is to become as like as possible to England in
religion and everything else, a theory which one finds underlying a great deal of the Unionist oratory, though in England it
has to be modified when the Duke of Norfolk is on the platform, as he is not merely a Catholic but a very rich man, finds
a very lukewarm supporter in Mr. Hewins, when he states:—

> "Most of the difficulties, of an economic character, in
> the financial relations between England and Ireland arise
> from the differences of economic structure and organi-
> sation between the two countries. If Ireland were a highly
> organised, populous, manufacturing country, the present
> fiscal system would probably work out no worse than it
> does in the urban districts of Great Britain. But whatever
> be the virtues or the demerits of that system, it was
> certainly not framed with any reference to the economic
> conditions which prevail in Ireland."

And, as a summary of the general effect of the Union, I
doubt very much if either Mr. Redmond or Mr. William
O'Brien would care to improve much on this:—

> "This economic estrangement and relative decline of
> Ireland must necessarily be a source of weakness to the
> United Kingdom. It practically means that the Union is
> merely political, and therefore unstable."

The following quotations from the body of the work
describe the condition of some of the leading industries during
the period that Ireland enjoyed legislative independence. A
glance at them will show that the allegation so frequently

made, that Ireland owes all her prosperity to the Union, is
one of the most ludicrous instances on record of politicians
trading on popular ignorance, with the single exception of
those who at the next election after the reform of the calendar
in 1752, raised the party cry: "Who stole the eleven days?". It
should be noted that at this time the English duties were so
high as almost entirely to exclude Irish manufactures, so that
whatever prosperity there was in Ireland was in no way due to
her, but arose entirely from the condition of the country itself
and from trade with the rest of the world. Miss Murray
describes as follows the state of some of the leading industries
of that time, most of which have since disappeared:—

> The glass manufacture probably made more pro-
> gress during this period than any other Irish industry.
> Immediately after the withdrawal of the trade restrictions
> two glass factories were erected in Cork, one for making
> bottle and window glasses of all kinds, the other for making
> all sorts of plate glass. Very soon the glass manufactured at
> these factories was held to be equal to any made in
> Europe, while other glass made at Waterford equalled, if
> not excelled, the same kind made in Great Britain, in spite
> of the established skill of the British manufacturers. . . .
> Before 1782 Ireland had imported all her flint glass from
> England, but now she not only supplied by far the larger
> part of her own consumption, but also exported some to
> America. . . . Next to the glass industry, the Irish cotton
> manufacture seems to have made the most progress after
> the repeal of the commercial restrictions. As early as 1783
> the Lord Lieutenant wrote that the printing of cottons
> had been brought to great perfection in Ireland. . . . In
> 1784 the Manchester cotton manufacturers attributed the
> great decrease in their trade with Ireland not only to the
> non-importation agreements which were then in existence,
> but also to the fact that the Irish were beginning to
> make for themselves such articles as fustians, cottons, and
> calicoes. The success of the Irish cotton trade alarmed the
> Manchester merchants, and the English cotton manufac-

turers began flooding the Irish markets with their goods selling them at reduced prices, in order to crush out the new industry. But these attempts do not appear to have succeeded, for there continued to be a general decrease in the amount of English cotton goods exported to Ireland . . . American importers stated that Irish corduroys were equal to the best British. Altogether, the prospects of the industry were hopeful. There was a good deal of enterprise connected with the manufactures. The best machinery was imported from England. Besides Brooke's factory at Prosperous, there were in a few years cotton factories at Slane, Balbriggan, and Finglas in County Dublin. Several English manufacturers set up other factories in County Waterford. . . . The cotton manufacture was now well established in Ireland, and its success seemed necessary to the prosperity of the country. . . . There was now a large cotton manufacture at Belfast, and during the closing years of the century the whole cotton industry became so prosperous that it threatened to rival the linen manufacture, and many linen weavers began to take to cotton weaving. At the time of the Union the cotton industry ranked next to the linen in value, and there were in existence thirteen cotton mills capable of working up 500,000 pounds of cotton, while much capital was invested in the industry. . . . All this time the linen manufacture continued to develop satisfactorily. The exports of plain linen cloth increased enormously from 1780 to 1796, the comparative fall during the last four years of the century being, of course, due to the general condition of the country. A thriving trade in coloured linens to the American States and the British plantations was opened up. Nearly all the coloured linen exported was sent to these places, for it was still excluded from the British markets by duties equal to a prohibition, whilst most of the Continental nations imposed heavy duties on the importation of these articles. A fair amount of cambric and lawn was also sent to America and the plantations, and at the beginning of the war with France it seemed likely that a demand might arise in Great Britain. . . .

Thread stockings and a considerable amount of mixed linen silk and cotton goods were also exported. The Irish foreign trade in linen goods was now far superior to that of Scotland, in spite of the encouragement which the latter country had received for nearly a century. In the article of plain linen cloth alone Ireland exported well over 46½ million yards, as against 23 million exported from Scotland.

"Some progress was made in the silk industry but little was exported, only a few pounds of manufactured and thrown silk and a few pairs of silk stockings every year. . . It was in the manufacture of poplins and other mixed goods that the Irish excelled. During this period there was a flourishing cabinet manufacture in Dublin and its neighbourhood, which gave employment to a considerable number of persons. . . ."*

In order to encourage the brewing industry the Irish Parliament diminished the duty on beer and added to the spirit duty. Miss Murray goes on to explain how:—

". . . as a result of these new regulations the recent decline in the Irish brewing industry was checked, and the output of beer and porter has continued to increase up to the present day. The progress of the brewing industry was not, however, coincident with a decline in the Irish distilling industry, in spite of the new taxation. Small distilleries disappeared, but the large ones increased their output, and the total amount of spirits distilled steadily rose. In 1780 the total produce of the distilleries was 1,227,651 gallons. This had increased to 3,499,596 gallons in 1782, just as the new policy of encouraging the breweries was being adopted; but in 1798 the total amount of spirits distilled increased to 4,783,954 gallons. . . . The efforts of the Irish Parliament to develop Irish resources in another direction met with greater success. Irish fisheries now sprang into importance by means of a careful system of bounties and a wise system of inspection of all fish exported. In 1778

* Miss Murray, p. 276 ff.

only forty fishing vessels had existed in Ireland, but in 1781 there were 333 fishing vessels eligible for bounty. In the following year this number had increased to 700, while there were three large ships of 200 tons each too large to receive the bounty, and many other vessels which carried less than the requisite number of tons. . . . The Irish Parliament was anxious to secure a good reputation in foreign markets for Irish goods. British witnesses testified that Irish herrings were sought after more than their own because of the unimpeachable character of all Irish fish. Often the West India fleet leaving the Clyde would go to Cork to ship Irish herrings. Irish fishermen went to different parts of Scotland to teach the people fish curing, while others went further afield and established 'a great fishery on the banks of Newfoundland', which, in 1785, 'increases daily.'. . . The same system of inspection which was applied in Ireland to fish was also applied to beef and pork, and the English Inspector-General of Exports and Imports stated that, in his belief, Ireland was in no small degree indebted to this regulation for the superior quality and character of her meat and the higher price which it fetched in every part of the world."*

Miss Murray's final conclusion would be startling, were it not that one of the principal arguments of the Ulster leader has insensibly paved the way for it. Her summing up is:—

"A study of the commercial and industrial history of Ireland during those twenty years from 1780 to the Union certainly shows that material progress was being made, and that the Irish were beginning to evince a spirit of industrial enterprise. Of course, many checks and drawbacks had to be encountered, and it was difficult for Ireland to compete successfully with those other nations which had such a long industrial start. The effects of the commercial restrictions could not but remain in the country, even after the restrictions themselves had been removed. This is why the

* Miss Murray, p. 286 ff.

foreign trade in woollen goods could not keep at the high level it had attained in 1785; it was one of the chief reasons why Irish manufacturers were possessed of such little capital and Irish artisans of such little skill; and it was the main reason why in later years Irish industries dwindled and decayed under the stress of British and foreign competition brought about by the new policy of Free Trade. But that so much progress was made in spite of the still existing commercial inequality with Great Britain says something for the elasticity of the country and the new spirit of enterprise which commercial and political freedom had awakened among the Irish people. From 1704 to 1782 the general export of Ireland increased from one to thirty-two, but in fourteen years, from 1782 to 1796, it rose from thirty-two to eighty-eight. We hear little of the old complaint of want of employment in the towns, except during two or three years of localised distress, for the growing manufactures kept all hands at work. At the same time, there is some reason to believe that the condition of the peasantry changed slightly for the better. The extension of tillage made their position less precarious, and it was not until after the Union that the evils due to the too sudden increase of arable farming began to appear. The famines which had occurred so frequently all through the century, disappeared for the time being, and the new national feeling did something to establish more humane sentiments towards the peasantry. The class of resident landlords was larger than it had been since the beginning of the century, and especially during the Volunteer movement Irish landlords wished to appear at the head of a prosperous tenantry. On the whole, this short period of legislative independence in Ireland was by far the most prosperous period which the country had ever experienced. The Irish Parliament included among its members many brilliant and capable men, who knew by what means they might best promote the prosperity of their country. The pity was that they had only a short twenty years in which to work, and that when the Union took place the industrial life of the Irish people was not fully or firmly enough established to benefit by the new connection. From the material point of view the Union achieved nothing for Ireland, simply because the two countries were too different in their economic life to allow of both reaping equal benefit from the operation of the same commercial system. Almost directly after the Union there began a decline in Irish trade and industry, slow at first, but afterwards very rapid, a decline which only quite recently has begun to be arrested. It is indeed doubtful whether, even at the present day, Ireland is much richer than she was in the years before the Union. Her population is a little less, the percentage of the population employed wholly or partially in manufacturing industry is less, there is a greater gulf fixed between agricultural and industrial pursuits, so that the mass of the people are thrown far more entirely upon the land. On the other hand, the material condition of the Irish poor has certainly improved in recent years, although this improvement is by no means commensurate with the progress which has been made amongst the lowest working classes in Great Britain.*

In other words, after 113 years of the blessings of the Union and the advantages of English wisdom and experience in administration, Ireland is just about as rich as she was at the time that measure was passed. In fact in some ways she is relatively poorer, since then she was, at any rate, able to stand on her own legs, while now we are told that the consequence of any loosening of the bond which unites her to England will be financial ruin. Let anyone compare Miss Murray's statement, "it is indeed doubtful whether, even at the present day, Ireland is much richer than she was in the years before the Union," with the following extracts from the reported speeches of Sir Edward Carson, in which he presents a new version of Dr. Johnson's remark that the finest prospect in Scotland is the road leading to England:—

"I believe to cut ourselves off from a wealthy country like Great Britain, to divide our exchequers, and keep the

* Miss Murray, p. 293 ff.

poorer exchequer for ourselves, leaving the richer on the other side, is simple madness in the interest of the prosperity of our people."

. . . .

"Well, that Bill had at least one valuable provision in it, because it was to advance £1,000,000 towards furthering the completion of the building of the necessary labourers' cottages. But do you think if he goes on with Home Rule next year, and the English people say that we are going to be separated and our Exchequer is separate—do you think we will ever get that £1,000,000? Do you think we will ever get any more money for the completion of land purchase? I would say to those who have this matter at heart: Get the Bill now, because as sure as we are here, and as sure as Home Rule is proceeded with, you will never get another 'bob' from the Imperial Exchequer towards any scheme that may be necessary for the betterment of our people."

It will thus appear that unless the Ulster leader has been exaggerating, Miss Murray's conclusion is very much an understatement of the case. If these are the advantages of the Union, that while all the rest of the civilised world has been increasing enormously in wealth, Ireland remains just where she was more than a hundred years ago, what great objection can there be on the financial side to giving other methods and other persons a trial? They may possibly do better, and can hardly do very much worse. Besides, quite independently of the question of national self-respect, this system of living on doles from England is one that cannot go on indefinitely. The British taxpayer is getting decidedly impatient of the policy of being continually called on to put his hand in his pocket in order to bribe every party in Ireland in turn, and whether the Home Rule Bill becomes law or not, the day is not far distant when Ireland will have to live within her income, and when that day arrives, those who were led by the hope of material benefit in the shape of a continuous influx of English gold to shut their eyes to all abuses and resist all innovations, may find that their policy has been a short-sighted as well as a selfish one, and that even from the point of view of their own interests it would have been better to have been more patriotic.

We have seen that during the eighteen years that she enjoyed legislative independence the condition of Ireland was one of very considerable prosperity. It is, however, sometimes alleged and still more often implied, that as a consequence of the mismanagement of the Irish Parliament the national finances were in such a ruinous condition that the union with the wealthy Exchequer of Great Britain, so elegantly and touchingly referred to above, saved the Irish Government from bankruptcy. The following extracts from Miss Murray's book will show what are the real facts:—

"During the first eleven years of legislative independence the expenditure of Ireland kept fairly level, averaging about one and a quarter millions per annum . . . In 1783 the deficit had been much larger, but it was successfully reduced through the efforts of the opposition party in the Irish House of Commons, and for the next ten years the condition of the finances was flourishing.

"The equilibrium maintained between revenue and expenditure during these years says a good deal for the financial policy of Parliament, when we remember that just at this time new sums were being spent in encouraging trade and manufactures, and in developing the natural resources of Ireland. . . . From 1785 to 1794 when the cost of the French war began to be felt, the annual deficit was never higher than £89,434 (British), and was generally very much less, while in 1790 there was an actual excess of revenue over expenditure amounting to £85,397 (British).

"No economy was effected by the Irish Parliament at the expense of England; on the contrary, generosity and loyalty were shown.
. . . .

"It has been seen in the account given of the Commercial Propositions how anxious Pitt was to secure from Ireland some fixed contribution to the general expenses of the Empire, such contribution to be applied either to the support of the Imperial navy or to the reduction of the

British debt. The Irish Parliament had shown itself quite willing to make some settled contribution, conditional on an equilibrium between revenue and expenditure in years of peace, but unconditional in time of war. But the jealousy of the British manufacturing interest had forced Pitt to modify the propositions, greatly to the disadvantage of Ireland; and in consequence they had been thrown out by the Irish Parliament, chiefly on constitutional grounds."*

During all this time the power of the Irish Parliament to effect useful reforms was considerably lessened by the fact that many of its own members were the corrupt instruments of the Executive, over which it had unfortunately no control; as Miss Murray goes on to show:—

"In 1790 the number of placemen and pensioners in Parliament was declared to be equal to one-half of the whole efficient body. The pensions on the Irish establishment, exclusive of military, were in 1789 £105,739, and it was said that fresh pensions to the amount of £16,000 had been granted since March 1784, besides additional salaries to sinecure offices in the hands of members of Parliament; while during the same period the whole civil list had increased by £31,000 . . . The long additional salaries to sinecure or utterly insignificant offices were granted in order that the names of the recipients should not appear in the pension lists, so that a sort of inferior and corrupt pension list existed. What Grattan and his party wanted was to check this extravagance and corruption on the part of Government by means of legislation . . . But Government resisted all these proposals with great energy, and it was not till 1793 that the Irish Parliament managed to pass its three great measures for limiting the powers of the Executive."†

Two of these, the Responsibility Bill and the Pension Bill, fulfilled to some extent the object for which they were intended. Not so the third:—

* Miss Murray, p. 296 ff.   † Miss Murray, p. 298 ff.

"The Place Bill excluded from Parliament revenue officers, placemen, and pensioners; all members who accepted offices under Government were to vacate their seats, although they might be re-elected, and every member of Parliament before he took his seat was to swear that he did not hold any pension or office which might incapacitate him from sitting. . . .

"The Pension and Responsibility Bills put Irish finances for the first time theoretically under the control of the Irish Parliament and also increased the real financial power of the Commons. But the Place Bill, from which so much was hoped, achieved nothing, for it was perverted by Government to corrupt uses . . . The actual enactment of the Bill in 1793 may at first have purified the Irish Parliament in some slight degree, but there is no doubt that later on the Bill was perverted to corrupt uses, and it was their power of changing borough members without appealing to the constituencies by a dissolution which enabled the Irish Government to carry the Union.

"In the financial year 1792–93 the condition of Irish finances seems to have been good. When the Chancellor of the Exchequer made his annual statement to Parliament in February, 1792, he stated that the unfunded debt was decreasing, and that the country was experiencing that improvement in the finances which he had expected, and in the hope of which he had deferred any application to Parliament for an extraordinary supply to discharge arrears . . . The increase of revenue foretold by Sir John Parnell took place, but in 1793 the war with France began, and the even course of Irish finances changed. . . .

"In consequence of the French war, and later on of the Rebellion also, the expenditure of Ireland increased enormously after 1793. It has been seen that from 1782 to 1793 the Irish revenue and expenditure fairly balanced each other, and that expenditure did not materially increase. But from 1793 to the Union expenditure increased at a very rapid rate. This increase was chiefly under the head of military services, and the total expenditure for the year

ended Lady Day, 1800, was as much as five times greater
than that for the year ended Lady Day, 1793.

"From 1782–83 to 1792–93 the sum expended annually
on military services amounted on an average to £585,000
(British). From 1793 to 1797 the increased military expenditure due to the French war raised this amount greatly,
and in the year ended Lady Day, 1797, the large sum of
£2,032,000 (British) was spent on military services alone.
In 1797 the cost of the Yeomanry force, established to
suppress the disorders in Ireland, first appears in the public
accounts, so from this year till the Union a further increase
in Irish military expenditure took place, an increase
caused, not by the French war alone, but also by the
Rebellion. In the year ended Lady Day, 1800, £4,596,762
(British) was spent on military services. If the military expenditure during these seven years, 1793–94 to 1799–1800 had
been at the normal rate of £585,000 per annum mentioned above, it would only have amounted for the whole
period to £4,095,000 (British). Actually it amounted to
£18,050,941 (British), thus exceeding the normal amount by
about fourteen million. A further expenditure was made
on military services in the three quarters of a year from
Lady Day, 1800, to January 5th, 1801, of over £2,300,000
(British), so that, roughly speaking, during the seven and
three quarter years since the commencement of the war
with France over sixteen millions (British) was spent by
Ireland on military services in connection with the war and
the Rebellion.

"Under these circumstances the Irish national debt rose
from an insignificant amount to a very large sum. On
Lady Day, 1783, the aggregate amount of the Irish funded
and unfunded debt had only amounted in British currency
to £1,917,784, and this amount had only increased by
£334,983 (British) by Lady Day, 1793. But from that date it
naturally began to grow enormously, and on January 5th,
1801, the aggregate Irish debt stood at £28,551,137 (British),
or over £26,500,000 more than it had been eighteen years
before. Nearly the whole of this increase took place in the

last eight years of the period, and was directly due to the expenses of the French War and the Irish Rebellion.

"It was therefore little wonder that the condition of Irish finances just before the Union was held to be appalling, and the financial difficulties under which Ireland laboured were seized upon by Lord Castlereagh in order to press for a legislative Union with Great Britain. He even underestimated the revenue of the country in order to prove his case that bankruptcy was inevitable if a Union did not take place.

"It is as well to emphasise the fact that the commercial and financial distress which existed in Ireland during the last four years of the eighteenth century was due to the specific causes which have been mentioned. There was little decline in the prosperity of the country until the end of 1796, and this though an expensive war was being carried on. Castlereagh himself acknowledged that during the first three years of the war with France, Ireland had been regularly improving in commerce and revenue, even though eight millions had been taken from her circulating capital at different periods. Naturally, however, it was impossible for this improvement to continue when the Irish disturbances broke out. Credit was bound to collapse and industry to be dislocated, and we can only be surprised that the statistics of exports and imports do not show even a greater fall than is actually the case and that so considerable a revenue was raised from the country."*

It thus appears that it was the Irish Parliament which was economical and the English Executive which was extravagant; that in spite of this extravagance and the strain of foreign war, the finances of the country remained fairly prosperous until civil war broke out, and that it was the latter which was mainly responsible for the great increase in Irish debt. Of course it will be very hard to hold the member of a Provisional Government responsible for debts incurred by it when some of them know law as well as the Attorney-General himself, even were it not run on the principle of limited liability, but in view

*Miss Murray, p. 300 ff.

of the very heavy expenditure incurred in the last civil war in Ireland, it would seem advisable that the underwriters should limit their liability also, and that the leaders of the Unionist Party should give the heads of the Provisional Government and the financial magnates clearly to understand that they will be responsible up to a sum of say £5,000,000, but not a penny more. This suggestion, of course, only applies to the amount to be thrown on the taxpayers, and does not refer to the party funds, which may be used in any manner that may appear desirable, so far as the present writer is concerned. I am following the later precedents and assuming that the burden will be borne by the taxpayers in general as a symbol of Imperial equality and an indication that Ulstermen still preserve intact their cherished birthright, but if by any chance the earlier method should be resorted to, and this expenditure be treated as a purely Irish charge, the "hard-headed men of business" who have any business left may find that too heroic methods of endeavouring to escape taxation defeat their own object and only lead to its increase.

There is one more possibility which those who are going into the civil war for the sake of their pockets would do well to contemplate. Should the royal assent be refused to the Bill for taking over the liabilities of the Provisional Government, or should the outbreaks in Ulster assume such a form that there will be a difficulty in drawing any very firm line of distinction between them and ordinary rioting, and the English Unionist leaders be tempted to take advantage of this technicality to repudiate their obligations, there will be nothing whatever to show there has been a civil war, and consequently the ordinary law will apply, and compensation for all malicious damage will be thrown on the rates of the locality in which it has taken place. Should this contingency arise, the whole cost of both sides in whatever disturbances take place, instead of being thrown on the broad shoulders of the British taxpayer, will be thrown on the comparatively narrow ones of the ratepayers of the three or four counties taking part in it, which is an aspect of the matter I would commend to the attention of those who think that on the worldly side they can make everything right by insurance. In addition to insuring their own property, they would do well to insure themselves also for the share of their neighbours' losses they are quite likely to be called upon to bear.

EDITOR'S NOTES

1 J.J. was aware of the general ignorance of Irish history, owing to the failure to teach it in the schools. He felt he had to embark on some remedial education for his target Ulster Protestant readership, in this and the next two chapters.

2 This is William O'Connor Morris, not to be confused with the chronicler of foxhunting and pop-historian Maurice of the same names. The former has some 17 serious historical works on record, covering the Land Acts, the Napoleonic Wars, the French Revolution, Hannibal's expedition against Rome (where I suspect J.J. first encountered him during his classical studies), and a *History of Ireland* 1494–1868, to which his *Ireland from* 1798 *to* 1898 is a sequel published in 1898 by Innes, London. Its target readership was primarily the English, whose knowledge of Irish history was even more deficient then than it is now.

3 I have been unable to trace any further publications by Alice Murray, who would appear to have foreshadowed subsequent work by George O'Brien. J.J. picked on her work, with its LSE origin, and Hewins preface, as an impeccable Unionist source for Home Rule supporting arguments.

CHAPTER VIII

IRELAND FROM 1800–1870.—THE ACT OF
UNION.—ITS FINANCIAL PROVISIONS.—
EFFECT ON THE CONDITION OF IRELAND.—
THE LAND QUESTION. —THE FAMINE.—POLICY
OF BRITISH LEGISLATION IN REGARD TO
IRELAND.—THE LAND ACT OF 1870.

I do not propose to take up time by a detailed account of the
methods by which the Act of Union was passed, but I cannot
refrain from giving one or two quotations from Lecky
("Leaders of Public Opinion in Ireland," second edition) with
reference to that subject:—

> "It is a simple and unexaggerated statement of the fact,
> that, in the entire history of representative Government
> there is no instance of corruption having been applied on
> so large a scale, and with such audacious effrontery." (p. 177)
>
> "The measure of Pitt centralised, but it did not unite, or
> rather, by uniting the Legislatures it divided the nations. . . .
> The Union of 1800 was not only a great crime, but was
> also—like most crimes—a great blunder." (pp. 192–4)

I shall now pass on to an examination of how far the financial
arrangements were just or advantageous to Ireland.[1] Here
again it is only necessary to quote from Miss Murray, who
summarises them as follows:—

> "1. Each country was separately to defray the expenses
> arising out of the payment on the interest or sinking fund
> for the reduction of the principal of its own pre-Union
> debt.

"2.(1) For the next twenty years the ordinary expenses of the United Kingdom in peace or war should he defrayed by Great Britain and Ireland jointly according to the proportion of 15 to 2; that is, Great Britain was to defray $15/17$ or 88.24 per cent, and Ireland $2/17$ or 11.76 per cent of the whole expenditure.

(2) At the end of twenty years, unless Parliament had determined that the joint expenditure of the United Kingdom was to be indiscriminately defrayed by equal taxation in both countries, the respective contributions of Great Britain and Ireland were to be fixed in such proportions as would seem just and suited to the respective resources of the two countries.

"3. Irish revenues were to constitute a consolidated fund on which the payments for Ireland's pre-Union debt was to be a first charge; the remainder of the revenue was to go to meet Ireland's share of the joint expenditure.

"4. The respective contributions of Great Britain and Ireland were to be raised by such taxes in each country as Parliament might think fit to impose, but no article in Ireland was to be taxed at a heavier rate than in England.

"5. If, after Ireland had defrayed the charge for her pre-Union debt and her proportional contribution to the expenses of the United Kingdom, there remained a surplus of her revenue, such surplus could be applied in any one of the following ways—viz., (a) in remission of taxation, (b) for local purposes, (c) in making good a deficiency of Irish revenue in time of peace, (d) in building up a reserve fund not exceeding five millions to relieve the Irish contribution in time of war.

"6. All debt incurred by Parliament after the Union for the service of the United Kingdom was to be regarded as a joint debt, and the charge of it was to be borne by the two countries in the proportion of their respective contributions.

"7. If in the future the separate debts of Great Britain and Ireland should be liquidated, or if their values should be to one another in the proportion of their respective contributions to imperial expenditure, Parliament might, if it thought fit, declare that all future expenses of the United Kingdom should be defrayed indiscriminately by equal taxes imposed on the same articles in each country subject only to such exemptions and abatements in favour of Ireland as circumstances seemed to necessitate.

"These financial provisions were not favourable to Ireland, but, even commercially speaking, Ireland stood to gain little from the Union."*

Then follow some details which it is unnecessary to quote, and she proceeds to the following general criticisms:—

"All this shows how little Irish affairs were understood in England. . . . None of the commercial terms of the Union gave any preference to Irish goods over foreign as the Commercial Propositions had done, and so even Irish linens were to have no security against the rivalry of foreign linens in the British markets. At the same time, the opening of the British markets to Irish manufactures could benefit Ireland little. Almost all the articles on the importation of which Great Britain had hitherto imposed very heavy duties could be worked up more cheaply by herself, and it was not possible for the Irish merchants to export these articles with any profit to England. . . . Great Britain and Ireland were too dissimilar in economic conditions to have the same commercial system, and this had been practically realised by Lord Castlereagh when he advocated the retention of the Irish protective duties on the importation of cotton goods. Irish manufacturers were bitterly opposed to the Union because they thought that under its arrangements of free trade between Great Britain and Ireland, Irish commerce would be ruined, and Irish industries would decline. And it is certainly true that

* Miss Murray, p. 332, ff.

Ireland, unlike England, was not in a position to profit
through free trade, and therefore she was not in a position
to profit, commercially speaking, from the Union. The
commercial advantages conferred on Scotland by her
Union with England were often cited at this time in order
to prove that benefits would likewise be conferred on
Ireland. But the cases were not analogous. For one thing it
was many years before Scotch trade and industry began to
progress even in a slight degree, and Ireland's material
progress during the eighteenth century seems to have been
as great as that of Scotland. But what is far more important, for nearly a century after the Union with Scotland
Scotch trade and industry were fostered and encouraged by
bounties and protective duties. Scotland had entered into a
Union when the ideas of protection reigned supreme in
England, and her infant industries received the policy of
protection necessary to their firm establishment. But now,
when Ireland was united to Great Britain, the new idea of
free trade was coming to the front, and by surrendering
her separate Parliament Ireland lost all chance of
artificially fostering her native industries. Free trade under
certain conditions cannot be an advantage. It could not be
an advantage to a poor country like Ireland, in which
industries were in their infancy, and which existed side by
side in the closest commercial intercourse with a rich
country where industries had long flourished. . . . As regards
the financial arrangements there also seems no doubt that
Pitt meant to do the fair thing by Ireland. But the whole
Union scheme of finance was founded upon a fallacious
basis; the arrangements were mistaken in themselves, and
time was to prove that they were unjust in their effects.

"The standards taken by Lord Castlereagh as the basis
for his comparison of the respective resources of Great
Britain and Ireland could have established nothing. It was
unfair to take the three years preceding 1799 as a basis for
comparison, for the presence of a large military force in
Ireland naturally caused a great increase in the consumption
of dutiable articles in that country. Moreover, in the

comparison of the respective resources of the two countries
certain sources of revenue were omitted, such as stamp
duties, post-office receipts, and the salt tax, all of which
would have shown a smaller proportion for Ireland. Again,
Lord Castlereagh's actual estimate of Irish exports and
imports was afterwards proved to be inaccurate. He com-
puted their annual average value as nearly eleven millions,
whereas the official statistics presented to Parliament in
1834 only made out the average in this period to be eight
and a quarter millions. But putting aside all inaccuracies
and misstatements, it is impossible to believe that any
approximate estimate of the comparative resources of the
two countries could have been obtained by merely
comparing their respective exports and imports or their
consumption of dutiable commodities. This was especially
true of two countries like Great Britain and Ireland, whose
economic conditions were so dissimilar, and whose popu-
lations differed in habits and customs.

"In estimating the proportion of Imperial expenditure
which Ireland should bear, Lord Castlereagh had tested his
conclusion by examining whether the ratio of 7½ to 1
which he had established would correspond with the ratio
of past expenditure, exclusive of debt charge, of Great
Britain and Ireland. He excluded all debt charges because
the pre-Union debts were to be kept distinct, but this
exclusion had the effect of rendering his reasoning fallacious.
In such a calculation as Lord Castlereagh was attempting
debt charges should certainly have been included both in
time of war and in time of peace, for war necessitates
borrowing, while in years of peace the debt charges incurred
in time of war must be redeemed. If the debt charges of
the two countries had been included in the estimate of their
expenditures, the average annual British expenditure during the seven years of war taken by Lord Castlereagh was
£43,034,000, and that of Ireland £3,089,501, so that the
expenditure of Great Britain was to that of Ireland during this period not 9 to 1, as was calculated, but 14 to 1.
Again including debt charges in the single year of peace

immediately preceding the war, taken by Lord Castlereagh, the expenditure of Great Britain was £19,251,563, and that of Ireland £1,395,950, thus giving a proportion not of 5¾ to 1, as was calculated, but of nearly 14 to 1 also. So by leaving out debt charges in an estimate of the peace and war expenditures of Great Britain and Ireland, the proportion of Irish to British expenditure was falsely raised. Lord Castlereagh did not compare the total expenditure of the two countries; he compared only selected parts of their expenditures. At the same time a calculation of the peace expenditure of a country based on the figures of a single year was bound to be worthless, while it was unjust to Ireland to estimate her average annual war expenditure from the expenditure of a period which included not only a foreign war, but also an invasion of Ireland and an actual rebellion.

"The clause in the financial article providing that indiscriminate taxation might be imposed when the British and Irish debts should become to one another in the ratio of their respective contributions to Imperial expenditure was, as Foster had pointed out, exceedingly curious. An increase in the indebtedness of Ireland must lead to increased taxes. How, then, would Ireland be better able bear equal taxation with Great Britain than at the time of the Union? But the explanation is that neither Pitt nor Castlereagh thought for a moment that in the future the ratio existing between the British and Irish debts would be raised by an enormous increase in the Irish debt, while at the same time a small increase took place in the British debt. What they both expected was that the British debt would decrease by the system of liquidation, while the Irish debt would at least not increase; then that the scale of British taxes would rapidly descend to the level of Irish, and consequently that indiscriminate taxation might be adopted without fear of injuring Ireland. Neither Pitt nor Castlereagh looked forward to almost fifteen years of almost continuous war. But the long war with France vitiated all their calculations and estimates. The miscalculations made by the framers of the Act of Union were chiefly due to their failure to see the future increase in the expenditure of the United Kingdom, and for this failure they can, of course, hardly be blamed. But we have seen that the calculations themselves were inaccurate and founded upon fallacious reasoning, so that even if a long war had not followed, it is almost certain that Ireland would still have found herself overburdened. As it was, however, the huge expenses caused by the war exaggerated and intensified to a high degree the injustice to Ireland which would in any case have existed."*

It thus appears that the framers of the Act of Union acted on information of an extremely limited character as to Ireland's resources, and which only happened to be incorrect by one-third, the error of course being to the disadvantage of Ireland, that some most important items for purposes of comparison were omitted, and that one clause acted in exactly the opposite manner to what we will hope was the intention of its framers, and made the increase of Ireland's debt a ground for increasing her burdens, a state of things which has gone on to the present day, and had only involved up till 1910 an amount, estimated by Lord MacDonnell at £325,000,000, as a contribution to the Imperial Exchequer over and above the cost of governing the country. One can understand an Englishman being rather pleased with a transaction over which his country has done so well, at least until the last year or two, though even he must feel that some of the sordid details are better forgotten, but that an Irishman, whether an Ulsterman or not, should be unable to find any better subject for his enthusiasm goes to show how extraordinary are the limitations of human nature, and how the tendency on the part of savage tribes to worship stocks and stones often survives in civilised races, in the form of veneration for paper and parchment.

I have dealt at somewhat disproportionate length with the material condition of the country during the eighteen years it

* Miss Murray, p. 335 ff.

enjoyed legislative independence, because the allegation, and to an even greater extent the assumption, is often made that Ireland owes all its prosperity to the Union, while the facts are that at the time of the Union, except for the effects of civil war and misgovernment, the country was fairly prosperous, and for more than fifty years afterwards its course was one of steady retrogression. An examination of the course of Irish history since the Union will make it quite clear that the misfortunes which Ireland has suffered during that period, and the comparatively little progress which she has made at the end of it, are almost entirely due either directly or indirectly to the system of government which was then established. The prospect of Catholic Emancipation was held out by Pitt as a bait to win the support of Irish Catholics for the measure. In the opinion of O'Connor Morris, the Irish Protestant historian whom I have already mentioned, Pitt was distinctly pledged to accompany the Act of Union by a full measure of Catholic Emancipation. Having secured the passing of that Act partly as a result of that promise, he deliberately threw over his pledges, sheltering himself behind the admitted hostility of the King, which he must have known about all along. But that was probably a mere subterfuge, as the King, according to O'Connor Morris, always gave way to the will of a resolute minister. Pitt made no serious attempt to overcome his hostility either then or subsequently. As a nominal protest he resigned office for a short time. But in the words of O'Connor Morris:—

> "The subsequent conduct of Pitt cannot be justified in the mature judgment of impartial history. He let his master know after a few days that he would not urge the Catholic claims again in the reign; he steadily supported an anti-Catholic Ministry . . . when he returned to office in 1801 he completely abandoned the Catholic cause."*

For the next twenty-five years the promised gift was withheld. In other words, while the Catholics who formed half of the British Army were fighting and laying down their lives for the

* O'Connor Morris, p. 60.

Empire in the Napoleonic wars, their fellow Catholics at home were denied the ordinary rights of citizenship. The Chief Whip of the Unionist Party, if he had lived in those days, so far from being able to hold his present high office, would not even have had the Parliamentary franchise.

The history of the movement for Catholic Emancipation does not end here. The agitation was carried on with gradually increasing vigour until it was finally successful; in any case, it was bound to succeed sooner or later. So long as it seemed possible to ignore this movement, the policy of successive British Governments was to withhold this gift. When the agitation on the subject began to threaten the foundations of the State, and when the alternative to Catholic Emancipation was a civil war in which the Catholic half of the British Army would probably have mutinied and arrayed itself against the other half, what was refused to justice was surrendered to expediency. The circumstances under which this Act was passed are typical of practically every Act passed since the Act of Union to ameliorate the condition of Ireland. Reform, as a rule, has only taken place when its delay would have rendered government impossible. A Unionist M.P. writing in the *Nineteenth Century* admirably describes this characteristic of the Catholic Emancipation Bill:—

"What scope there would be for a philosophic pen in winding up a history of Catholic Emancipation! For it is an epitome of the policy of Ireland's governors—robbery followed by cruel persecution; then a gradual growth of public opinion, strong enough to irritate, but too weak to force the hand of the Ascendancy of the day. Then agitation, exasperation, outrage, promises of reform, failure to fulfil them, and crass ignorance and senseless brutality vying with one another in the government of the disordered country. Then increased agitation, crime, and coercion, a greater volume of public opinion, and growth of menial fear in the rulers of Ireland; and lastly after many years of insult and indifference, redress forced from authority, not through a consciousness of justice inexcusably delayed, but under the influence of menace and menace alone."

British statesmanship, or what went by that name in those days, is directly to blame for the betrayal of Catholic Ireland in that matter. The large increase which took place in the amount of Irish taxation was a direct and inevitable consequence of the Act of the Union itself, but as Irish taxation was and has been increased even beyond what was contemplated by those who framed that Act, and in defiance of its terms, the blame for this must be laid at the door of the successive British Governments which either connived at or deliberately brought about this increase. The total amount taken from Ireland in overtaxation as estimated by a competent authority is at least £200,000,000. That the gross amount of Irish taxation was largely increased (quite apart from overtaxation) immediately after, and as a result of, the passing of the Act of Union may be seen from the following quotation from Miss Murray:—

> "From 1801 to 1816 the total expenditure of Ireland amounted to £148,000,000, or more than three and a half times the sum expended during the previous fifteen years."*

As much of the expenditure which was thus unfairly saddled on Ireland by the terms of the Act of Union had to be met by loans, "between the years 1801 and 1810, while the total British debt less than doubled itself, the Irish debt almost quadrupled, having grown from £32,215,223 to £112,634,773, as against an increase in the British debt from £489,122,057 to £737,422,469."†

When the Act of Union was being passed, those who framed its financial terms did not, it is to be hoped, contemplate the possibility of the war with France lasting so long, and thus costing so much, as it ultimately did. The enormous debt which Ireland was forced to contract was due to the cast-iron provision that the contribution to Imperial revenue should be two-seventeenths of the total amount it was necessary to raise. What Ireland could not raise by taxes she was forced to raise by borrowing. The Act of Union contained a clause that when the respective debts of Great Britain and Ireland were

* Miss Murray, p. 373.   † Miss Murray, p. 392

in proportion to the amount of revenue contributed by each, the two exchequers might be amalgamated, and the taxation of the two countries assimilated, subject to such exemptions and abatements in favour of Ireland as circumstances seemed to demand.* This state of affairs came about not, as was anticipated, as a result of a great diminution of the British debt, but as a result of a relatively much greater increase of the Irish debt. By the amalgamation of the exchequers Ireland was saved from national bankruptcy, but no relief was brought to the individual Irish taxpayer. Taxation was henceforth to be indiscriminate as between Great Britain and Ireland, always subject to the exemptions and abatements mentioned above. Under this arrangement the taxes of the two countries have been gradually equalised, and the exemptions and abatements almost entirely abolished, regardless of the relative taxable capacity of the two countries, and the suitability or otherwise of the British fiscal system to Ireland.

One of the chief motives of those who desired the passing of the Act of Union was commercial jealousy. Miss Murray says with reference to a public declaration made in Great Britain in 1785 that "a real Union with Ireland under one legislature would take away every difficulty" in the commercial relations of Great Britain and Ireland which were then under discussion:— "This declaration is noticeable as being one of the first of the many suggestions which were soon to follow for a legislative Union between Great Britain and Ireland. Its ruling motive was commercial jealousy and a wish to make the Irish people pay the same taxes as the British."*

The British commercial interests that desired an Act of Union and the increase of Irish taxation obtained both; nor were they disappointed in their further hope that this would lead to the decay and gradual extinction of the Irish industries whose competition they most feared. Not only was capital which is so necessary for the growth and expansion of industry drained from the country by the exorbitant amount of Irish taxation, and the heavy loans which were necessary to

* Miss Murray, p. 248.

meet it during the French war, but a fiscal system maintained entirely in the interests of Great Britain helped to complete the ruin of many of the Irish industries which had flourished under the fostering care of a native Parliament.

Free trade, except for certain 10 per cent. *ad valorem* duties of a mutually protective character, which were finally abolished in 1824, was established between Great Britain and Ireland by the Act of Union. The result was that every Irish industry except the brewing, distilling, and linen industries dwindled and decayed, until most of them became practically extinct during the first fifty years of the Union. It is customary to point to the linen industry as one which has grown and flourished under the present regime; but it must not be forgotten that that industry also made considerable progress under a free Irish Parliament. Moreover, at the time of the Act of Union the cotton industry rivalled it in importance; fifty years later the former had ceased to exist. The linen trade prospered under the new fiscal system, because it had no cross-Channel rivals to fear, and had been firmly established at the time of its adoption.

After 1800 the woollen industry gradually decayed, and until quite recently was almost extinct. About forty years of the blessings of the Union were enough to complete the ruin of the Irish silk industry. The glass industry met with a similar fate after a period of about the same duration.

The influence of taxation on industry is very great. Capital is necessary in order that the industries of a country should develop and be in a position to adapt themselves to changing markets and new methods of production. Credit is just as important as capital, and in fact is only another name for capital. The first half of the nineteenth century was a period of industrial expansion and changing methods of production. The factory system was coming in, and new machinery involving considerable initial outlay was being adopted. Great Britain was a country where industries had long flourished and where much capital had been amassed. She was able to adapt herself to the new circumstances, and thus her industrial prosperity went on increasing. Many of the industries which had flourished under the free Irish Parliament were of recent origin. They had had less time to amass capital, and consequently were less able financially to adapt themselves to new requirements. Nevertheless all might have gone well if a fiscal system suitable to them had been retained, and if the government of the country had been such as to enable capital to be amassed and credit maintained. Not only was the fiscal system of the United Kingdom progressively modified in the interests of Great Britain and against those of Ireland, but the financial system established by the Act of Union, and which lasted for the next seventeen years, was of such a kind that Ireland was compelled, as already explained, to raise by taxation and borrowing such an enormous amount as her share of the total expenditure as to be threatened with national bankruptcy. The drain on the resources of a poor and ill-governed country was enormous, and the consequence was that the credit of Ireland became so exhausted that in 1815, according to Miss Murray, "it was thought impossible to obtain in Ireland even £1,000,000 by way of public loan." The capital which ought to have been retained in the country in order to further industrial enterprise was diverted to other purposes, which, however productive of warlike glory, were entirely non-productive in the industrial sense, and were in fact economically disastrous to the people of Ireland. To expect infant industries to grow and flourish under such conditions was to expect the impossible.

The industries of a country can be seriously handicapped by exorbitant taxation. An unsuitable fiscal system, quite apart from the amount of taxation, may be even more disastrous. The Irish manufacturers seem to have been able to control to some extent their own markets as a result of the 10 per cent. *ad valorem* duties which were established by the Act of Union, and which were actually retained until 1824. During this period the woollen, glass and cotton industries were maintained, though they show a tendency to decline as compared with the previous period. After 1824 this tendency is more pronounced, and by the year 1850 these industries were practically extinct. The system of complete free trade as between Ireland and Great Britain which was adopted in 1824 left these Irish industries completely at the mercy of their British rivals. The cotton in use in Ireland had, as already mentioned, experienced what it might expect if its Manchester rivals were placed in a position to crush it. It was temporarily saved by the adoption of a prohibitive duty by the Irish Parliament, and the maintenance of a protective duty under the Union for the first twenty-four years must have helped to enable it to exist. When this was removed, the contest became too unequal, and it gradually succumbed.

It is unnecessary go to into details with regard to the other industries which disappeared; a few extracts from Miss Murray's book will show that in general their disappearance may be attributed to the unsuitable fiscal system which the Act of Union imposed on them. They are as follows:—

"Free trade, which has resulted in developing to such a great extent the manufactures of Britain, has done much to decrease the industrial life of Ireland." . . .*

"The industrial history of Ireland during the nineteenth century shows how impossible it was for Irish manufacturers to compete with British once the two countries were commercially united, and all custom duties on articles going from one country to the other gradually abolished. It also shows the advisability of a country possessed of little industrial development fostering and protecting its infant manufactures until they are firmly established in order to prevent them being crushed out of existence by the competition of other countries. But Union with Great Britain necessitated the application of the new free trade principles to Ireland just at the time when Irish industries should have met with encouragement and protection." †

In consequence of the destruction of industrial life the Irish people became more and more dependant on the land; and as the land was thus their sole means of support, and the system of land tenure was far from ideal at this time and for

* Miss Murray, p. 344.   † *Ibid*, p. 351.

long afterwards, the question of the relations of landlord and tenant became one of life and death for the Irish people. In a country like England, where industrial life is well developed, if a man cannot get land, or cannot get it at a rent he can afford to pay, he can turn his hand to something else, and need not despair of earning a living in the land of his birth. In Ireland at this time there was no such option; the tenant had to take land on what was nominally a contract system, but the practical working of which was such that if he was to live at all in his own country he must pay, not the rent he could afford or the rent the land was worth, but the rent his landlord chose to ask. In the absence of industrial life, the competition for farms was very great, and rents were high accordingly. In England the landlord let "farms," in Ireland he let "land" only. In England the "equipment" which was necessary in order that the tenant should farm his land at a profit was provided by the landlord. In Ireland the tenant was compelled to provide this "equipment" himself. In many cases the tenant by the improvements he effected acquired what was morally a joint ownership of the land. Yet in the eye of the law the landlord's title was absolute, and he could, and often did, confiscate the tenant's improvements, either by raising his rent or by evicting him and taking possession of the improved farm himself. Only in Ulster was the tenant's position to some extent improved by the existence of what was called the "Ulster Custom." Under it the tenant was enabled to sell to the incoming tenant the interest he had acquired in the land as a result of his own industry, and the landlord usually allowed the sale. But even in Ulster the only sanction of this custom was public opinion, and if the landlord chose to evict the tenant or confiscate his improvements by raising the rent, he had a perfect legal right to do so. In fact the law went out of its way to put a premium on dishonesty and cruelty on the part of a landlord, and to penalise any member of the class who displayed what are usually regarded as the characteristically Christian virtues.

A number of subsidiary causes tended to aggravate the inherent evils of the Irish land system. Tillage was encouraged by the high price of corn in the English market, and this high price was due to the Corn Laws which were maintained up till 1845. By tillage a farmer can live on a smaller farm than would be required if he only went in for grazing. As a result of the Relief Act of 1793 the forty shilling franchise had been extended to Catholics, and landlords were tempted to multiply the number of "forty shilling free-holders," as they were called, in order to gain political influence. No limit was placed to the progressive sub-division of holdings. In consequence of all this, in the words of O'Connor Morris, "the land was split up over immense and ever growing areas, into little patches, often of the minutest extent, the abodes of dense, teeming and poor multitudes." At the same time a process of consolidation of farms was going on. It was thought that the existence of larger farms would tend to promote more scientific methods of agriculture. The landlords became afraid that if they allowed the continued existence of very small farmers in too large numbers their rents would become insecure. The country thus became what many parts of the three southern provinces are to-day, a country of very small farms side by side with very large farms. Unfortunately the consolidation of farms was often combined with the eviction of the occupiers of small farms in order to make up the larger ones, and the "clearance system," as this was called, became a term of odious import. The forty shilling freeholders had been the backbone of the movement for Catholic Emancipation. One of the clauses of that Act abolished the forty shilling freehold franchise. The result provides an illustration of the inadvisability of acting entirely on preconceived theories without a knowledge of the concrete facts to which they are being applied, and their probable ultimate consequences in the circumstances of the case.

A great deal might be said against the policy of creating forty shilling freeholders, but their abolition gave a further impetus to the process of consolidating farms by the eviction of small holders, which was already going on. The landlord had no further interest in retaining tenants of this class. By the time of the Famine this tenure had entirely disappeared.

Those who had formerly been forty shilling freeholders, if they had not been evicted, had sunk into the position of mere tenants-at-will. British statesmanship, or rather want of statesmanship, is directly responsible for the result.

The condition of Irish agriculture thus went from bad to worse during this period. A Commission known as the Devon Commission was appointed, and reported in 1845. The report throws a lurid light on the condition of Irish farmers and agricultural labourers. It stated:—

"That the agricultural labourer of Ireland continues to suffer the greatest privations and hardship; that he continues to depend upon casual and precarious employment for subsistence; that he is still badly fed, badly clothed, and badly paid for his labour. . . . When we consider this state of things, and the large proportion of the population which comes under the designation of agricultural labourers, we have to repeat that the patient endurance which they exhibit is deserving of high recommendation, and entitles them to the best attention of Government and of Parliament. Up to this time any improvement that may have taken place is attributable almost entirely to the habits of temperance in which they have so generally persevered, and not, we grieve to say, to any increased demand for their labour."*

In many parts of the country his only food was the potato, his only drink water. The very small farmer was little better off. His chief, and practically his only, food was the potato, while the sale of the family pig went towards the rent. As Miss Murray says, ". . . the condition of the whole class of farmers was deteriorating, and they were continually in the hands of the local moneylenders."

Ulster was rather better off, but even here the state of the agricultural population was not at all satisfactory, in which connection I quote once more from Miss Murray:—

* Report of the Devon Commission, quoted by Miss Murray, p. 366

"Even in Ulster, which was by far the most prosperous of the four provinces, on account of a better system of land tenure and the employment given by the linen manufacture, comfort was only comparative. . . . Throughout the rural districts of Ulster the people were suffering from the withdrawal of the linen manufacture to the towns."

Miss Murray goes on to explain how in general the poverty of the country districts was added to by the growth of the factory system and the concentration of the industry in the towns:—

"At the beginning of the century an agricultural family could earn a considerable addition to its income by spinning woollen or linen yarn, and even making the yarn into cloth. Now the decline of the woollen industry, and the revolution in the manufacture of linen, had hit these small spinners and weavers severely. Flax ceased to be grown except for home use, and men who had supported themselves partly by weaving were forced to depend entirely on their wages as agricultural labourers."*

This was the state of the country in the year preceding the famine; the Devon Commission was a Commission of landlords, yet they reported that the condition of agricultural Ireland was about as bad as it could be, and that legislative reform was necessary. It was left for the famine of the two following years to provide its terrible solution for the problem of the destitution of the very small farmer and the agricultural labourer; the recommendations of the Devon Commission for the improvement of Irish land tenure were prejudiced by the English point of view of its members. They practically ignored the moral title which the Irish tenant had already obtained by improvements effected, and considered that complete justice would be done if he obtained compensation under strict conditions for improvements effected in the future. The whole attitude of successive British Governments to the Irish land question for many years later followed on the lines of this report. Its object was gradually to substitute the English

* *Vide* Miss Murray, Ch. XVI., *passim.*

system of land tenure for the system which had grown up in Ireland, regardless of the amount of wrong and loss inflicted on the Irish tenants in the process.

I shall reserve for the present the discussion of the various Land Bills which were introduced later on to improve the position of the tenants, merely remarking by the way that although the Irish land system was rotten to the core, seventy years elapsed from the passing of the Act of Union, and twenty-five from the report of this Commission before any serious attempt was made to grapple with the problem.

The State of Ireland in 1845 may be briefly summarised as follows:— Many industries had disappeared; industrial life was less widely distributed than hitherto. The price of agricultural produce was kept unnaturally high by the Corn Laws, which also helped to encourage tillage and keep up rents. At the same time a process of consolidation of farms was going on, often involving great hardships in the way of evictions. The great majority of the agricultural population were very small farmers and agricultural labourers, whose staple food was the potato. In fact the potato was the food of fully a third part of the Irish people, and was almost their sole means of subsistence.

Naturally the partial failure of the potato crop in 1845 and its complete failure in 1846, caused wide spread ruin and starvation.

"The loss in money was estimated at sixteen millions sterling; this may afford some idea of what the results were in a country already impoverished, and always very poor. Even in the best and most prosperous districts, society was disorganised in a short time; there was a general calling in of debts and demands; the landed gentry received but a fraction of rent; hundreds of farmers of the better class became bankrupt; thousands of peasants fled from their homes in despair. In less fortunate counties the consequences were, of course, more grave; but in districts which had suffered the year before, and in all those which were more or less backward, the condition of affairs became soon appalling. Famine advancing slowly from the coast-line, from Donegal southwards to Kerry and Cork, and gradually making its way inland, threw its dark shadow over a third part of Ireland; starving multitudes were lifted up from the land and tossed to and fro to seek the means of prolonging life; and thousands sank into unknown graves."*

Some of the methods used by the Government in coping with this calamity were typical of British statesmanship at its worst. In 1845 Peel set on foot a system of unproductive works, half the cost of which was to be borne by local bodies. In the next year the famine was much worse, and Lord John Russell, the new Prime Minister, on the plea that the local bodies had been wasteful, passed a "Labour Rate Act" which imposed the whole cost of unproductive works on the local bodies which voted them. However, the state of affairs was so bad that the local bodies voted such works wholesale regardless of the cost. The result was that many of the local bodies became bankrupt.

After the famine was over a law known as the "Rate in Aid Act" was passed, which compelled the solvent Irish Unions to make good the financial loss of those which had become insolvent through the operation of the former Act. On this law O'Connor Morris passes the following comment:—

"If the principle of this scheme was legitimate it ought not to have been confined to Ireland, it should have been extended to England as well. . . . This measure was simply grotesque injustice; no serious excuse was ever made for it."†

In other words, in spite of the imperial equality with Great Britain which the Union is supposed to have brought about, and which is now so touchingly referred to as "our cherished birthright", the predominant partner applied the principle "bear ye one another's burdens" to Ireland only, so that from the point of view of burden bearing in this case the Act of Union might as well never have been passed.

* O'Connor Morris, p. 152.   † O'Connor Morris, p. 169

The English Government tried another remedy which, although temporarily a relief, had ultimate consequences which were disastrous and ought to have been foreseen. They extended outdoor relief to Ireland, but imposed a stringent test of poverty of an arbitrary and artificial character. No one holding more than a quarter of an acre of land was eligible for relief. In the words of Lord Dunraven ("Legacy of Past Years," pp. 224 ff.):— "Instead of tiding them over an emergency, finding them in seed, and endeavouring to help the people to help themselves, the British Parliament deliberately turned every starving family out of their holding, and forced them, for a morsel to put in their mouths, to abandon the only means they had of subsistence in the future."

As O'Connor Morris puts it:—

"Peasants were compelled in thousands to give up their little holdings, in order to qualify for relief; emigration, already large, set in on an enormous scale, and became ere long that exodus of the Irish people which has so powerfully affected the state of the country. The petty occupiers of the soil, in fact, were dispossessed by the State in multitudes; for one victim at the hands of landlords there were probably fifty through the operation of the law."*

The State did not even rob for its own benefit, but for that of the landlord, and in its imbecility went out of its way to extend the principle that to him that hath shall be given. It is impossible to conceive any Government of Irishmen, however undemocratic, being guilty of such combined stupidity and cruelty.

All this time Ireland was producing large quantities of corn, which were being exported to England from the starving country. Not only did the Government take no steps to prevent this export, but actually it facilitated it. A French writer, M. Paul Dubois,[2] "Contemporary Ireland," p. 70 ff., says:—

"During the most critical period of the famine, in 1846 and 1847, Ireland exported corn; barley, oats, and cattle in

* *Ibid.*, p. 155

far greater quantities than would have sufficed to feed the people. It was not want of foodstuffs that caused the famine. But the produce of the land was used up in paying the landlord's rent. There was famine in the midst of plenty. It was an artificial famine, for, as Mitchel declared, 'the exact complement of a comfortable family dinner in England is a Coroner's inquest in Ireland—verdict, starvation!'"

Thousands perished by starvation; hundreds of thousands fled from the doomed land and made their way to other parts of the world, particularly the United States.

"The Irish exodus, as it was rightly called, was almost everywhere a scene of many woes. In many places families of peasants of the better classes toiled painfully in troops along the roads, fleeing, with their household stuff, as before an invading army. Crowds of the victims of harsh ejection, or of the more pitiless measures of the State, could be seen huddled in spots where there was a chance of shelter, on their way from their ruined homes to the nearest seaport. . . . The sufferings of these multitudes in the long voyage across the Atlantic, were simply appalling . . . The emigrants were abandoned to the tender mercies of merchants not subject to control by the State; as the demands of misery far exceeded the means of support the consequences may be easily guessed at. The emigrants were crowded into the worst kind of vessels, without sufficient supplies of even the coarsest food, without regard to health, comfort, or even common decency, and thousands perished in the terrible transit. . . . The Government might have controlled the greed of merchants; they might have insisted on regulations being made to secure life and health for their crowds of emigrants; . . . Nothing perhaps contributed so much to the fierce resentment which burned in the hearts of thousands of Irishmen as the apparent neglect of the State in this matter; it left the bitterest memories, which still survive."*

* O'Connor Morris, pp. 167–168.

The immediate result of the Irish famine was the repeal of the Corn Laws. The ultimate results of this measure were not felt in Ireland until the seventies, when the competition of the wheat-growing districts of the New World began to tell. This state of affairs was aggravated by one or two bad harvests, and the suffering which ensued in Ireland was the immediate cause of the agrarian agitation which for the first time won from the British Government the Magna Charta of the tenant's liberties, popularly known as the "Three F's."* This will be referred to in greater detail later. For the present I shall content myself with remarking that the net result of the two successive fiscal systems which were applied to Ireland since the Union was, first, the destruction of many Irish industries; secondly, an unnatural encouragement of tillage for the first forty-five years, with disastrous results to the Irish land system, and finally a sudden and unlooked for depression of Irish agriculture owing to the adoption of free trade, from the effects of which Irish agriculture has only recently recovered.

Rents had been abnormally high owing to the high prices of agricultural produce before 1845. After the famine the ruined peasantry were no longer able to pay these high rents, and were scarcely able to pay any rent at all. Many peasants were evicted in consequence, but numbers of landlords were ruined owing to the non-payment of rent. British statesmanship had thus another chance to distinguish itself; it took the chance, and in 1850 passed a law called the Encumbered Estates Act which was one of the most glaring examples of the inability of the Parliament at Westminster to legislate for the economic necessities of Ireland. Its general principle was plausible enough; it was thought that if the landlords whose estates were very much encumbered could be supplanted by a class of solvent landlords, the results would be beneficial to Irish agriculture and to the country as a whole. Its application was in the best and most approved "rule of thumb" style which has nearly always characterised the attempts of Great Britain to legislate for Ireland. All these estates were thrown on the market at once, with the result that they were sold in

* Fair rent, free sale, and fixity of tenure.

many cases for much less than their real value. Again quoting from O'Connor Morris:—

"Lands at rentals of hundreds of thousands were brought into a half-closed market. . . . Estates valued a few years before at more than twenty years' purchase, sold for half or even a third of that sum; many honourable families of the landed gentry which, but for the law, would have been saved, disappeared from their ancestral homes; . . . Confiscation, however, did not stop at what was above; it made its evil effects felt in what was below. In the case of most of these estates, as throughout Ireland, the occupying tenants had improved their farms, and had acquired con-current rights in them; these rights, sometimes amounting to a joint ownership, were ruthlessly destroyed by the provision of the Act which gave purchasers a perfect title exempt from such claims. . . . Nine-tenths, certainly, of the estates that were sold fell into the hands of needy Irishmen of the mercantile or the shop-keeping class, without the associations peculiar to landed gentry; and their conduct was natural to such a class. Many of these purchasers bought cheap to sell again in time, and became jobbers in land of the worst type; but the immense majority bought to retain their possessions, and proved themselves to be the true successors of the previously almost extinct middleman, the historical oppressor of the Irish peasant. The means by which these speculators made their bargains were charac-teristic and deserve notice. They usually borrowed half the purchase money, and instantly raised their tenants rents in order to meet the accruing interest; and as the tenants had no rights under the law, they were compelled to submit to what was a wrong in almost every instance. . . . The Encumbered Estates Act, and all that has flowed from it, ought to be a warning to British statesmen not rashly to meddle with the Irish land, a subject they have meddled with, nevertheless, from the days of the Elizabeth to the present hour, usually with the result of making bad worse."*
No further comment is necessary.

* O'Connor Morris, pp. 172–173.

In 1853, when Ireland was still prostrate as a result of the famine, Mr. Gladstone, who has now the reputation of having been a friend of Ireland, was sufficiently English and unstatesmanlike to think that the proper time had come to assimilate further the finances of Ireland and Great Britain. He extended the Income Tax to Ireland, and between 1853 and 1860 he and his successors more than trebled her spirit duties. "The taxation of Ireland, still a very poor country, was increased by a sum of nearly three millions and, compared to that of Great Britain, was largely raised."*

Mr. Gladstone was cynical enough to represent that he gave Ireland a set off for the Income Tax by releasing her from a questionable debt of £4,000,000 which had been contracted in connection with Famine Relief, and which really ought to have been an Imperial charge. Up to 1898 the amount paid by Ireland for this boon was £23,000,000; so it is more than doubtful if, had she been a free agent, the arrangement would have been accepted, but under the Union she had no choice in the matter. In this way the British Government drove a coach and four through the financial provisions of the Act of Union, and the chief exemptions and abatements which she was guaranteed under that Act were thus abolished. This state of chronic overtaxation has continued ever since.

In 1895–6 the Financial Relations Commission reported that whereas the taxable capacity of Ireland was only $\frac{1}{21}$ of that of Great Britain, her revenue was actually $\frac{1}{13}$.

As before mentioned, it has been estimated by a competent authority that the amount contributed by Ireland in overtaxation, that is to say in taxation in direct violation of the terms of the Act of Union, since the passing of that Act is at a moderate estimate £200,000,000. The Financial Relations Commission agreed that, financially speaking, Ireland has gained nothing from the Union, and may have lost much.

"The population of Ireland was larger at the Union than in 1896, agriculture was more profitable, for the

* O'Connor Morris, p. 191.

repeal of the Corn Laws had not yet impoverished the Irish agriculturalist, the Irish foreign trade was larger, there were more manufactures in the country, and therefore the income of Ireland could not have been less at the Union than it was ninety years later. But under an Irish Parliament, in a year of peace, taxation was a little over £1,000,000; in a year of war and rebellion it only reached £2,300,000. In the war times after the Union Irish taxation rose to £4,500,000 per annum, and in 1896, after a long period of almost continuous peace, it stood, at nearly £7,000,000."*

Quite apart from overtaxation, the fiscal system of the United Kingdom has been progressively modified in the interests of Great Britain. and without regard to those of Ireland.

The repeal of the Corn Laws was a great boon to the manufacturing interests of these countries, but as those of Ireland were only a small fraction of the whole population, its evil effects far outweighed the benefits it conferred. In 1853 Mr. Gladstone extended the Income Tax to Ireland.

"The additional yield from the Income Tax in Ireland enabled Gladstone to carry out further reforms in the way of reducing taxes on necessaries and the materials for manufacture, reforms which, like the previous ones of Peel, were calculated to benefit the inhabitants of a manufacturing country but could have little effect on the people of agricultural Ireland."†

Thus once more the material interests of Great Britain were fostered without any corresponding advantage accruing to those of Ireland.

I believe it is possible to trace nearly all the problems which have agitated public life in Ireland in recent times to the passing of the Act of Union. I have already shown how the industrial life of Ireland was to a large extent destroyed thereby. The capital which might have been employed in

* Miss Murray (summarising report of Financial
Relations Commission), p. 399.
† *Ibid.*, p. 385.

industrial enterprise, and which was necessary to enable Irish manufacturers to adapt themselves to the introduction of new methods, was drained away in ever-increasing taxation. The Irish corn trade was kept in a condition of unnatural prosperity by the system of Protection which prevailed up to 1845, and then by a sudden change of fiscal policy a period of depression was brought about. The Irish people had been made more and more dependent on the land, and as a result of legislation in the interests of England, it became more and more impossible for the land of Ireland to support the Irish population. The Irish question is henceforth a land question, and the land question owes its paramount importance to the effect of the Act of Union in making the land the sole means of sustenance of the majority of the Irish people. The system of land tenure in Ireland was, as already pointed out, far from ideal. After the repeal of the Corn Laws, the rackrents which could formerly be obtained owing to the keen competition for land and the high prices of agricultural produce, could now be enforced only by the threat of confiscation and eviction, which the state of the law enabled the landlord to carry out if he wished. Up till now the Act of Union itself was the chief agent in bringing about the evils which ensued. But after this the British statesmanship which connived at, and indeed actively assisted, the Irish landlord in his exactions, is chiefly to blame for the maintenance of the Irish land system with its evil associations. And it was mainly due to the system under which Ireland was now governed, and to the non-existence of a strong and independent Irish party in the House of Commons in those days, that the evil results of the Irish land laws, though they called to heaven for redress, should have been treated as if they simply did not exist.

The Devon Commission found the state of Irish agriculture profoundly unsatisfactory. Years elapsed before any legislation was passed to amend that state of things, and though it must be confessed that Deasy's Act of 1860 was on the lines of the Devon Commission recommendations, it, like the report of that Commission itself, was completely wrong in the cure it sought to apply to the evils that admittedly existed. It endeavoured to substitute the English system of contract for the equitable system of custom which tended to prevail in Ireland. It refused to allow compensation to the tenant for improvements unless made with the landlord's consent. In future no improvements were safe unless made under the terms of a contract express or implied. The Act effected no useful purpose, and its principal result was to simplify and cheapen the process of eviction.

Since the date of this Act real attempts have been made with some degree of success to redress the most glaring anomalies of the Irish land system; in addition, the Church of Ireland has been disestablished and disendowed in 1869. The verdict of history is that these reforms were just and necessary, yet it is unfortunately true that had it not been for the fear lest if these concessions were not granted, a worse thing would happen, they would have been sought in vain.

This is mainly due to the fact that Westminster is so far away mentally if not physically, and most of the English members of Parliament move in such a different atmosphere, and are so much occupied with the interests of a totally different class from those of the great majority of Irishmen, whatever their religion, that nothing short of an earthquake will secure their attention, or persuade them that all is not well with Ireland, or might be if the Irish only tried to imitate the British a little more energetically.

The Disestablishment of the Irish Church was admittedly a legislative outcome of the Fenian agitation which convulsed the country from 1864 to 1867. In the forty years which followed Catholic Emancipation twenty-three Bills in favour of the tenants were thrown out by the British Parliament. During the same period forty-two Bills to maintain an unjust system and keep down agitation found their way to the Statute Book. But agitation could not be kept down while grave and palpable wrong remained. O'Connor Morris thus describes the immediate antecedents of the Land Bill of 1870:—

"Five-sixths probably of the occupiers of the soil in Ireland had sunk into the class of mere tenants-at-will;

even the Tenant Right of Ulster had, in some instances, been nibbled away by a certain class of landlords; and at the same time the joint ownership, often morally a fact, but legally ignored in the courts of justice, had gradually been more and more developed. Harsh evictions, also, had become more frequent; and these had been attended with their ordinary results—not a few frightful cases of agrarian crime."*

The Land Act of 1870 gave legal sanction for the first time to the principle of Tenant Right. The tenant was to receive compensation for disturbance, and compensation for improvements, realisable when he was quitting his farm. The Act, was, however, vitiated to a large extent by a further attempt to modify the Irish land system on the lines of the English. It enabled the tenant to contract himself out of its benefits. They might generally be exchanged for a lease of thirty-one years. In thousands of cases tenants accepted these leases, thereby abandoning their rights under the Act, and often this was done under undue pressure. Mr. Gladstone in introducing this Bill spoke with scorn and derision of the principle of the "three Fs":— Fair rent, free sale, and fixity of tenure. He considered that his Bill was a final settlement of the Irish land question, and that when it became law the last would be heard of the agitation for the "three Fs". Mr. Gladstone showed himself in this respect to be, not the broadminded and sympathetic statesman which he is traditionally represented to have been, but a mere self-satisfied English legislator attempting to solve in an offhand manner a question whose many bearings he did not fully appreciate. The faults and shortcomings of this measure were such that within eleven years it had to be supplemented by a Bill in which the "three Fs" were enshrined, and by the irony of fate, it fell to Mr Gladstone to introduce that measure.

* O'Connor Morris, p. 210

EDITOR'S NOTES

1 J.J. makes the classical nationalist case using impeccably unionist
   sources.
2 Louis Paul-Dubois, *Contemporary Ireland* (Dublin, Maunsel, 1908).
   There is an introduction by T. M. Kettle M.P., in which he
   defines the Paul-Dubois position as '. . . definitely for Ireland and
   against England . . . for the Gaelic League and against linguistic
   imperialism, for the ploughed field and against the grazing ranch,
   for Home Rule and against the Act of Union. . .'. Paul-Dubois
   acknowledges help from T. P. Gill, Rev. F. J. Hogan and the
   Maynooth authorities, and Sir Horace Plunkett; also J. F. Taylor
   K.C., the late W. E. H. Lecky, A. E. Clery, J. M. Hone and G. F.
   H. Berkeley. The intellectual basis of pre-1914 all-Ireland Home
   Rule thinking needs exploration, especially as regards its inclusive
   non-sectarian character.

CHAPTER IX.

IRELAND FROM 1871 TILL THE PRESENT DAY.—
THE LAND ACT OF 1881.—CRITICISMS OF IT.—
EXTENT OF PREVALENCE OF DUAL OWNERSHIP
IN OTHER COUNTRIES.—THE IRISH LAND PURCHASE
BILLS. THEIR OBJECTS AND WORKING.—
RECORD OF ULSTER UNIONIST PARTY.

The compensation for improvements given by the Bill of
1870 failed to meet the requirements of the case, because,
except in the case of the Ulster Custom, this compensation
could only be given when the tenant left his farm. This was
what he could not afford to do, and, in many cases as well, he
was prepared to submit to any terms rather than leave his
home. Again, an evicted tenant had to take legal proceedings
in order to make good his claim for compensation for
disturbance, and in the nature of things he was generally
unable to afford the expenses of such proceedings. Moreover,
when he did succeed in making good his claim, the landlord
usually recouped himself by raising the rent on his successor.
This power of arbitrarily raising the rent made the provisions
of this Bill to a large extent futile. It was useless to compel the
landlord to give compensation for improvements when he
could indirectly confiscate them by increasing the rent.
Moreover, the Act of 1870 made compensation for disturbance
payable only when the tenant was being dispossessed by a
notice to quit. It was not as a rule payable when he had to go
owing to non-payment of rent, so that a bad year produced
the same sort of cumulative misfortunes as those which took
place during the famine period. The crisis came in 1879,
when, owing to a bad harvest, tenants were in many cases

unable to pay their rents. This involved a confiscation of Tenant Right, and evictions for non-payment of rent under these circumstances increased. A Bill to remedy this state of affairs was introduced and passed the House of Commons in 1880. It was summarily rejected in the Lords. The result was that the activity of the Land League increased, and agitation, accompanied in many instances by crime, spread in many parts of the country. "In the two years, 1880 and 1881, the agrarian outrages in Ireland, which in 1879, a bad year, were little more than eight hundred in number, reached the appalling total of nearly seven thousand."* Mr. Gladstone, who was then Prime Minister, first tried coercion, and then concession. He introduced and passed the Land Bill of 1881 of which the principles he had before denounced formed the basis. It legalised for the first time the principles of Fair Rent, Free Sale, and Fixity of Tenure. This is another example of a British Government conceding to fear what it had refused to justice. Mr. Gladstone with characteristic frankness has admitted as much:—

> "I must record my firm opinion," he said in 1891, "that the Land Act of 1881 would not have become the law of the land if it had not been for the agitation with which Irish society was convulsed."

So much odium has been cast on this Act, and it has been so calmly assumed by the Unionists that the condition of dual ownership to which it gave legal sanction is something so monstrous that hardly any sacrifices on the part of the British taxpayer are too great to get rid of it—at a price, the landlords' price—that I have thought it advisable to consider the question whether dual ownership is anything so very extraordinary, or whether this is only another instance of the blind leading the blind, and the familiar being treated as the universal. My conclusions might seem to point in the direction of advantage having been taken of popular ignorance, but in view of the fact that equal ignorance is permissible in

* O'Connor Morris, p. 250

members of Parliament and even Cabinet Ministers, I shall in all cases of doubt take the more charitable view. The most convenient book of reference on the subject, which is entitled "Systems of Land Tenure in various Countries," has the misfortune to be issued by the Cobden Club, but seeing that it came out nearly forty years ago, before the progress of Tariff Reform had reduced that institution to its present desperate shifts, and contains contributions by such respectable and distinguished persons as the Hon. G. C. Brodrick, uncle of Lord Midleton, late Secretary of State for War in the Unionist Government, Sir George Campbell, K.C.S.I., formerly Lieutenant-Governor of Bengal, Sir Robert Morier, a distinguished British Diplomatist, and M. Emile de Laveleye, a Belgian scholar and writer on economic subjects, presumably free from any English party bias, it will not be taking any very great risk if its statements are accepted on matters of fact. Before going into details, I might also point out that where land is rented from a landlord for agricultural purposes, in the nature of things there must always be a certain amount of dual ownership if the tenant is not to be robbed of whatever improvements he may make, and is to take any pride or interest in his work, and not simply regard himself as a contractor whose only object is to make all the money he can while he has the chance; and having gone as near as he safely can to exhausting the soil, go off elsewhere when his term expires.

Of the foreign countries I propose to deal with, France is naturally the first. While in theory the state of the law is more in favour of absolute property than one might expect, in practice there are two circumstances which render this of far less importance than in the British Isles. One is that as a matter of custom leases are usually renewed to a good tenant. The other is that industrial life is widely distributed in that country, and if a man cannot get land at a suitable rent, he can turn his hand to some other occupation. Even in France, however, there was no such arbitrary and absurd rule as that of the English law which in Ireland used to give to the proprietor everything that is put upon the land, and in certain cases the outgoing tenant gets compensation for his unexhausted improvements. Where he did not, he did not make them, and irrigation not being one of these, one consequence was that France has occasionally suffered severely from disastrous droughts. In France also there existed a large quantity of common land, estimated by Professor Cliffe Leslie at nearly ten million acres, in the possession of various local bodies. If dual ownership is bad, what must be the state of centesimal or millesimal ownership, and yet France has not merely staggered along under the burden, but shares with England the reputation of being one of the richest countries in Europe.

In Germany, being composed of a large number of states, the details of the transition from the feudal to the modern system of land tenure naturally varied in each, but as the general principles followed were usually the same, it will be sufficient to describe the Prussian legislation of 1850. A consideration of it should give pause to those who sometimes refer to the Emperor William as the *Deus ex machina* who will, if the necessity arises, deliver Ulster from the fate to which Home Rule would subject her. If one of the conditions of deliverance is the application of the Prussian land legislation to Ulster, those landlords without whose presence no Unionist gathering at the present day seems to be complete, will feel not merely that the money spent on rifles has been wasted, but that they are very much in the position of the frogs who exchanged king Log for king Stork. Up till 1850 there existed certain feudal dues to which the landowners were entitled. In that year the Prussian Legislature not merely passed a law commuting them into money payments, but committed a further outrage by applying to them the iniquitous principle of compulsory purchase, and fixing the price at eighteen times the amount of the rent charge. No conferences here, or bonuses increasing in proportion to the number of years purchase the landlord succeeded in wringing out of the tenant, or pleasing spectacle of landlord and tenant settling their differences amicably at the expense of the general public. Had this Prussian legislation of 1850 been taken as the model for the Irish land legislation of 1903, every Irish farmer would long since have become a proprietor, millions of pounds of the taxpayers' money would have been saved, and Ulster would not have been penalised for its loyalty by its supposed friends in the way it has been. If any negotiations with Germany have been entered on by the Ulster leaders, it is to be hoped that there is a clause in the contract making it quite clear that it is only the German army and navy that is wanted, not the German land laws; otherwise those who have hitherto successfully resisted compulsion may unconsciously be the means of bringing it about.

Should any Ulster landlord, in his disgust at the legalised robbery of his class that has taken place in Germany, turn to Russia as a country in which democratic forces have as yet made little progress, it is to be feared an even greater disappointment awaits him. The Russian peasants were originally serfs of the landowners. By the legislation of 1861, they were not merely freed from this position, but the landlord was compelled to hand over to them in hereditary copyhold against the payment of rent, an amount of land of which not merely the minimum was fixed in regard to quantity but in regard to quality also, and the law required that as a general rule the best land should be handed over to the tenants. Nor was this all. Not only was the landlord compelled to give up the best of his land to the tenant at a rent, but the tenants as a body were given the option of buying out their farmyards with or without their holdings, as they preferred, at 16⅔ the amount of the rent, that is at what we should call 16⅔ years' purchase. Where all did not agree to do so, any particular tenant who so desired could assert his own right of purchase by paying one-fifth more. Four-fifths or three-fourths of the amount necessary to effect the purchase, according as the sale was a complete or partial one, was advanced by the State. Being only an ordinary Ulsterman and not an Ulster leader, it is no part of my business to endeavour to turn the thoughts of those susceptible to my influence towards foreign countries, but I fancy there are a good many Ulster farmers who, having waited in vain for nearly thirty years for an opportunity of purchasing their holdings, would, if they knew the above facts, almost wish themselves Germans or Russians.

In Belgium the ideal of the earlier English legislation in connection with the Irish land question, has as a rule been attained, and the relations between landlord and tenant based entirely on contract. The result has been that the agricultural population are as a rule very poor, that the landlords rarely give leases for more than nine years lest they should have to wait too long before being able to raise the rent, and that in the period between 1830 and 1866 the average rent per acre increased by 78 per cent. Even in Belgium, however, the outgoing tenant has to be compensated for certain unexhausted improvements, so that there is still some falling short of the ideal of absolute ownership.

In the Dutch province of Groningen there exists a tenure called the Beklem-regt, which is the very essence of dual ownership, under which the rent can never be raised, and subject to certain payments on transfers, the tenant can do pretty well whatever he pleases with the land so long as he does not diminish its value. The results of this system, instead of bearing out the dismal prophecies in regard to the consequences of dual ownership, are thus described by M de Laveleye:—

"Thus, instead of tenants with the fear of losing their holdings always before their eyes, and ground down by ever-increasing rents, this system, derived from the Middle Ages, has created a class of semi-proprietors independent, proud, simple, but withal eager for enlightenment, appreciating the advantages of education, practising husbandry not by blind routine and as a mean occupation, but as a noble profession by which they acquire wealth, influence, and the consideration of their fellow-men; a class ready to submit to any sacrifice to drain their lands, improve their farm buildings and implements, and looking for their well-being to their own energy and foresight alone."

Similar tenures have existed in Portugal and Italy, and with regard to the former country, in the province of Minho, where it was specially prevalent, it was found the produce per acre of land was a good deal more than double that of the province of Alemtego where it did not exist, though the latter province is naturally much more fertile.

It is curious that the criticisms of the principle of dual ownership and the attempt to correct the supposed evils produced by it were entirely confined to Ireland, and in another part of the Empire those evils were left to work their way unchecked among a population more than fifty times as great. An examination of Sir George Campbell's article on the Indian land tenure shows that dual ownership is there the rule rather than the exception.[1]

His summary of the tenures in the various provinces is as follows:—

"The present distribution of tenures in the different provinces may then be stated to be (speaking generally) as follows:— Oude being at one extreme with an aristocratic system, which gives the land to nobles and financiers; Madras and Bombay at the other, with a system which gives the land to the people.

"*Oude.*—Great Zemeendars, almost complete owners, with few subordinate rights.

"*North-west Provinces.*— Moderate proprietors; the old ryots have fixity of tenure at a fair rent.

"*Punjab.*—Very small and very numerous peasant proprietors; old ryots have also a measure of fixity of tenure at fair rent.

"*Bengal.*—Great Zemeendars, whose rights are limited. Numerous sub-proprietors of several grades under them. Ancient ryots who have both fixity of tenure and fixity of rent. Other old ryots who have fixity of tenure at fair rent variable from time to time.

"*Central Provinces.*—Moderate proprietors. Ancient ryots who are sub-proprietors of their holdings at fixed rents for the term of each settlement. Other old ryots have fixity of tenure at a fair rent.

"*Madras and Bombay.*—The ryots are generally complete proprietors of the soil, subject only to payment of revenue."

It will thus appear that in every province except Oude dual ownership is the normal condition of things, if it is borne in mind that in most of Madras, Bombay, and the Punjab the Government is the landlord, and that a peasant proprietor simply means a tenant who has no landlord between himself and the Government. In Oude, however, the land is owned by large landowners, as against whom their tenants have few rights; Sir George Campbell's verdict on the system prevailing in this province is that it has not been a success, in spite of a great deal of official and unofficial sympathy and assistance at the commencement. The following passage, describing the state of things at the time he wrote bears a painful resemblance to certain unfortunate passages in Irish history:—

"So far from improving the country as capitalist landlords, it has been necessary for Government to come to the assistance of the aristocratic system by lending the Talookdars money to stave off their creditors and protecting them from legal procedure. They have made free use of the power to raise rents and evict; notices of ejectment have been annually served by tens of thousands. Sub-proprietors and ryots have attempted to resist, and a war of classes has prematurely arisen, involving questions which elsewhere have not been reached in several generations."

It would therefore seem that the advantages of absolute as compared with dual ownership are by no means obvious, while its disadvantages are sometimes painfully apparent, and it is notorious that whatever party has been in power at home, the whole tendency of Indian legislation in recent years has been in the direction of affording further protection to the tenants, that is of increasing the dual nature of the ownership instead of attempting to get rid of it.

The chief criticisms to which the Land Act of 1881 has been subjected are something of the following nature:—It stereotyped a system of dual ownership under which the landlord was little more than a rent charger on his own estate. His power to use his position for the improvement of the lot of his tenants was taken away. Moreover, the

procedure for fixing a fair rent was often of a haphazard
character and tended to paralyse industry and reward
thriftlessness; though it was instrumental in reducing rents
which were in many cases too high, it made little or no
distinction between rackrents and rents which were more
equitable, but, in point of fact, caused a wholesale reduction
of Irish rents by about 20 to 30 per cent. In that way the
landlord whose rents were excessive fared relatively better
than the landlord whose rents were already equitable, as little
or no distinction was made between them in the reductions
which took place.

The first part of the criticism would have been more to the
point if the improvement of the lot of the tenants had not so
often taken the form of ensuring that they lived the simple life
by depriving them of the means of living any other. The
second part deals rather with the administration of the Act
than with the principle of it, and in any case is by no means
confined to the situation created by it. Under a system of pure
contract the hard and grasping landlord will in the nature of
things come off better than the kind-hearted and generous
one, while if he continues to do so here, it is only due to the
incompetence of the officers entrusted with the duty of fixing
the rent. If the thriftless tenant profited more than the
industrious one, this also was due to the imperfection of the
instrument, and in any case the discouragement to thrift is less
than under a system by which the proceeds of it are automatically confiscated. While there is much to be said for the
creation of a system of peasant proprietors so long as it is
done in a businesslike way and at a reasonable price, this
should not blind us to the enormous improvement in the
condition of the Irish farmer effected by the Land Act of 1881.
The economic improvement was for a long time not marked,
as the fall in rents hardly kept pace with the fall in prices, but
the social and political benefits were enormous. A phrase
which in most cases would be merely a piece of rhetorical
exaggeration could be truthfully applied to Mr. Gladstone
when in addressing an Ulster audience a speaker said:— "He
found you slaves and he left you free men."

At the time of the passing of the Land Act of 1881, Nationalist opinion, as expressed by Parnell, was in favour of State-aided purchase of Irish land. This doctrine was heretical while its only advocates were Parnell and his followers. Since 1903 it has been the gospel of the Unionist Party in regard to Ireland. Nevertheless even before 1881 tentative efforts were made by the State towards assisting a number of Irish tenants to become the owners of their farms.

The Unionist Party is accustomed to take to itself all the credit for the beneficent policy of land purchase. But it was not adopted until the legislation of the Liberals had substantially lowered rents. Was the guiding principle concern for the tenant's interest, or a desire to allow the landlord to get back something of what he had lost? In subsequent pages I shall quote facts and figures which will show that this question can have only one answer.

The Unionist Party adopted the principle of voluntary land purchase in 1885. In that year the Ashbourne Act was passed, and by it £5,000,000 was advanced to enable tenants to purchase their holdings. O'Connor Morris says in this connection:—

> "Instead of paying as hitherto part of the purchase money, the tenant was to have the whole sum lent to him by the State, repayable by a terminable annuity much lower than an ordinary rent. The transaction, therefore, was not, in a real sense, a purchase; it was, properly speaking, a gift akin to a bribe."*

O'Connor Morris doubtless means that it was a bribe to the tenants. It was equally a bribe to the landlord. The tenant was bribed to buy by the prospect of paying less as an annuity instalment than he had paid in rent, unless he bought at an absurdly high figure. As the process was to be voluntary on the landlord's side, he had to be bribed to sell by obtaining a good deal more than the value of his land. This is the characteristic vice of the principle of voluntary land purchase,

* O'Connor Morris, p. 303.

which runs through the Wyndham Act of 1903 to an even greater extent than in the case of this Act. As I shall now explain, both Acts were so framed that it would pay the tenant to buy at a price much higher than the real value of his land, and the question as between him and his landlord was not in the least what the land was worth, but how much he could be induced to pay, and what retaliatory measures he was likely to take if the landlord refused to sell.

The economic absurdity underlying all the Unionist Land Purchase Acts is so glaring that it is to my mind absolutely incomprehensible how they failed to awaken a storm of protest. It requires very little mathematical or technical knowledge to see that under normal circumstances when a payment in perpetuity is to be commuted into a payment for a term of years, during that term of years the amount paid should be greater than before. What happened in this case was that owing to the fact of the Government being able to borrow at a lower rate than private individuals can, it could afford to buy out the land and repay itself by instalments which were actually less than the previous rent. So far so good; the Government could buy out every acre of land in the country with advantage both to itself and the tenant, on one condition, *that it did so at the market price.* But that was just what the Unionist Government did not want to do, but rather its object was to let its friends the Irish landlords get back something of what they had lost through the operation of Mr. Gladstone's Land Acts. A German or a Russian Government undertaking a scheme of this kind would have taken care to fix the price, or provide machinery to do so. Not so the British Unionists. The sacred principle of freedom of contract must be preserved, with the dice loaded in favour of the landlord. Had the estates been sold in the ordinary way, it is very doubtful if many of them would have fetched more than 20 years' purchase. Where one was sold out under a Purchase Act where the instalment was 4 per cent. of the purchase price, until 25 years' purchase was reached, the tenant would have to pay no more than before. Where the instalment was $3\frac{1}{4}$ per cent., anything less than $30\frac{3}{4}$ years' purchase would still afford some profit to the tenant as compared with not being able to buy at all. The landlords, in the absence of a compulsory clause, took full advantage of these facts, and demanded prices not according to what the estates were worth, but according to what there was a prospect of the tenants being induced to give. To make absolutely sure that no landlord should sell too cheap, and give the last Gilbert and Sullivan touch to an already absurd situation, the Wyndham Act of 1903 gave a bonus to the landlord at the expense of the British taxpayer, and this bonus was in proportion not to the rental but to the purchase money, so that the more was got out of the tenant the more was got out of the taxpayer, and any landlord who sold at a reasonable price lost doubly. The so-called Purchase Acts were really Landlords' Endowment Acts, and only served the former purpose incidentally so far as it was involved in serving the latter.

It must, however, in fairness be admitted that the possibilities of the situation were only gradually appreciated, or else it required the confidence engendered by a long spell of office and the majority secured in the khaki election,[2] to give the courage requisite for taking full advantage of them. In the Purchase Acts of 1885, 1887, and 1891, the instalments were fixed at 4 per cent. of the purchase money, so that a tenant who agreed to a term of more than 25 years' purchase would have to pay more than his former rent. As the whole attraction of the scheme from the tenants' point of view was to get a reduction of rent, this was never done, and the average price of the land sold under the Ashbourne Act was only about 18 years' purchase (Bonn: "Modern Ireland and her Agrarian Problem," page 138, footnote).[3] So long as the instalments remained at 4 per cent., the absence of compulsion is important rather as retarding sales than as increasing the price, and the Unionist Ministry cannot be very severely criticised for their failure to include it, in view of the fact that not merely did their Irish supporters in the House of Commons not use their influence in this direction, but when in 1896 a proposal was made by the Government itself to apply the principle to properties in the Landed Estates Court, whose duty it was under certain circumstances to sell the encumbered property in its charge, the present Ulster leader opposed the Bill which contained it as a "betrayal", and criticised its terms most scathingly. In a letter to *The Times* of July 23, 1896, Sir Edward, then Mr., Carson left no doubt as to the class of the Irish people whose interests he and his fellow Irish Unionists had at heart in their criticisms of the Bill. In this letter he wrote:—"I say nothing now of the manner in which *those of us who represent landlords' interests* in the House have been treated by our friends."*

The election of 1895 had been fought in Ireland entirely on the question of Home Rule. No sooner was the Union safe than these Ulster Unionist members made it perfectly clear that on land questions they were in the House of Commons to represent, not the interests of the Ulster tenant farmers who had returned them by their votes, but those of the class to which they themselves almost exclusively belonged. Sir Edward opposed this Bill as of a socialistic and revolutionary character. The then champion of orthodoxy has now become a revolutionist himself, and I greatly fear, as I have indicated some way back, that there is considerable likelihood that the Provisional Government which has by this time been set up, will have to go a good deal further in the direction of socialism than the Land Bill of 1896 went, if a considerable proportion of its subjects are not to die of starvation during the first fortnight of its existence.

The attitude of the Ulster leader is essentially the same to-day as it was in 1896. Circumstances, however, and consequently the methods it is advisable to use, are different. In 1896, the Union being safe for the time being, he was free to consult the interests of his friends the landlords; at present, the Union being again in danger, he desires to save the Union doubtless in order that in future he may be able once more to promote the same interests he admittedly had at heart on that occasion. In each case the fixed idea to which everything else must give way is that the Irish landlords must be preserved in

* The italics are mine.

their rights and privileges at all costs, and as for the rest of the population, where not deserving of extermination as hereditary enemies, it should be extremely thankful if it is allowed to live on the crumbs let fall from the rich man's table. If there is to he a civil war, it is to be hoped that the rank and file, especially the agricultural classes, clearly understand what they are fighting to establish, otherwise the splendour of the victory, if there is one, may be dimmed, as in the case of the Balkan allies, by the outbreak of hostilities among the conquerors.

It is customary in Unionist circles to speak with bated breath of the Wyndham Act of 1903 as the finest flower of British statesmanship, and to allege that if the wicked Liberal Government had not killed it by the modifications introduced in the Act of 1909, Ireland would now be an earthly paradise, and the very thought of Home Rule would be indignantly repudiated lest the ideal perfection of the situation should be marred. Let us examine how far this description of the measure and its results can be accepted as correct. Friendliness and harmony are rather at a discount at present, but when it is considered desirable to praise those virtues, it is pointed out that it was in connection with this measure that almost for the first time in history all parties were united. The Act was the sequel to a conference, the proceedings of which I must frankly admit form the strongest argument in favour of the Union of any I have yet seen, since in this case it provided a milch cow whose productiveness was only equalled by its docility. The landlords were there to get as much as they could for their land. The Nationalist leaders were there to get a substantial reduction on the payments to be made by the tenants. How were these conflicting interests to be reconciled? The difficulty might well seem insuperable, but it was triumphantly overcome. In regard to the manner in which the problem was solved I shall again quote from the German historian already mentioned, who writes as follows:—

"If the payments of the tenants were to be reduced by 15 per cent. to 25 per cent., and the gross income of the landlord to be reduced by only 10 per cent., on the basis of

3 per cent. investments, it is clear that there must be a gap to be filled up. This gap was to be filled by the Treasury of the United Kingdom, by means of a bonus to be accorded to the landlord in the interests of the pacification of Ireland."

That the harmony thus established failed to be permanent is in no way surprising. Austria and Russia have not ceased to quarrel because they agreed on the partition of Poland, and as it is no part of the policy of the Irish Party to consult the interests of the British taxpayer while they are kept at Westminster against their will, while the landlord classes instinctively look on him as their natural prey, an agreement on this point means no more than it did in the analogous case I have alluded to. The Nationalists took what they could get, and the landlords got what they could take. This turned out to be considerable. Under this Act the period of repayment was extended, and the instalments reduced to $3\frac{1}{4}$ per cent. of the purchase money. The effect of this on raising the price of the land has already been pointed out. A zone system was also introduced, by which if the reductions on purchase were between 10 and 30 per cent. on second term rents, and 20 and 40 per cent. on first term rents, the Estates Commissioners were bound to make the advances at once, whereas in other cases a tedious investigation was necessary. This meant in effect the establishment of a legal minimum price of 21.53 and 18.46 years' purchase respectively, or practically of 21.53 since most of the rents by that time had become second term. Then on the top of all this was the bonus of £12,000,000, which was given in proportion to the price realised, so that the landlord might have a double inducement to hold out for a high figure. And as if to remove any possible doubt that the object of the framers of the measure was to subsidise the landlords, not to benefit the tenants, there was another ingenious provision, which I shall leave it to the German historian to describe. Bonn, at page 141, English translation, writes as follows:—

"The landlord, however, is permitted to sell his residence and demesne, not to the tenants, but to the Land

Commission. He can afterwards buy them back from the Commission by means of an advance which they will make him, but which it must be observed may not exceed one-third of the total value of the estate. The landlord has never drawn rent from this demesne, but on an estate of the value of say £20,000 he has perhaps encumbrances amounting to some £10,000 for which he is paying interest at 5 per cent. For every £1,000 of net rental he, therefore, received only £500. Now let us suppose that he sells his residence with the estate and receives £5,000 for it. With this £5,000 he pays a part of his old debt and contracts a new one at 2¾ per cent. interest; that is to say, instead of paying £250 interest he pays only £140, thus saving £110."

In other words, lest the pressure of his necessities should induce any landlord to sell to the tenants at a reasonable rate, the Government steps in, obligingly buys his residence and demesne land, and then sells it back to him at what is, so far as he is concerned, little more than half-price, since it reduces his liabilities by that equivalent. In this way a certain proportion of the money which the deluded British taxpayer had been induced to vote under the impression that he was establishing peasant proprietors in Ireland, not merely did not go to establish them, but was utilised so as to prevent their establishment by relieving the landlords of the necessity of selling their tenanted land, and consequently raising the price of all such land sold, and causing the money left to be devoted to this purpose to go a much shorter way than it otherwise would.

The most superficial consideration will show that the inevitable result of all these provisions was to inflate artificially the price of Irish land sold under the Act. It was calculated when the Wyndham Act was introduced, that the £100,000,000 which it contemplated advancing would suffice to bring about the transfer to the tenants of all the agricultural land remaining in the bands of the landlords. Under the Wyndham Act £85,410,602 has actually been, or is about to be, advanced. The Act of 1909 has added £11,225,234 to that figure. Even now, however, one-third of the land of Ireland still remains unsold, and the cost of selling it is estimated at £60,000,000. If there was any accuracy in the calculations of the framers of the Wyndham Act, it would seem that a considerable proportion, say half, of £60,000,000 has been simply wasted, though perhaps the Party responsible for that Act would dissent from this view on the principle that "It's not lost what a friend gets." In other words, the Irish landlords who have sold, have got anything up to £30,000,000 more for their land than it was worth.

The most annoying thing in connection with this enormous squandering of public money is that it was entirely unnecessary, even in the interests of the landlords themselves. One reason why many landlords were unwilling to sell except at a prohibitive price, was that where estates were entailed, the purchase money could only be invested in trustee securities, which only as a rule yield from 3 to 3½ per cent. Had this provision been relaxed, investments could have been found at 4 and possibly even 4½ per cent., which would have been safe enough for all practical purposes, and the price could have been reduced in a corresponding degree without loss to the existing owner. A foreigner would have expected that a government which called on the taxpayer to make such sacrifices and incur such liabilities in order to bring about a certain result, would have taken all the subsidiary measures requisite to ensure that result being attained—in fact the German author I have quoted criticised this portion of the Act rather severely—but this presupposes a logical completeness in English legislation the absence of which is its greatest pride. Besides if once the voice of logic or reason had been allowed to begin to make itself heard, it would have gone on to demand a compulsory clause, and to take some steps to check the inflation of value created by the operation of the Act, and that would have been downright socialism. It was rather hard on the tenants whose lands were not sold, but the sacred principle of property was at stake, and as those who were hit hardest were Ulster loyalists, they had the satisfaction of knowing that they were being martyred for the cause.

Consequently it was left to the Act of 1909, and to that introduced during the last session, to remedy this and the other glaring administrative defects of the Wyndham Act, after that measure of frenzied finance had collapsed under the weight of its own extravagance. The absence of compulsion did not matter very much in the south and west, as the custom which used to prevail in some of those parts of shooting at a landlord who showed too marked a disregard for the interests of his tenants, and the other practices incidental to a land war, made a large proportion of the landlords only too glad to sell out when the opportunity was afforded them of being able to do so on favourable terms. In Ulster, however, where except in backward places like Donegal, the people not merely do not shoot at their landlords, but send them to represent their interests, as they fondly believe, at Westminster, the situation was different. The landlords there are quite content with the existing arrangement of things, and in a great many instances have elected to remain. As long ago as 1905, Bonn, the German author I have frequently had occasion to quote, foretold this, when he wrote:—

"There will, however, always be a number of properties whose owners will decline to sell. These will be precisely those estates whose tenants pay their rents regularly and will not be led into acts of disorder—that is to say practically the Ulster tenantry."

In order to verify the extent to which this has happened, I have thought it advisable to examine the most recent statistics on the subject. They are complicated somewhat by the fact that holdings above a certain size do not come within the scope of the Act, and also, if I may be allowed to say so, by the other fact that nearly half of the population of Ulster is Nationalist, and in Nationalist districts the attitude of the landlords and tenants towards each other is very much the same as in the South and West. These circumstances make the figures I have obtained all the more striking.

A recently published return for the period up to 31st March, 1913, gives the area, poor law valuation, and purchase money of (*a*) lands sold, and (*b*) lands in respect of which proceedings for sale have been instituted and are pending under the Irish Land Purchase Acts; also the estimated area, poor law valuation, and purchase money of lands in respect of which proceedings for sale have not yet been instituted. The details are given for counties and provinces as well. From this return it appears that 12,202,591 acres of land have been sold, or are in process of being sold, under those Acts, and that 6,577,219 acres have not been sold, and no negotiations for their sale are pending. That is to say 65 per cent. of the land of Ireland has been affected by already existing Land Acts. What are the figures for the respective provinces? In Ulster 2,989,866 acres have been, or are about to be, sold, whereas 2,173,198 acres do not come in either of these categories. The total number of acres of land in Ulster is thus 4,963,064; 65 per cent. of this is 3,225,991. But the amount of land actually sold or about to be sold in Ulster is less than this by 436,125 acres. Thus the proportion of land sold in Ulster is rather less than the average for the whole of Ireland in the proportion of 56 to 65. Let us take the figures for the other provinces. The total number of acres of land in the other three provinces is 13,816,746. Sixty-five per cent. of that is 8,980,884 acres. But the amount actually sold, or about to be sold, is 9,412,725 acres. That is to say over 68 per cent. of the land of the other three provinces has been, or is about to be, sold, as against 56 per cent. in Ulster. These facts speak for themselves. Moreover, this is not all. In Ulster practically every holding comes within the terms of the Land Acts previous to 1909, while in Leinster and Connaught, and to a lesser extent in Munster, there are many large grazing farms and holdings so large as to be excluded from the scope of the 1903 Act. By that Act no holding worth more than £5,000, or in exceptional cases £7,000, might be sold. If we take it that practically every holding with a poor law valuation of £200 and upwards is worth upwards of £5,000, we can see to what extent the figures ought to be re-arranged in order to bring out the true proportion. In Leinster there are according to the last Census return 2,078 such holdings with a total area of 858,567 acres. In Munster there are 920 with an acreage of 368,744. In Connaught there are 397, with a total area of 236,760 acres. In Ulster there are only 553, the total area being 184,940 acres.

Let us make the necessary corrections by excluding the lands not eligible for sale and then compare the results obtained. They work out to 58 per cent. and 76 per cent. respectively. In other words only about three-quarters as much land has been sold in Ulster as would have been if it had kept pace with the rest of Ireland. This is the reward of loyalty and industry, and all those virtues which their leaders and their newspapers are never tired of telling the Ulster people they possess, and that the rest of the population are conspicuously without. And more wonderful still, the only chance of getting this state of things remedied is by a measure introduced by a Government against whom they are even now preparing to take up arms, and which is kept in power by the assistance of the "hereditary enemies." When this is the manner in which Ulster farmers are treated by their friends, apart from all moral considerations, it seems rather a waste of energy to kill their enemies, much more to undergo a long and laborious training in order to be in a position to do so. When their friends behave as their enemies, would it not perhaps be advisable to wait and see if after all their supposed enemies are not their friends? They cannot well be less so than those who have hitherto posed as such.

It is usually asserted that the Liberal Government by the Land Act which they passed in 1909 killed land purchase. It is more correct to assert that the Act was killed by its own financial absurdities. The £100,000,000 which Mr. Wyndham fondly hoped would complete the sale of Irish land was nearly all used up by 1909 and less than two-thirds of Irish land was sold. Owing to the reasons given above, the prices paid were very much inflated, and consequently the money available was used up in buying out landlords who found it convenient to sell, and did not go so far as it would have gone had there been a compulsory clause and machinery for fixing a fair price. Moreover, by a clause in the Wyndham Act which for sheer cynical audacity eclipses all the others, the cost of the flotation of Land Stock fell ultimately on the Irish rates, so that the tenant who was deprived of the privilege of being able to buy, might at least participate indirectly by helping to pay for the land of those who did have the opportunity. However, the stock fell so much in value, and the liability of the rates mounted to such an extent, that it became imperative to relieve them, which was done by the Act of 1909 passed by the Liberal Government. The Act of 1903 was a failure in the congested districts of the West, where holdings are uneconomic, and a tenant could not afford to pay the price which the landlord would be willing to accept. On such holdings a peasant proprietary could no more thrive than did the tenant farmers they would be replacing. There were in 1902 upwards of 200,000 holdings of the class technically known by this name, that is to say, with a poor law valuation of under or a little over £4. In this case the problem is one not of the mere purchase of a tenant's holding, but of the purchase of untenanted lands and their resale in lots to the occupiers of uneconomic holdings. The Congested Districts Board was founded in 1891 to deal with this situation. It had no compulsory powers of expropriation and consequently the progress of the work was so slow that in 1903 it had only dealt with some 44 estates. By the Land Act of 1909 the requisite powers of compulsory expropriation were given to it, but that good friend of Ulster, the House of Lords, threw out the compulsory clause so far as it applied to the rest of Ireland, and since then land purchase in the congested districts has proceeded rapidly. Mr. Birrell introducing the new Land Bill said:—

> "Then came the much abused Act of 1909, and the result of that Act was in the very part where land purchase hardly moved at all. The Congested Districts Board had been able to purchase for the relief of congestion and the improvement of the people 1,485,774 acres of land. Since the passing of that Act land purchase had proceeded in the West even faster than it had in any other part of Ireland"

This was the result of the existence of a clause compelling the landlords of untenanted lands to sell their land at a fair price, in order that they might be distributed among the occupiers of the uneconomic holdings in question.

The Congested Districts Board is a fairly large and expensive Government department, yet the party which is now trying to make political capital out of the fact that the administration of the Insurance Act has to be paid for, kept it practically idle while they were in office rather than give it the powers necessary to secure its efficiency.

Some of the most glaring defects of the Unionist measures have been or are in process of being corrected by the legislation of the Liberal Government, and because they do not go on pouring money like water into the lap of the Irish landlords, but insist on getting value for it in return, the latter and their phonographs in Westminster have actually had the effrontery to raise the cry that the Liberals have killed land purchase. They are so accustomed to consider themselves the centre of the universe that it never even crosses their mind that the interests of the rest of the nation may have to be considered as well as theirs. The whole guiding principle of the Unionist land purchase schemes has been admirably summarised by a French writer, M. Paul Dubois,[4] who in his book "Contemporary Ireland" writes thus about the Land Act of 1903:—

> "Emanating from a Government friendly to the landlords, it hides badly, under an appearance of impartiality, clever attempts to place the landlords in a position of advantage to raise in their favour the price of the land."

The record of the Ulster Unionist members and their leader, whose only connection with Ulster that I have been able to discover, is that he comes there sometimes in order to address political meetings, and latterly to perform functions of a semi-regal character, has not been particularly brilliant in regard to the question of land purchase. Has it been any better in regard to anything else? The Ulster Unionist members are returned mainly by the votes of Ulster farmers and workingmen. When one eliminates from their ranks lawyers, landlords, and distillers, how many of them are left? How many of them have interests which coincide with those of their constituents, or rather how few of them have any that are not directly opposed to theirs?

So far as the province they are supposed to represent is concerned, what have they ever done beyond endeavouring to keep everything as it was before, with an occasional sop to the landlord and the liquor interest when the party leaders at Westminster so decreed? They are at one with the rank and file of their party in Ulster only in their opposition to Home Rule; even in this particular they are only able to maintain the zeal of their constituents at fever heat by playing on their religious fears and repeating parrot-like the cry, "Home Rule means Rome Rule," a belief which they may or may not hold in their hearts, but of which in any case a slight acquaintance with history, a little breadth of view, or in the last resort a brief interview with the present Chief Whip of their Party ought to suffice to disabuse them. Whether Home Rule means Rome Rule or not, everyone knows ritualism is essentially Romish, yet the Ulster Unionists helped to pass an Education Bill in 1902 which was a surrender to the ritualistic tendencies of the Church of England. Lest I should seem to be exaggerating, I add a quotation from a sermon by Rev. W. J. Hanson preached at Albertbridge Congregational Church on the anniversary of "Ulster Day" in obedience to the orders of the Ulster leader, his criticism of the general tendency of the Act for which Sir Edward Carson himself voted ought to be of interest to those Ulster Protestants who regard him and his party as the bulwark of their faith. The reverend gentleman is reported to have made use of the following remarks:—

"But why should I bring you centuries back that you might see the workings of Rome, for is it not in the memory of even the youngest her doings within the last few years? Think of the Education Act, an Act which practically hands over the whole education of the youth of England to Ritualists, and the next generation will be under the yoke of Ritualism. *It was no friend of Protestantism that did that.* Think of a Nonconformist child as the result of that Act being marched from his school and made to bow with other Ritualistic children before a crucifix. You may say that he can refuse through his parents, but a law that makes it even possible that Protestant children would be asked to do so in a Protestant country is iniquitous in the extreme, and should not be tolerated."

The Ulster Unionist members were "no friends of Protestantism" in 1902. Neither are they friends of temperance reform—a cause with which most Protestant denominations are closely associated. In fact their attitude on this question is notorious, and used to call down on their unrepentant heads the wrath of the General Assembly of the Presbyterian Church in the days when that body still possessed some vestiges of independence, and had not yet been transformed into a Unionist Club.

It is unnecessary, however, to enter into further details about the manner in which they have misrepresented the interests and flouted the desires of the general body of their constituents. I pass on to discuss their attitude towards the general question of the Government of Ireland, and their policy with regard to the present Home Rule Bill.

EDITOR'S NOTES

[1] The reference is to the Cobden Club compilation mentioned earlier in the text. I detect here also perhaps the influence of the older brother James in the amount of attention given to India.

[2] An election won by the Tories in a wave of Boer War jingoism.

[3] Moritz Julius Bonn wrote extensively on imperialism and colonisation, his first being *Modern Ireland and the Agrarian Problem* (Dublin and London, 1906). Of the ten titles on record in the TCD library the last, in 1961, is with Alan Denson and is a reminiscence of George Russell (AE) together with a collection of the latter's writings. He wrote critically in the 1930s on the economics of the Depression, and in the 1950s on European integration. He would appear to have been an agrarian economist of the Left, with co-operativist leanings, somewhat similar to J.J.

[4] See note 2, ch. 8, p. 135.

CHAPTER X.

ATTITUDE OF ULSTER UNIONIST PARTY ON
GENERAL QUESTION OF GOVERNMENT OF
IRELAND.—UNSTATESMANLIKE CHARACTER
OF THEIR OPPOSITION TO THE HOME
RULE BILL IN THE HOUSE OF COMMONS.—
SUGGESTED IMPROVEMENTS IN THE BILL
ITSELF.—THE FINANCIAL QUESTION.—EFFECT
OF OLD AGE PENSIONS ACT.—NEED FOR
READJUSTMENT BETWEEN IMPERIAL AND
LOCAL EXPENDITURE.—ADVANTAGES OF
HOME RULE TO IRELAND, TO GREAT BRITAIN,
AND TO THE EMPIRE.—CONCLUSION.

The Ulster Unionist leaders speak as if the existing system of
Irish Government were perfect and all that is required to
make the country into an earthly paradise is a paltry sum of
not more than £60,000,000 to buy out the remaining Irish
landlords at whatever price they choose to demand, and a
recognition on the part of the Irish people of their own inferi-
ority, and of the ability of England under all circumstances to
manage their affairs much better than they can themselves.
This is the view put forward in Ulster, but it is by no means the
one accepted in London, of which the following extract from
a leading Unionist paper, the *Globe*, may be taken as typical:—

"In determining to dismiss Lord Loreburn's proposal
from their minds Unionists must not fall into the error of
assuming that the government of Ireland can be left in the
state in which it is at present. For good or for evil, the
situation in Ireland has been utterly changed by the recent

course of politics, and it is of no use for Unionists to shut their eyes to the fact. Castle government is hopelessly discredited, and can no more be restored to the credit it once possessed than Humpty Dumpty to his wall. We must be prepared to initiate large, and even generous, reforms in the machinery of Irish administration."

The writer, of course, goes on to say that all this can be done without any concessions to the principle of Home Rule, but he does not explain how, and his reference to Humpty Dumpty irresistibly suggests two other characters in the same book, Tweedledum and Tweedledee, the differences and distinction between whom he would do well to study with some care, as they are apparently of the same nature as those between the scheme of reform which the Unionists may ultimately be forced to adopt, and that which they are now prepared to plunge the country into civil war in order to prevent. Shakespeare may have been a very great genius but when he wrote the lines:—

> "What's in a name? that which we call a rose,
> By any other name would smell as sweet,"

he failed completely to foresee the importance of terminological distinctions in modern political warfare.

In making the following statement I fear I shall run counter to the prejudices of all existing parties who understand the rules of the game as it is played at present, and cannot do more than form a rough guess as to what would be the effect on their prospects of altering them, but it seems to me that a great deal of the violence of political conflicts at the present day is due to the system of single member constituencies, and the absence of a second ballot, which often results in a state of things in which the tail wags the dog. Does anyone outside their own ranks seriously believe that the present Ulster Unionist members really represent the Ulster electors to whose interests they are opposed on almost every conceivable question? In most instances they owe their seats simply to the fact that of two evils people choose what seems the lesser, and though the Protestant farmers fear and distrust the landlords, they fear and distrust the priests rather more, and consequently whoever has captured the party machinery has only to raise the cry, "Do not split the Protestant vote," and his success is assured; when the election is over, his constituents often complain bitterly about the manner in which he disregards their interests and favours those of his own class, till the next election comes round, and after a repetition of the same process he is again elected. In constituencies like North Antrim, however, where there is not a very large Catholic population, the risk of letting in a Nationalist can be neglected, with the result that the electors there sometimes take the bit in their teeth, and indicate that they expect something more from their representative than to be able to shout at all times and places, "We will not have Home Rule."

A second ballot, by which no candidate would be declared elected unless he had an absolute majority of the votes recorded at the election, would do a good deal to remedy this state of things, and still more could be done by a system of proportional representation, as indicated by Lord MacDonnell in the address delivered by him before the Literary and Scientific Society of the Queen's University, Belfast on February 23rd, 1911, where he says:—

> "The Irish Parliamentary Parties of today—the Nationalist and Unionist—are recruited for a special object—the Home Rule battle at Westminster, and do not represent the various phases of local feeling in Ireland on public questions. If I may, without offence, say so, moderate opinion finds no representation and no expression amongst them. But, if the opinion of moderate men who are now permitted to take no part in politics, but who exist in large numbers in Ireland, cannot be represented in due proportion in the proposed Assembly, then I should despair of the good effects which I expect from co-operation between all classes of Irishmen for their country's good. But I do not despair, because I believe that in the system of proportional representation we have found the means of

securing in the proposed Legislative Assembly a full and true expression of all shades of political thought. It was, therefore, with extreme pleasure that I noted the cordial reception given by Mr. Redmond and by the Irish Nationalist Press to Lord Courtney of Penwith's recent letter to Mr. Sexton on proportional representation for Ireland."

He then goes on to explain the working of the system, the essence of which is that the elector expresses his second and third choice and so on, and votes given to a successful candidate in excess of the number required to secure his return, or votes given to a candidate in a hopeless minority, are not wasted but are transferred to the candidate next in sympathy with the elector. The system necessitates larger constituencies than the present, returning each a number of members. Under Lord MacDonnell's scheme each elector would have only one vote, which would where necessary be transferred as indicated above. The only drawback to the scheme is that it is a little complicated, and it seems to me that the very similar results might be attained in a simpler way. Let a return be made to the old system of representation in which the unit in the country was the county, except that where the county is so large that it would on a basis of population return more than five members it might be divided. Let each voter have as many votes as there are vacancies, and let him either distribute these or concentrate them as he pleases. The result would be that in each division any minority of at all respectable proportions could make sure of getting at least one candidate in, but this would be the least of the benefits conferred by this method. Under the existing system it is generally the policy of the candidate to vilify in every way possible the members of the opposite party, and phrases like "hereditary enemies," "rebels, "traitors," etc., which leave a sting behind them, and do a great deal to create bad feeling, are freely bandied about. Under the proposed system it would be to the interest of the candidates not to abuse, but to conciliate the minority, since, where the minority were not strong enough to return a candidate of their own, the one who approached nearest to them would be most likely to receive their concentrated vote, and, consequently, unless he entirely alienated the sympathy of the majority, would have the best chance of success. Such a system, especially if combined with a second ballot, would do a great deal to bring the weight of political influence from the circumference to the centre, and restore that influence of moderate opinion the absence of which is the greatest difficulty in Irish politics. If there is a conference on the Home Rule question, I would earnestly commend some such scheme to its consideration, even though it might involve the political extinction of some of those who under the present system occupy the position of leading lights.

It would also do a good deal to allay the apprehensions of Protestants, who as a rule do not know Irish and do not want to learn it, if a statutory provision were inserted in the Bill that the official language should be English, and that a knowledge of Irish should not be a requisite for employment in the public service except in counties or districts where a certain proportion, say 20 per cent., of the population were Irish-speaking. Certain American and Colonial precedents show that what are nominally educational tests can be twisted to serve a political purpose, and while there is every reason to hope that an Irish Parliament would have more sense than to attempt anything of this nature, it would help to allay distrust if the possibility of such a policy were placed outside the sphere of practical politics by being made *ultra vires*.

The financial clauses of the Bill are not as favourable to Ireland as they might be, and for this the Ulster Unionists are largely to blame. Their policy has, in fact, been not to make the Bill better, but to make it worse, so as either to disgust the country with it or to render it unworkable if passed. This is an extremely dangerous policy, and there is in history one very striking example of its consequences which, if known to them, might have made them pause. It was precisely similar tactics on the part of one of its leading citizens that led to the downfall of the Athenian empire. The Athenians determined on an expedition against Syracuse, which was certainly as unjustifiable as any Ulster member ever conceived Home Rule to be. One of their leading statesmen, Nicias, was opposed to it, but seeing that the people were set on it, tried to force them to abandon the project by exaggerating the number of men and ships that would be required if it were to have any chance of success. Contrary to his expectations they readily voted the extra forces required, so that practically the whole fighting strength of the country was sent on this enterprise. The expedition met with disaster and was almost annihilated, and the consequence of the line that Nicias took was that what would otherwise have been an ordinary reverse became an irremediable disaster. The analogy is, of course, not complete, but the lesson of its essential features is obvious. If the Ulster Unionist members had the slightest idea of statesmanship, they would not in the manner they are doing risk everything in opposition to Home Rule, but would at least allow for the off chance, and try to arrange that if the Bill becomes law, it will be as little mischievous as possible. If the financial provisions are unjust to Ireland, Ulster will suffer just as much as the rest of the country whether she is under the Dublin Parliament or not, seeing that her prosperity is inextricably bound up with that of the other provinces, the inhabitants of which are among her best customers.

It seems to me that the financial arrangements as they stand at present, and as they will have to stand unless there is a settlement by consent, are of a somewhat unsatisfactory nature both from the Irish and the English point of view, and, in attempting to reconcile two conflicting systems, the framer of these clauses has succeeded to the extent of including most of the disadvantages of both and not very many of the advantages of either. The one was complete fiscal autonomy, for which from the Irish point of view there is a great deal to be said. The existing system of indirect taxation, especially in regard to the Excise duties, is unsuitable to Ireland, the inhabitants of which, while generally much poorer than the inhabitants of Great Britain, have a tendency to consume a relatively larger proportion of highly taxed articles like tea and spirits. It is admitted that under the existing system the quantity of alcohol in spirits is taxed four times as heavily as that in beer. It is idle to reply, as a British statesman once did, that the Irish have no grievance, as they can drink beer instead of spirits. The argument would hardly have seemed so conclusive to its author had he been told he could drink gin instead of champagne, and if steps had been taken to force him to make the alteration. Quite independently of the question of individual preference, it is largely a question of climate and constitution, and to many people beer even of good quality is absolute poison. Even if beer possessed all the virtues which it is assumed to possess, the fact remains that, in spite of the good advice tendered to them, a considerable number of people are being driven by the present high rate of duties on spirits to the use of substitutes such as ether and methylated spirits, about the deleterious nature of which there can be no doubt. If Ireland had the control of her own taxation, the most obvious duty of an Irish Chancellor of the Exchequer would be to reduce somewhat the taxation on tea and spirits, and increase considerably that on beer and stout, thus adapting the incidence of taxation to the habits and customs of the people. The drawback to this would be that it would involve a Customs barrier between Ireland and Britain, and anyone who has experienced the delay, trouble, and inconvenience that have to be experienced in landing in a country where there is a Customs examination, as compared with the simplicity of crossing from Ireland to Great Britain or *vice versa* under present conditions, will agree that this is not an obstacle lightly to be set up. A point was made by the Unionists of the possibility of a danger, which seems to me largely imaginary, of Ireland's concluding informal commercial arrangements with foreign Powers, with the result that this criticism was met by allowing Ireland under Home Rule to increase, but not to lower, Customs and Excise duties. In other words, Ireland, which is admittedly a poor country, is left with the alternative of either just barely being able to make ends meet, or increasing those taxes which press most hardly on the great mass of the people. Income Tax cannot safely be increased, as the immediate effect of doing so would be to drive out of the country nearly all the persons of independent means who at present find it convenient to reside there because living is cheaper than in England. If any variation whatever is made in the Customs duties, it means just the same restrictions and formalities in travelling and in forwarding goods and parcels, as if the whole fiscal systems of the two countries were different. As compared with the existing scheme, it seems a pity that the principle of complete uniformity of Excise and Customs duties within the British Isles was not accepted. No doubt Ireland has suffered greatly from equality of taxation with Great Britain in the past, but whatever damage has been done is done, and things have more or less adapted themselves to the existing conditions, and unless complete fiscal autonomy were granted, which seems impracticable, the benefits of any variations in Customs and Excise duties would seem to be greatly outweighed by the hampering of trade and obstruction to communication with Great Britain and the rest of the world which they would necessitate.

In the Bill as it was read a first and second time the Irish Parliament was given power to lower, as well as to raise, Customs duties. The former was a valuable provision, but owing to the outcry of the Opposition it was abandoned. The Government would have done well to have eliminated the power to raise Customs duties as well, and thus avoided the necessity of the complex arrangements which a Customs barrier would involve.

It is puzzling at first sight why the Government adopted so parsimonious a policy in framing the financial clauses of the Bill, and went out of its way to create machinery in order to make the amount of subsidising that seemed necessary as small as possible. The answer is that the Liberals have become disgusted with the extravagance and waste which characterised the Irish policy of their predecessors. (I have quoted some examples of it in the discussion of their land legislation.) Not only so, but the Liberals have incidentally greatly increased Irish expenditure by passing the Old Age Pensions Act, by which Ireland has benefited much more than any other part of the United Kingdom, owing to the fact that the number of her people over 70 years of age is based on a decreasing, not an increasing population, and consequently bears a greater proportion to the remainder than in any other part of the three kingdoms. The result was that the former surplus of Irish revenue over expenditure became a deficit, and after having received not less than 325 million pounds from Ireland since the Union, the British Government found that it was likely to lose, and lose heavily, if the present system was continued. From the Irish point of view there is nothing to be said in principle against the policy of spending vast sums of Imperial money in Ireland provided an adequate result is obtained. It is some satisfaction to an Irishman to find that after more than a century of overtaxation, the Union has turned out to be not quite so profitable to England as it was at first. But to go on spending money in maintaining a system of government which is as inefficient as it is extravagant, is neither good business nor good statesmanship. The Irish naturally complain about the incapacity of the Irish Government as it is carried on at present, but they have no interest in making it less expensive. If they succeeded, the saving would go to the British Treasury, and would not directly benefit Ireland.

On the other hand, under a system of self-government the Irish would have every incentive to reduce the present exorbitant cost of Irish Government, where that could be done without loss of efficiency. Everyone is agreed that the present system of governing Ireland is an extravagant one, but to bring it home more vividly, I append a quotation from the report of Lord Farrer, Lord Welby, and Mr. Currie, who were members of the Financial Relations Commission. They wrote:—

"The expenditure of Belgium may be compared not unfairly with that of Ireland. In Belgium, as in Ireland, government is centralised, and the functions of administration are extended. The imports and exports of Belgium, excluding transit trade, are valued at £117,000,000 in 1893; those of Ireland are guessed at £45,000,000. In short, if Ireland is said to be poor, Belgium is beyond question prosperous, wealthy and progressive, yet the charge of

Civil Government in Ireland for 1892–93 was £4,544,000, while the charge for like purposes in Belgium in 1893 was £2,600,000. We therefore state the case much against Belgium if we reckon in broad figures her expenditure to that of Ireland as 3 to 4½. That is, Civil Administration in Belgium (population 6,300,000 in 1893) cost less than 10s a head, in Ireland 19s 7d or double. Looking to special items, we find that the salaries provided in the Belgian estimates for the fifteen judges of the two courts of justice are barely £6,000 per annum, while Ireland pays her Lord Chancellor £8,000."

Under these circumstances there is nothing surprising in the fact that most of the Ulster leaders are lawyers. They are as interested as the landlords who have not sold in maintaining the present system. It is true that the Lord Chancellor's salary has been since reduced, and he now has to endeavour to make ends meet on a paltry £6,000 a year. The moral, however, is obvious. The policy of the Unionists is, so long as the British taxpayer can be got to stand it, or can be kept from finding out how his money is being squandered, to maintain the present costly methods of governing Ireland, and supplement them by a system of subsidies on an even larger scale than before, and probably not much different in character, if they are going to complete the "beneficent policy of land purchase" on the same lines as those on which they managed it formerly.

The Liberals, however, have discovered that the Union has begun to cost Britain money, and have become alarmed about the growing difference between the amount of Irish revenue and the cost of Irish services. They have followed the right lines in attempting to solve the problem by giving Ireland a Parliament of her own and an Executive responsible to it, and consequently the power to effect economies in Irish administration. This, however, will only be possible when vested interests have been provided for. Meanwhile they have furnished her with every incentive to be economical by giving her the bare minimum that will pay for the present cost of

Irish services, while at the same time they hold a lien on all Irish revenues, and will automatically divert any natural increase in the yield of already existing Irish taxes to paying off part of this deficit. Unfortunately this involves that the growing cost of the Services which have been transferred—in few or none of which as it happens are economies possible, or at any rate not immediately—must be met by increased Irish taxation. Instead, therefore, of resolutely facing the fact that the Irish Parliament must be subsidised by a certain amount at first, and arranging to do so, while at the same time providing for the growing cost of Irish services—no economies can be effected for a number of years for the reason already given—by giving Ireland a share in the natural increase of the yield of the taxes at present levied in this country, every effort seems to have been made to make the amount of this subsidising as small as possible, and to divert to Imperial purposes the whole of the natural increase in the yield of the present Irish taxes, and in some cases to make the Irish Parliament itself contribute to paying off the deficit, if it increases the yield of certain Imperial taxes by more than 10 per cent.

The course adopted is greatly to be regretted, but what has been done illustrates once more the way that Ireland suffers through the dissensions of her people, and the fact that the manner in which she is used as a football for English political parties, generally renders it impossible for her own representatives to unite even in defence of the most obvious interests of their country. The Government had to deal with an Opposition who were quite prepared to shut their eyes to the fact that their own policy in regard to Ireland is infinitely more expensive to the British taxpayer, and who were determined to make every ounce of political capital possible out of the fact that any subsidy is given at all, and trust to the shortness of the public memory to secure forgetfulness of the fact that the necessity for it was mainly a legacy left by themselves. Even if the Liberals had not inherited so many other disastrous legacies from their predecessors as to render necessary considerable economy, they were practically forced in self-defence to cut down the grant to Ireland to the lowest possible limits, in order to avoid providing their opponents in Great Britain with a dangerous if rather dishonest weapon. Had the Irish Unionist members had any regard whatever for the interests of their country, that is if they acknowledge it to be such, they would at least have called a truce over the financial clauses of the Bill, and joined with the Nationalists in insisting that these should be more favourable to Ireland, instead of conniving at a policy of persuading the British elector that he is being robbed for the benefit of the Irish one.

As a matter of fact there are other ways, not inconsistent with Liberal principles, by which the Government might have arrived at a solution of the financial difficulty, without devising means to make future generations of Irishmen of other classes pay back to the Imperial Treasury something of the money which has been squandered by the late Unionist Government in endowing the Irish landlords, and thereby providing an illustration of the principle "*quicquid delirant reges plectuntur Achivi.*" Most of the trouble has been caused by the fact that English legislation hardly ever looks ahead of the immediate problem it has got to deal with, and that unless some steps are taken towards readjustment, Mr. Lloyd George, so far from being the terrible Socialist he is supposed to be, bids fair to be the best friend the landlords ever had, though possibly an unconscious one. It is occasionally mentioned as a gratifying fact that the operation of the National Insurance Act and of Old Age Pensions is reducing the amount of pauperism, but what never seems to have struck anybody, and which, if its bearing on the problem had been considered by the framers of it, might have radically altered the whole financial scheme of the Home Rule Bill, is that in doing so a burden which has hitherto been borne by the owners of immoveable property, that is land and houses, is being lifted off their shoulders and thrown on those of the general community, with the result that if nothing is done to check the process, their property will increase in value by the equivalent of the tax of which they are relieved. I have before me a summary of the latest returns relating to pauperism and old age pensions for the three kingdoms. From these it appears that the total amount paid in Old Age Pensions in England-Wales in 1911–12 was £7,948,016, and that the number of paupers over 70 years of age had fallen from 229,000 in 1906 to 57,700 in 1913. Those receiving outdoor relief had fallen in the same period from 168,000 to 8,500. In Ireland the estimated cost of Old Age Pensions for 1913–14 is £2,618,000. The Irish figures in regard to pauperism are less striking, as they do not separate persons over 70 years of age from persons under it, but refer to all classes in receipt of poor-law relief. Even here, however, the reduction has been considerable, and, including outdoor relief, and sick, aged and infirm in workhouses, the total reduction last year as compared with 1906 was over 24,000. It must also be remembered that the present tendency is to turn the workhouse hospitals more and more into general hospitals for the treatment of such cases as cannot conveniently be treated at home, and that since the introduction of the Insurance Act a large number of patients who would formerly have been treated free, that is at the expense of the ratepayers, now pay their way for whatever time they spend in such hospitals. The average cost per pauper was in England and Wales £16.65, in Scotland £14.73, and in Ireland £12.67. If, therefore, there has been a diminution of even 300,000 paupers, that represents a saving to the rates, that is ultimately a benefit to the owners of immoveable property, of nearly £4,000,000 a year, which is far more than the amount by which Ireland's expenditure exceeds her income.

If it is thought that this saving to the rates is a saving to the community at large, I would refer to an authority of the unimpeachable character of Dr. Bastable, Professor of Political Economy in the University which returns Sir Edward Carson as its Senior Member. Professor Bastable in his "Public Finance," second edition, page 370, says:—"Other charges are often shifted to rent while it can hardly ever transfer its peculiar burdens." With regard to houses he holds that, in so far as they are manufactured articles, a tax by increasing the cost, limits the supply, and thus falls on the consumer, that is, the occupier. We all know, however, that in the country the poor-law valuation on the house is only a small fraction of the total valuation of the holding, and that in towns the expensive item in regard to a house is the site value.

It may, therefore, be taken as a sound general principle that ultimately the main portion of the burden of local rates falls on the landlord, and that under a system of free contract, anything which tends to reduce rates will ultimately tend to increase rent by an equivalent amount. Of course, in the case of those holdings in Ireland that have become the property of the tenants under the Land Purchase Acts, the reduction in rates will come as a windfall to them, but unless they have been thoroughly demoralised by the system of State pauperisation which has become the cornerstone of Unionist policy in regard to Ireland, they must not expect the interests of the rest of the country to be sacrificed to theirs, and after suffering so much at the hands of the landlord, ought not to join with them in a selfish outcry against anything which would prevent their being given an unearned increment at the expense of the community at large. As a matter of fact, so far as the Irish farmers are concerned, I believe it would be to their advantage in the long run to pay higher rates, if by doing so they could avoid the necessity of the imposition by the Irish Parliament of any additional Customs or Excise duty; and leave it with a little more financial margin to undertake works of public improvement. A Customs barrier between Great Britain and Ireland by hampering the trade between the two countries will tend to reduce the price of farm produce and increase that of goods imported into Ireland. If the Irish Parliament has any money at all to spare, it may be taken as fairly certain that one of its first acts will be the nationalisation of the Irish railways, the rates on which are a public scandal, and are throttling the whole agricultural and industrial life of the country. There are two alternative policies of railway management, high rates and small traffic, and low rates and large traffic. The Irish railway companies in their timidity and selfishness have adopted the former. A State-managed system would adopt the latter, which would probably lead to quite as good returns on the capital expenditure as the present method, after the period of transition had been passed, and by reducing the amount of freight to reasonable limits, would enable the Irish farmer and manufacturer to buy cheaper and sell dearer. A tax which would lead to this result would in no sense be a loss, but would be of the nature of a most productive investment.

If, therefore, it is borne in mind that the effect of Old Age Pensions, Labour Exchanges, the Insurance Act, and similar pieces of ameliorative legislation of recent years, is to a large extent to throw on the taxes expenditure which was formerly borne by the rates, the obvious conclusion would appear to be that any scheme of finance which does not recognise this fact and allow for it, is based on insecure foundations, and that the state of things that should be legislated for is not that which happens to exist at the moment, but that which may be expected to exist when the necessary arrangements and adjustments have been made. The obvious course is to throw back on the rates the equivalent of the amount of which they are being relieved by these new branches of Imperial expenditure, which can easily be done by reducing the grants in aid in proportion to the decline of expenditure on poor relief. If this were done, the difference between expenditure and income would become somewhat less in the case of Ireland, and owing to the saving effected in the rest of the United Kingdom the Government could afford to deal with the financial aspect of Home Rule on a broader basis, and dispense with the cumbrous arrangements to which the possibility of differential Excise and Customs duties gives rise. The financial relations might with great advantage to both countries be arranged on the basis of identity of Excise and Customs duties. Even if there were great apparent loss at first, an additional expenditure of even several hundreds of thousands of pounds annually would be preferable to the setting up of a Customs barrier within the British Isles, and would probably involve less loss in the long run.

In the same way the Post Office might very well be kept in the hands of the Imperial Government, as is done in other countries where there are federal institutions, and one of the principal grounds of criticism on the part of the Unionists removed. Apparently the main reason for making it over is that in Ireland it is run at a loss, which it is desired to cut in order to get Irish expenditure and income to approach each other more nearly. If this state of affairs already existed, the Government would no doubt legislate according to general principles and fixed standards, and would not be having recourse to measures which appear to contradict these, but are supposed to be rendered necessary by the special circumstances of the case. Yet, even in view of the present deficit on the Irish revenue account, which must be considerable for some time even if the plan I have suggested is adopted, as in the matter of Customs and Excise, so in that of the Post Office, uniformity is so important that a very considerable additional expenditure would be a lesser evil than a departure from it.

An outcry has been raised about the naval and military danger of having the Post Office under divided control, and though this is largely based on the assumption that Ireland will always continue to be unfriendly, and such dangers as those have been greatly reduced by the discovery of wireless telegraphy, this would seem to be a case where the criticisms of the Opposition might be met, not only with no loss of principle, but with a decided improvement in the symmetry and efficiency of the measure. If this were done they could hardly grumble at the additional expense of what they claim to be an Imperial necessity, though people who in the same breath demand a General Election and refuse to be bound by the result of it, are possibly capable even of that. However, the change would seem worth making in whatever spirit it is received. I am making no attempt to conceal from myself or from my readers the fact that the present Bill is capable of improvement in many respects, particularly in its financial provisions. Even, however, if it should become law in its present form, I am satisfied that the advantages which will ensue will far outweigh the disadvantages. The latter will become more obvious when the Act is put into operation, and will no doubt be removed by subsequent legislation before any great harm has been done. On the other hand, the policy of civil war which is the alternative to the present Bill will, if persisted in, most certainly lead to irremediable disaster. If property is destroyed, or life is lost, or trade and commerce ruined, and civil war usually involves all these consequences, no subsequent legislation can make good the damage thus inflicted, except in the case of compensation for property destroyed, and that only partially. The Bill, as it stands, is infinitely better than civil war under the auspices of a Provisional Government. It is also better than the maintenance of the present system. Looked at from the point of view of comparative politics, or even from that of the institutions of our own Colonies, the present system is a monstrosity which even the most pronounced Unionists do not attempt to defend. Each province of Canada and India, and each of the Australian and South African colonies has its own legislature, and the British Isles, which have more legislative work than all the others put together, have to content themselves with one, and then find a good deal of the time of that one being taken up with answering questions about the conduct of the police in some insignificant Irish village, or explaining the reason why certain transfers of civil servants drawing salaries of about £80 a year have taken place. The consequence of the tremendous congestion arising from there being only one legislature in the country, and so much of its attention being occupied with parochial affairs, is that everything has to give way to Government business, and the private Bill has almost been squeezed out of existence. For nearly every scheme of local improvement or development an Act of Parliament is necessary, but the people who suffer may be clamouring for the change, the money to effect it may be forthcoming, and yet the scheme may fall through, or have to be postponed for years, simply because Parliament cannot spare five minutes to give it legal sanction. Even where in the end a private Bill is got through, the cost is prohibitive. I have heard of one case of the improvement of an Irish harbour where the expenditure that had to be incurred in getting the work sanctioned came to more than that on the work itself. Were there a

Parliament in Dublin the expense of such Bills would be reduced to at most one-fifth of what it is at present, and besides, the money would be spent in the country. Nor is it always merely a case of the cost involved, or the inability of Parliament to find time to attend to such Bills. The recent experience of the wealthy and aggressively loyal Corporation of Belfast, who lost much money in promoting a Bill the most valuable parts of which were eliminated by their friends the House of Lords at the instigation of the local railway companies, will be fresh in the memory of my Ulster readers. It is hardly quite fair to say the House of Lords is not a representative body; it is, however informally, the representative of—vested interests. Anything, therefore, that threatens vested interests, even though it should only be with legitimate competition or legitimate taxation, has very little chance of getting through that august assembly except under the provisions of the Parliament Act. Nor again, is it merely private Bills that suffer under the existing system; Government business also has to be neglected or hurried through in a manner that is extremely unsatisfactory, though with characteristic lack of logic those who are most bitter in criticising these deficiencies are the very people who are most wedded to the system that renders them inevitable. If there is one British statesman more than another that possesses the confidence and respect of all parties and of the country at large, it is Sir Edward Grey. And yet what has he to say on the subject, when looked at from the Imperial point of view in which it must naturally present itself to the Minister for Foreign Affairs? In his speech at Berwick I find the following. (I again quote my good friend the *Irish Times*, which gives a comparatively full report in spite of the fact that he is a political opponent, but hesitates between *oratio recta* and *oratio obliqua* in a manner which might be rather puzzling to a schoolboy who was required to turn the passage into Greek or Latin):—

"Home Rule had become a necessity, on the purely practical ground of the interests of English and Scottish and Imperial politics. Parliament would become increasingly incapable of transacting satisfactorily the important business of the United Kingdom unless Home Rule became law. They were told that Ulster would resist the Home Rule Bill to such an extent as to create civil war and bloodshed. It does not make a settlement by consent any easier to be confronted with all the language we have heard on behalf of Ulster during the last few weeks, he proceeded. They are appealing to us on the other side now to realise how much better and pleasanter a settlement would be by consent than a settlement carried by force. We do not want to disregard that appeal, but it does not make it easier if the language of menace and threats of civil war are used. It is an exceedingly bad precedent, because if the minority in Ireland are to use threats of civil war, what is to be expected of the majority in Ireland if Home Rule fails?

"Well, bloodshed is exceedingly unpleasant. Civil war is detestable and abominable. Can it be avoided? They say it all depends upon the government—that it can be avoided but it depends upon the Government and the Liberal Party whether it can be avoided. Well, that is not an aspect of the case upon which I am going to dwell to-night. I say, on the other hand, I think it can be avoided, but it depends upon Ulster and the Conservative Party whether it can be avoided. Agreement should be possible, but it depends not merely upon one side being conciliatory and reasonable, but upon both sides being conciliatory and reasonable. If there is to be agreement there must be some sort of compromise, and I should like to clear the ground of something which will make agreement impossible. Ulster says it is going to fight. Now, I should ask Ulster, not what is Ulster going to fight against, but what is Ulster going to fight for? Is Ulster going to fight for the continuance of the existing state of things? I think about a year ago they were arguing that Home Rule must be dropped, and that when it was dropped they were prepared to co-operate with the House of Commons in dealing with Irish land, education, and every sort of reform Ireland wanted. That is exactly what we cannot have. We cannot have the time of the House of Commons taken up with these things. They have got to be dealt with in Ireland by Irishmen for Ireland. Ulster's position is that Home Rule means the destruction of Ulster, or the Protestants in Ulster. I reply that equally from the British and Imperial point of view the continuance of the existing state of things as regards the House of Commons means destruction to us.

"To resist Home Rule Ulster says is a matter of life and death to them, and we say that to put an end to the existing state of things is a matter of life and death for us, and we must resort to methods that are needed to put an end to the existing state of things, and if violence is to be used to resist Home Rule in order that the existing state of things may be maintained—then you must meet violence by violence. They say that under Home Rule they are going to be withdrawn from the British flag. Well, of course, they are not going to be withdrawn from the British flag. But the flag depends upon this—that the great affairs of this country—the questions of Imperial defence, of foreign policy, of colonial policy—should be well managed. To be well managed the Prime Minister and his Cabinet must have time to give attention to them, to think about them; and the House of Commons must also have time. If you continue the existing state of things you will prevent not only the present Government, but any future Government, and any future Prime Minister, from being able to discharge the great affairs of State as they ought to be, and prevent the House of Commons from doing it, and that is the way the flag will be brought down. If the flag is to be upheld it must be by great Imperial affairs being well managed. If they are to be well managed the Imperial Parliament and the central Government must be set free to attend them."

Another advantage which will commend itself to everybody except those who will have to adapt themselves to the new conditions will be that after Home Rule becomes law, Ulster members of Parliament, and Ulster politicians, will no longer find it good policy to indulge in indiscriminate vituperation of

the rest of the country. One of the many evil legacies of the
Union is the necessity, or at least the advantage, of playing to
the British gallery, and the consequent temptation to try and
make out the native Irish population to be rogues and rascals
and, as compared with the peaceful and law-abiding citizens
of Ulster, little better than savages, to protect the latter
against whom the might of Britain is always necessary. Of
course, this strain is not always adopted, and at times it is
varied by the announcement that the people of Ulster are
really very warlike, only they usually prefer making money to
fighting, but that, if they are sufficiently roused, they are
quite prepared to march to Cork, and, if necessary, to oppose
in armed conflict not merely the rest of Ireland, but England
and Scotland as well. All this sort of talk keeps up an
exaggerated hostility, which as a rule prevents the faintest
chance of any Irish question being settled on its merits by the
persons most competent to deal with it, each of whom is much
more occupied in trying to persuade a sufficient number of
British members to join with him in crushing the other side,
than in attempting to convince those Irish members who
do not agree with him. If Home Rule brought no other
advantage, that of compelling the Irish Unionist members in
future to observe the ordinary rules of courtesy towards their
opponents, and putting an end once and for all to such
language as that which has characterised Sir Edward Carson's
recent campaign, would be one of no trifling importance,
and would remove one of the most powerful causes of disunion
among the people of Ireland.

There is one more advantage which Home Rule would
bring, which is of a nature to appeal to the statesman and
administrator rather than to the man in the street, though it
is to be hoped that the efforts of the jingo press to educate the
country on the subject of the "white man's burden" have
prepared the way for his understanding it. Briefly it is this,
that the present system has all the disadvantages peculiar to
an arrangement the reverse of that described in the phrase
"Heads I win, tails you lose." While England insists on governing the country according to her own ideas, and in

disregard of the wishes of a large section of the population that she should allow them to govern themselves, however well she does it, and however much she may spend out of her own pocket in the process, she can expect no gratitude; it is simply taken as a matter of course since no one has a right to interfere in the affairs of another unless he does better than that other could have done himself, and to do well in such a case is merely a most elementary duty. When, on the other hand, England does badly, and we have seen what a ghastly mess she made of the Irish famine, and how she persistently went wrong on the land question for quite two generations, the righteous indignation which is everywhere felt against the officious bungler is directed against Britain and British statesmanship. Even if the British Government started with a clean slate, as it might do, if for instance it were to acquire a further portion of Africa, and its sole anxiety were to give the best administration possible for the money, it could hardly expect to inspire enthusiasm, but at the best it might hope for toleration or acquiescence, on the principle that it is better to bear the ills we have than fly to others that we know not of. When, as is usually the case, it is hampered, not merely by the limitations and inherited prejudices of its own legislators and administrators, but by the influence of the vested interests which have grown to look to England for protection, and the crowd of place-hunters who expect to be provided for at every change of administration, the chances of anything in the nature of even moderately good government fall almost to zero, and consequently all that England can look for so long as the present system lasts will generally be a mixture of anger and contempt. If these sentiments are felt to any great extent towards her own ministers in an Irish Parliament she can change them, and even if their successors are no better, the blame for their shortcomings will not fall on England. From the British and the Imperial point of view this is an extremely strong argument in favour of Home Rule. I am not now concerned with any theories that it is better that people should govern themselves badly than that they should be well governed by others, which I may say in their undiluted form

I do not accept, but am simply pointing out that in the nature of things the English government of Ireland can never be very good, and is often likely to be very bad, and that while its goodness evokes no gratitude, its badness gives rise to a feeling of fierce resentment, which instead of falling altogether on the statesmen responsible, is largely directed against Britain and the British connection generally. Human ingenuity could hardly devise anything more detrimental to the interests of both countries; British administration follows whatever course is set for it from Westminster in entire disregard of Irish public opinion, or even of Ulster public opinion so far as Ulster has any that is not imported ready-made, and Ireland retaliates by hating her rulers since she is not permitted to change then. Even Ulster occasionally grumbles bitterly, as the present writer can testify, when her wishes and interests are ignored in regard to such a subject as land purchase, but at election times all that is necessary is to raise sufficiently loudly the cry of "No Popery," and she returns to heel and obediently carries out the orders of her lords and masters, who recently in forming the Provisional Government have not even troubled to go through the farce of pretending to consult her.

When responsible leaders of the Unionist Party are in a statesmanlike mood, as they sometimes are, they hardly ever contend that some delegation of powers is not necessary if the Irish question is to be solved. The Ulster leader himself has expressed his willingness to consider favourably a scheme for the extension of the powers of Local Government in Ireland. The matter, however, ends there so far as he and his party are concerned, and a torrent of invective is directed against whatever scheme is proposed, without any attempt to put forward a better one. This is easy, and paying from the point of view of party advantage, but it does not bring a solution of the question any nearer, and I cannot imagine any solution which would not leave those who have been shouting so long "We will not have Home Rule," with a rather uncomfortable feeling that they have been fighting for a mere form of words. The more responsible Conservative leaders would like to see the question settled, but having played the Orange card so successfully for nearly thirty years, and there being a chance that it may again turn up trumps and give them another term of office, they cannot quite make up their minds to rid themselves of it, though they see quite well that it cannot serve their purpose for ever, and that the time is rapidly approaching when they must revise their policy and adapt it to the existing situation. In the meantime they have adopted the policy which they believe will pay best for the present, and are forwarding it to the best of their ability by a division of labour under which the leaders in Ireland serve out rifles to as many of the Protestant religion as can be got to take them, and imitate all the methods of the Catch-my-Pals in order to sweep the greatest possible number into their organisation, while those in England profess a great aversion to strife, but say that the people of Ulster are such terrible fellows that there will be no holding them in if the Government continues to pursue its wicked course. They conveniently overlook the fact that the British working man, or the people of Dublin, or Johannesburg, or Cawnpore would be equally terrible fellows if they likewise found kindhearted individuals willing to supply them for nothing with as many rifles as they cared to accept, and subscribe a million pounds to pay all their lawyers' and doctors' bills, at the same time assuring them that all the principal commanders on the other side had been gained over, and in any case they would soon be the Government themselves and would make it all right for them, so that there was really no danger unless through carelessness in handling their unaccustomed, and in the case of the Italian rifles and the Sniders, I must admit, rather clumsy weapons, they accidentally shot themselves or each other.[1]

The policy of the Unionist Party in general, and the Ulster section in particular, is thus neither statesmanlike nor patriotic. On the off-chance of being returned to power on a wave of anti-Nationalist feeling they are desirous of lighting the fires of civil war, not only in Ireland but in Great Britain and the rest of the Empire, and they regard the disaster which would ensue in the very improbable event of their success as an evil of lesser magnitude than that the present Home Rule Bill should become law, and they should be debarred the chance of themselves introducing the "large and even generous reforms" in the government of Ireland, or the considerable extension of local government, which Sir Edward Carson himself says he favours, and which would only be Home Rule under another name. Sir Edward Carson in his speech at Dungannon is quite explicit in his statement of the policy of "damn the consequences" which proved so unfortunate for his party on the question of the Budget. He is reported as having said—

> "If disaster follows—disaster, let me say, which will rend not only Ireland or the United Kingdom, but all his Majesty's dominions beyond the seas, into two parts, and two parties struggling against each other in a fratricidal fight at a time when we ought to be showing a great united front to all the nations of the world, the blame will not be with us. Yes, it is a terrible thing to contemplate, and Heaven knows I contemplate it frequently myself. But there is one greater disaster even than that horrible picture, and it is the disaster of so showing ourselves decadent descendants of our forefathers as to exhibit to the world such a poor spirit that we are prepared without a blow to surrender the freedom we have inherited."

This is only his naive way of saying that rather than appear in the undignified position he must if this agitation should fail, and the Home Rule Bill should become law and prove not altogether unsuccessful, thereby destroying his reputation as a prophet—he has long since lost any reputation for states- manship he may ever have possessed—he is prepared to get up a civil war all over the Empire, and place it at the mercy of the next strongest Power in Europe.

As a matter of fact the Ulster leader's threats of sedition and attempts to undermine the allegiance of the army are already bearing an evil harvest in India, and, particularly if successful, may lead to consequences which, to any real lover of the Empire, would indeed be "a terrible thing to contemplate." As I write I notice that Sir John Jardine, M.P. for Roxburghshire, formerly a judge in the High Court of Bombay, writes as follows to *The Times* of October 15[2]:—

> "The Unionist leaders in Ulster have played their last, their trump card, tampering with the Army in order to overawe the authorities constituted to uphold and enforce the laws. To my certain knowledge the seditious boastings made in Ulster are regularly printed over in India, and the doctrine of fighting against laws they dislike will be relished as delicious by all who are conspiring against our rule. This leads on to mutiny and massacre. In India we enforce the laws against sedition, and would never yield one inch to the threat that the Army is being tampered with."

As a further specimen of the patriotism of the Ulster leaders and the Imperial nature of the movement, I would call attention to the following statement of the sentiments of two of them, which I have not seen contradicted. Captain Craig, M.P., is reported to have told a *Morning Post* interviewer:—

> "There is a spirit spreading abroad, which I can testify to from personal knowledge, that Germany and the German Emperor would be preferable to the rule of John Redmond, Patrick Ford, and the Molly Maguires."

One of his colleagues, Mr. Chambers M.P., is stated to have said:—

> "That when the King signs the Home Rule Bill, he will no longer sing 'God Save the King,' but will say 'England I will laugh at your calamity. I will mock when your fear cometh.'"

I am not going to take up time in discussing the question of whether the King should act on the advice of his Ministers or of the leaders of the Opposition, or on his own judgment, though I do find it a little hard to reconcile the two latter methods with Parliamentary Government, but surely persons who in the past made so much capital out of their supposed loyalty and devotion to the Crown and Constitution, might bear for once with not getting their own way without calling in a foreign enemy, or might refrain from indicating in such a marked manner their displeasure with the King for acting in whatever way he considers to be his duty, even though they may have gone out of their way to suggest a better course?

In spite of the heroic methods which are being used in order to defeat this present Home Rule Bill, there is hardly any objection on the ground of principle to the policy it seeks to carry out; the whole opposition is based on the supposition that if a Dublin Parliament possessed any power, it would use it badly. But after all, on close examination it may turn out that the Nationalist members are no more the terrible fellows they are supposed to be than the Ulstermen are. No doubt in the course of the land war there was a considerable resort to violence, but does any Ulsterman, not a leader, even pretend to defend the state of things against which that war was directed, or has anyone who is a tenant ever shown the slightest compunction in sharing the fruits of the victory he not merely did not win, but in many cases allowed his then leaders to do their utmost to prevent? In this connection I quote from Mr. Erskine Childers:—

"Nobody denies the intense sincerity of Ulster Unionists. Nobody questions their loyalty to Great Britain; but do they themselves realise what 'loyalty' is beginning to signify? Two millions a year is the price at present being paid by Great Britain for the Union. The price is rising ominously fast. A day may come—*a day will come*—when Englishmen sweeping aside all the laboured sophistries about the 'prosperity' of Ireland and the necessity of regarding that country as a 'productive investment' for British gold, may, in a wholesome revolution towards common sense and economy, declare once for all that the system of debauching Ireland with subsidies must stop. Is Ulster going to wait till that humiliating ultimatum is pronounced? Or is she in a corresponding revulsion of feeling to anticipate it by co-operating with other provinces to forward Ireland's interests under a scheme of self-government? Ulster Unionists have not begun to consider that question. Yet if we Home Rulers must reexamine the foundations of our faith in the light of recent events, they should apply a still more searching retrospective test to the unreasoned conviction they inherit. Have they gained by resolutely opposing for a century almost every measure, religious or economic, designed for Ireland's good? With their privileged land system, dating from before the Union, was it fair or politic to stand aside from the long and terrible struggle waged by their less fortunate Roman Catholic fellow-countrymen to obtain the same essential privileges? Is it not even a little mean, while profiting themselves, at the eleventh hour, from the land reforms won by others—at God knows what cost of famine, degradation and expatriation—to join in the ignorant hue-and-cry against Irish Roman Catholics for 'criminality'? Is it fair, when they remember the black historical record of Protestant intolerance in Ireland, to taunt Roman Catholics with aiming at a religious tyranny which it would not only be physically impossible to assert, but which they have never shown the smallest symptom of desiring? And is it manly or sensible, or even *loyal*, for the lack of a little faith in human nature, to insist now on maintaining a form of government so demoralising to Ireland, and so burdensome to Great Britain?"

If force had occasionally to be resorted to in order to win reforms in the past, is not the whole *raison d'être* of Sir Edward Carson's campaign, not to mention that of the Suffragettes, that for a movement to get itself taken seriously, it must have force behind it? When one considers how iniquitous the Irish land laws were, and that until remedied they confiscated automatically the fruits of the tenants' labour and industry, the surprising thing is not that so much force was used, but so little.

Moreover, if the civil war succeeds, there seems every prospect that the rank and file of the Ulster army will find before long that it will be necessary to resort to the methods they have hitherto condemned when used by others; if they are not to be reduced to a position of subjection much more complete than any they are likely to experience under an Irish Parliament. I sincerely hope that when the war is over they will keep their rifles, whoever may have paid for them, as their sole protection against their own leaders. A rather indiscreet Unionist has somewhat prematurely revealed what the policy of the party is likely to be when they return to office. This extract, like many others, is taken from that *enfant terrible* of the Unionist press, the *Irish Times*, and is as follows:—

> "Mr. Bernard Holland, in a letter to *The Times* to-day, argues against Mr. Erskine Childers, that the hour is not yet ripe for a Federal Unionist solution. I see no possible, immediate, peaceful solution except that the nation should return a Unionist Government to power, who should repeal the Parliament Act, place the House of Lords upon a reformed and stronger basis, with fixed numbers, reform the House of Commons by making representation correspond exactly with population throughout the United Kingdom, and appoint a Commission to consider in what way provincial Legislatures and Administrations could best be formed within the United Kingdom; and what powers could best be entrusted to them."

In other words, the first task of the Unionists will be to render the House of Lords the supreme power in the State by abolishing the Parliament Act and depriving the Crown of the power of creating new peers, thereby removing the only constitutional means left of making it bow to the will of the people. Whether provincial legislatures do or do not exist under such conditions is a matter of no importance, since they will in any case be subordinate to the paramount authority in the body politic, which under such a regime would really be the House of Lords, and in this respect the House of Commons would be little better off.

The forces of reaction would thus obtain such a grip on the shoulders of the nation that nothing less than a revolution could shake them off, and the country would become as much at the mercy of the rich as it was in the eighteenth century, or as the United States threatened to be until recently. Then farewell to legislation for the uplifting of the masses of the people, whether in the form of Land Acts or Temperance Acts or Factory Acts, and Ulster can rest happy in the assurance that she has been the means of putting back the hands of the clock a hundred years, and reducing herself and the rest of the country to the same position of subjugation from which, in her own case, she was formerly delivered against her will.

As I write, the composition of the Provisional Government has been announced, and a study of the list of members goes far to confirm what I have said about the sort of rule that may be expected when, if ever, it succeeds in bringing the administration of the United Kingdom into line with its ideals. As might be expected, it starts off with an 'Upper House' which contains a lot of names very few people have ever heard of before, and whose connection with Ulster is thus described by a London paper:—

"Most of the titled ones are, or have been, large owners of land in Ireland, and several have benefited largely by sales to tenants."

This should put an end once and for all to the campaign of calumny that is going on against the landlord classes. Even when they have got their money and have been enabled, if they so desire, to clear out of the country on very favourable terms, they are ready at the call of duty to return to it, and lend their time and the influence of their titles—I will not say their names because, as I have explained, most of these are little known—to the task of governing it.

The list of members of the Lower House was too long for publication in most newspapers, but in spite of its length there seems to be entire unanimity on the fact that it does not contain the name of a single individual, who by any stretch of imagination could be described as a working man or a representative of the working classes. In fact, except that a few business men are thrown in for the sake of appearances, the

work of both houses could have been done equally well by a
local committee of the Irish Landowners' Association.

If the people of Ulster have no more regard for the Empire
than some of their leaders have, to judge from the extracts I
have quoted, there is one quality of which they must have
more for the simple reason that they could not possibly have
less, and that is a sense of the ridiculous. Let anyone consider
the history of the whole campaign, beginning with a Covenant
got up by the successors of the very persons against whom the
original historic Covenant was directed, and drafted with
such legal cunning that no two persons are agreed as to what
it means in any individual case, though its general effect is to
tie the members of all the Protestant Churches who allowed it
to be thrust on them to the chariot wheels of one political
party, and ending for the present with an improved version of
"The three tailors of Tooley Street," whose famous manifesto
beginning "We the people of England," has been thrown
entirely into the shade by the collection of landlords and
lawyers who call themselves, "We the Government of Ulster,"
and if he is honest with himself, I challenge him not to feel an
inclination to say, "Enough of this tomfoolery!" Should these
appeals be in vain, and I am compelled, however reluctantly,
to descend to that plane of material interests above which so
much of Unionist oratory seems to find it difficult to rise,
there are some considerations the people of Ulster would do
well to ponder before they risk as much as a single drop of
their blood or a single shilling of their property in resistance to
the lawful authority for the time being. Who are these people
who have constituted themselves judges and rulers over them?
Do they represent anybody but themselves and those classes
who have been their worst oppressors within the memory of
men still living, and who are quite as ready to oppress them
still if ever they get the chance? Who was the avowed champion of the Irish landlords at Westminster, and even against
his own party? The Ulster leader. Who was one of the first to
vote against the Old Age Pensions Bill? The Ulster leader.
Who helped to surrender English Nonconformists to the
tender mercies of ritualism in the primary schools? The Irish

Unionist members. Who threw out the most important portion of a Bill for the improvement of Belfast at the bidding of the vested interests? The House of Lords, which this movement is intended, and, even if not intended, cannot, if successful, fail to make, the supreme power in the Constitution. Their love for Ulster is rather of the nature of that of the walrus for the oysters in "Through the Looking-glass," which did not prevent him from eating them all up.

It thus appears that neither the mass of the British people, nor the Irish, whether of Ulster or not, have much to gain by the return of the Unionists to power, but on the other hand stand a very good chance of being deprived of most of the political influence they have obtained within the last fifty years, and of practically all chance of future legislation in their interests. Should Home Rule, however, turn out a success, or even not a very great failure, the gain would be immense. Ireland has been blocking the way for over 30 years, with the result that both British and Imperial legislation has been either neglected or attended to only by fits and starts. Home Rule would at once remedy this state of things, and give the rest of the three kingdoms a chance of receiving some attention, which in view of the state of things that exists in connection, for example, with the two questions of rural depopulation and infant mortality, he will be a bold man, who will deny that it sadly needs. Not less important would be the improvement in British relations abroad. Anyone whose memory goes back 20 or 30 years can remember a time when the favourite amusement of the United States was that known as "twisting the lion's tail," and when British Unionist statesmen had to put up with affronts which showed that meekness in the presence of somebody as strong as yourself is not a monopoly of any one political party. This was almost entirely due to the necessity on the part of American politicians of conciliating the Irish vote, which in those days of coercion was naturally hostile to Britain. All this is now changed, the attitude of the United States is infinitely more polite and friendly, and where any difficulties exist, they are due not to the Irish, but to the capitalists who display a tendency to construe international obligations in the way that best suits themselves, and in doing so not merely meet with no support from the Irish, but find them ranged on the British side; witness the following extract from the *Irish Independent*, a leading Nationalist paper, in its issue of 13th October last, *á propos* of the Panama Canal:—

> "The Americans have reason to be proud of their achievement, though the policy which the United States Government has adopted of taxing unduly foreign shipping using the canal will cause other nations to be rather reserved in their praise of this great work."

The same considerations apply to our overseas dominions,[3] though to a lesser extent, and there can be no doubt that the grant of Home Rule, unless embittered by civil war, would tend to draw together all parts of the Empire, and improve immensely its relations with the United States.

Is it, therefore, the part either of wisdom or patriotism to take up the attitude which Ulster is being encouraged, and cajoled, and frightened into taking up on this question, to plunge this country into civil war, destroy for the moment England's position in Europe, and postpone indefinitely if not for ever all chance of a complete understanding with the United States and with our own colonies, on account of dangers many of which are imaginary, and practically all of which could be obviated if she only had leaders who had the slightest capacity for constructive statesmanship, or who could do anything but repeat a few stock phrases in a manner that any moderately intelligent parrot might hope to equal after a few months training? War of any kind is a very terrible thing, and there are several European countries, of which Bulgaria is the latest example, whose experience shows that success by no means always attends the same side. Civil war is more terrible still, and, whichever side wins, leaves behind a legacy of hate which it takes the best part of a century to obliterate. If, as all the circumstances indicate, the proposed civil war will be indistinguishable from ordinary rioting, and the would-be warriors can be starved out without firing a shot, the arguments against entering upon it are even more conclusive.

I have endeavoured in the foregoing pages to throw a much needed light on the cause for the sake of which Ulster is being asked to fight, the character of the persons who have undertaken the task of ruling her while she does so, and hope to undertake that of ruling the Empire when she has finished if they have not split it into fragments in the meantime, the results which will almost certainly follow their success, and what their chances of success would seem to be. I have attempted to show that the course they are adopting is neither wise nor patriotic, but if the appeal to wisdom and patriotism is made in vain to those who are accustomed only to arguments addressed to their religious prejudices or their material interests, there are two questions which I would like to reiterate, and which the people of Ulster will do well to answer for themselves after a consideration of the record of their leaders when in office, and an examination of the mingled niggardliness, childishness and incompetence displayed in their military arrangements. One is whether it is worth the sacrifice of a single drop of blood in order to return to power persons, who when in office made such a selfish use of it, and displayed such indifference and often hostility to the interests of those who placed them there. The other is whether, however good the cause, a resort to force has the slightest chance of success, and is not doomed to result either in farce or failure. In both cases I ask, "Is it worth while?" and if my fellow-Ulstermen possess the common sense with which they are credited, and do not wish to give another illustration of the principle that those whom the gods wish to destroy they first make mad, I have little doubt about the answer.

EDITOR'S NOTES

1 At the time this was written the Larne gun-running had not yet
   taken place, and J.J. was in a position to disparage the quality of
   the equipment so far available to the Ulster Volunteers. After it
   took place, the situation was changed *de facto* and the Ulster
   Volunteers were in possession of modern equipment. The fact that
   it took place means that J.J.'s book failed in its main objective,
   which was to defend the constitutional Home Rule process from
   the machinations of the Tories out of office, and to oppose such
   gun-running politically with reasonable arguments.

2 This must have been 15 October 1913; the 'as I write' suggests a
   note added at the last minute by J.J. The book was reviewed in
   the local press on November 1913. He was working against time
   to try to stem what he saw as a rapidly unfolding disaster. The
   Curragh mutiny took place the following March.

3 J.J. was advocating the participation of Ireland, as a whole, on a
   partnership basis in the running of the British Empire. The
   transition to total independence would have taken place along the
   lines of Canada and Australia.

APPENDIX: THE TORY PRESS

FROM *THE SPECTATOR*, 1 NOVEMBER 1913[1]

AN EXAMPLE OF CONTEMPORARY TORY FULMINATION

What Civil War in Ulster Would Mean

STRANGE as it may seem, there are plenty of indications in the speeches of the Liberal leaders, and still more articles in the Liberal newspapers, that the Liberal Party have not as yet in the least recognized what civil war in Ulster would mean. No doubt the Cabinet have abandoned the idea that the Ulster people will quietly yield when they are told that submission to the will of the local majority is a principle too precious to be applied to the Irish Protestants of the north, and that they must be content to be ruled by the will of the local majority in the south and west of Ireland. In former days the Southerners argued that "Liberty is the kind of thing that don't agree with niggers". So now in effect we are told that autonomy is the kind of thing that don't agree with Irish Protestants. We must do the Government the justice to say that they are beginning to understand that the Ulster Protestants do not like to be told this. They know now that the Ulstermen mean business, and that if the Bill passes without exclusion they will have, as Sir Edward Grey says, to meet violence with violence. That is a step gained, but we feel sure that ordinary Liberals do not in the least appreciate the nature of the violence which will have to be used by them. They think that a whiff of grape shot and the killing of some two or three hundred men in the streets of Belfast is all that will be necessary. In fact, the party Liberal envisages a kind of rather strenuous Tonypandy or a repetition of the Dublin riots, but with Church of England clergy men and Presbyterian ministers instead of trade union officials as leaders.

We can assure them that they are mistaken. The problem they will have to solve next June, if the Bill is carried through without the exclusion of North-East Ulster, will be something wholly different. What they will have to face is the putting down of a hundred thousand partially drilled, but on the whole well organized, men led by capable leaders in whom they believe—men armed with a very efficient rifle, and possessed of an ample store of ammunition.[2] The ammunition, it should be noted, is not gathered in one magazine, which can be seized and destroyed by a *coup de main*, but scattered and concealed throughout the country. The Ulstermen have not put all their eggs into one basket. Their principle is one man one rifle, and each man the guardian and storekeeper of his own rifle.

At first people may be inclined to say that this arming and organizing of the Ulstermen will make their repression all the easier. It will incline them, we shall be told, to come into the open and try a pitched battle, in which they are sure to be hopelessly beaten. We are not in the secrets of the Ulstermen, but we know enough of them to feel sure they have grasped the truth that they are quite unable, even if they had the wish, to stand up to the British Army and beat it in a pitched battle. They may be a passionate people, but they are also a very cautious, and in some ways slow and dour people, and they recognize the value of those qualities. They will be quite content, in spite of their organization, to play a Fabian game in the north-east, to spread themselves throughout their mountains and bogs and by their lake sides, and let the Government attempt the work of disarming the villagers, or chasing them up and down the country while the more mobile bands ambush the Government supplies, cut the railways, and render difficult the feeding and movements of the troops.[3] The Ulstermen are prepared to keep on at a delaying campaign of this kind for two or three months. They will not like it, no doubt. How fully they recognize what they are in for is shown by their willingness to accept exclusion and the experiment of Home Rule in the rest of Ireland rather than have civil war. That they will endure all the horrors of civil war if exclusion is not granted to them rather than submit to a Dublin Parliament we have no sort of doubt. And here let us point out that it is idle for the government to say that they can be as Fabian as the Ulstermen, and that they have not the slightest desire to attack them. They will be obliged by the force of circumstances to take the aggressive rather than the peaceful line. As we have said again and again, though we do not in the least approve of or desire to encourage such action, there is no doubt that the moment the Bill passes there will be in all the Protestant centres a movement to drive away the Catholics. They will not be massacred, but do what the leaders will, the Protestant workmen and the Protestant majorities in the towns and populous areas will not consent to live with a Catholic and Nationalist population beside them. Fear and panic will have their usual effect. They make men cruel and ruthless. Protestants will argue that they cannot feel safe, when they take the field in their regiments, if their homes are left at the mercy of the Catholic minority. That minority will accordingly be expelled or, at any rate, an attempt will be made to expel them as traitors within the citadel. The Catholic minority will naturally resist and appeal for protection from the Government, and so the fight will begin. Next will come reprisals from the south and west, and still more in the places on the Ulster border where the Catholics are in a majority, where they will very naturally say that they have to mete out to the Protestants the treatment meted out by them to the Catholics. They will endeavour, in fine, to drive out the Protestants. These movements on the border will again be met by raids of Protestants, and especially of the Protestant mounted corps, to protect their co-religionists.

The fact that the Ulster civil war will begin in this way will make it very difficult for the Government to do what is always wise in cases of civil trouble, i.e. to keep their forces concentrated. The appeals for protection on the part of the Catholics, and the natural desire of the Imperial Executive to prevent reprisals, will produce a demand for troops not only throughout the six Plantation counties, but in Donegal, Cavan, Monaghan, parts of Tyrone and all along the southern borders of Ulster. The General will be overwhelmed with demands to send troops here, there, and everywhere, to prevent what will be called "massacres", and which, as blood becomes hotter, will almost deserve that description. "How utterly monstrous! How abominably wicked of the Ulster people to plan such things!" will doubtless be the comment of our Home Rule readers. We are not going to defend such deeds for a moment, but we know what would happen. That is why we are willing to sacrifice Unionist principles in order to obtain exclusion as the one thing which will prevent civil war—assuming, as we recognize we must, that the Government are too much entangled in their pledges to Mr. Redmond to take the better course of a general election or a Referendum.

The certainty that this struggle will begin not in a mere Belfast street riot or in a neat general action, such as many Liberals seem to suppose, but collisions throughout the whole province of Ulster and its borders, will make war come in its fiercest and most terrible form. It will also make it come in a form that will have tremendous and far-reaching consequences for the Government, though apparently these consequences are at present quite invisible to them. The Government, we are sure, will want to do their coercion with the least possible amount of cruelty. They are humane men, and, quite apart from any other considerations, will want not to shed any more of the blood of their countrymen than is absolutely necessary. But even if they were themselves without pity, they would know that a great effusion of blood might at any moment lead to reaction which would be fatal to them as an Administration. They will not then consent or be able to do what a Continental Power would do, and what in truth would be the kindest thing to do. They will not tell their generals to draw the first blood, and to be sure that a great deal of it is shed in the first few days in order to strike terror into the rebels. They will not give the order, *Frappez fort et frappez vite.* Instead of that they will try wherever possible to make so great a display of force that the rebels will be overawed, and be compelled either to evacuate the positions they may have taken up or else to surrender without a shot. They will, in effect, always want to confront one rebel with two soldiers. But if the Army is to be broken up into small bodies in order to give protection, and is to be widely scattered throughout North-East Ulster to save the Catholics, and spread broadcast on the borders to prevent the extinction of the Protestant minority, and, further, if this work is to be accomplished with the least possible amount of bloodshed, we are certain, whatever may be said now to the contrary by so-called experts, that two hundred thousand men will be required for the work. We tried dealing with the Boers on the cheap with forty thousand men, with the result that we had later to get together four hundred thousand men.[4]

As this war will have to be a kid-glove war, at any rate at the beginning, we are certain that the Government will not be able to wage it with fewer than two hundred thousand men. Now this means that in addition to the troops already in Ireland they will have to send about a hundred and sixty thousand men, or the whole of the expeditionary force. This again means that the whole of the Reserve will have to be called out and kept out for least three months. But consider the dislocation of trade caused thereby and the fury of the men at being recalled to the colours for such a purpose as forcing Dublin rule upon North-East Ulster! Further, the calling out of the Reserve, and the taking of the expeditionary force out of England and Scotland, will oblige the Government, unless they are willing to run greater risks than we believe they are, to order the embodiment of the whole of the Territorial Force. But a pretty mess that would result in. That the Territorial Force would obey the order for embodiment willingly enough in the case of a foreign war, is beyond doubt, but the grumbling over embodiment in the case of civil war, even though the men would not be employed in Ireland, will be most formidable.

Having got their two hundred thousand men and put them into the field in Ireland, do the Government recognize how quickly that force will become demoralized unless they are kept constantly springing at the throats of the rebels, that is, being constantly blooded? If they leave the soldiers scattered about in the Ulster villages and small towns, it will be absolutely impossible to prevent them fraternizing with the men, and still more with the women, and hearing stories of Catholic outrages, very likely untrue, but nevertheless stories which will make the ordinary Protestant Scotsman and Englishman "see red" and soon render him useless for the work which he will be called upon to do. Louis Philippe found out too late the danger of keeping troops hanging about for political reasons instead of sending them straight at the enemy. In '48 the army, if it had been at once let loose at the Paris mob, would have gone for them, and there would possibly been no abdication. They were kept inert for three or four days, and then it was found impossible to use them. They had not become Republicans in theory, but they found they could not shoot down on a Wednesday men with whom they had been chatting on the most familiar terms up till Tuesday night. A man will not consent to be a kindly, good-tempered, friendly soldier one day, and use a repeating rifle on his friends the next day with ruthless precision.

We shall say no more about the difficulties of employing English and Scottish Protestant troops against the Ulster Protestants—remember, the moment civil war begins it will be a religious war in esssentials. The possibility of something in the nature of what would be a technical mutiny among officers and troops is too horrible to discuss. Civil war is bad, but mutiny, however well-intentioned, is ten times worse. It is difficult even to describe the prospect without appearing to give encouragement where that is the last thing we wish to give. Unfortunately, however, all the facts seem to show that there will be a large number of officers who will find it impossible to reconcile the soldier's duty with what they conceive to be the citizen's duty. It is all very well for us to say, as we should say, that in that case the soldier's duty must come first. But what are we to reply if officers say that they cannot and will not be governed by abstract considerations, and that they will not give the order to fire on Ulstermen? And here it must not be supposed unwillingness to shed the blood of their fellow subjects will only be found among violent Loyalist officers and men. We heard only the other day of an officer—and there must be plenty such—who in politics is a strong Home Ruler, but who yet feels an abhorrence to shedding the blood of Ulstermen. However, we will for the moment dismiss these considerations and assume—as assuredly we should like to assume—that there will be no resignations and no trouble with the Army, except that inevitable trouble of fraternisation of which we have spoken above. Even in that case the Government will have to put two hundred thousand men into Ulster, and then in order to do so will have to call out the whole of the Reserve. They have not, apparently, imagination enough to understand this yet, and are still in the happy-go-lucky "whiff of grape shot" stage. They will find it out, however, before next June.[5] Let us hope that by then they will have come to the sensible conclusion that if they are to maintain their Irish policy it can only be done by the exclusion of the homogeneous Protestant and Loyalist Ulster.

EDITOR'S NOTES

[1] This article was timed to appear to influence the Tory conference. It is on record in the Irish Quaker archive in Dublin, as having been enclosed in a letter from Henry Harris, of the Friends Foreign Mission Association in London, to J. N. Richardson, Mount Caulfield, Bessbrook, dated December 1913, in which he enquired whether these questions had been discussed in committee. I intend to research the then position of Ulster Quakers, and whether action was taken on foot of this letter. Richardson apparently refused the use of his car for the transport of the Larne guns, and set up and staffed hospital facilities in Bessbrook for the anticipated civil war. (W. Ross Chapman, 'James Nicholson Richardson (1846–1921)', *Journal of the Friends Historical Society*, vol. 58, no. 1, p. 70.

[2] In November 1913 this was bluff; the Larne gun-running had not yet taken place, and the comments in J.J.'s book regarding armaments were valid. It is likely, however, that the author of the article was aware of the plans and the schedule, so he could bluff with confidence.

[3] This guerrilla warfare approach was subsequently adopted with great success by the I.R.A. from 1919 onwards. Why did they not take it up before 1916? Could it be that they had failed to absorb the military implications of the Ulster developments, just as they had totally underestimated the political?

[4] These arguments were picked up by the Germans; J.J. always held that the Germans inferred that with the British occupied in Ulster they could attack France via Belgium with impunity.

[5] This again suggests that the author had advance knowledge of the Larne gun-running plans.